The Local

A History of
THE ENGLISH PUB

The Local

A History of
THE ENGLISH PUB

PAUL JENNINGS

TEMPUS

For Felicity

First published 2007

Tempus Publishing Limited
The Mill, Brimscombe Port,
Stroud, Gloucestershire, GL5 2QG
www.tempus-publishing.com

© Paul Jennings, 2007

The right of Paul Jennings to be identified as the Author
of this work has been asserted in accordance with the
Copyrights, Designs and Patents Act 1988.

British Library Cataloguing in Publication Data.
A catalogue record for this book is available from the British Library.

ISBN 978 0 7524 3994 5

Typesetting and origination by Tempus Publishing Limited
Printed in Great Britain

Contents

List of Figures

Preface and Acknowledgements

This book is the product of over twenty years of researching and thinking about the history of the pub and drink. The greater part of that work has inevitably been in libraries and archives. But it has been informed too by my observations working in a pub for some years in the Lake District and helping out in an Irish bar on New York's Eighth Avenue, as well as from a customer's point of view. Those observations may have taken in some depressing places and some dispiriting behaviour, but the pub has also provided me with real pleasure. I recall fondly, for example, the Castle Hotel in Oldham Street, Manchester, the Albert Hotel in Keighley or the Princess Louise in Holborn, three very different establishments. It is this protean institution that I have sought to portray. I have approached it in a scholarly way, but I have also tried to write for a wider readership interested in this essential part of the country's history.

Over the years of research I have incurred many debts. More particularly for this book I should like to thank the staff of the J.B. Priestley Library of the University of Bradford; the Brotherton Library of the University of Leeds; the Local Studies Library at Bradford Central Library; the Bradford and Wakefield branches of the West Yorkshire Archive Service; the East Riding Archives at Beverley; the North Yorkshire Record Office at Northallerton; the Lancashire Record Office at Preston; and Southampton Archive

Services. For photographic assistance I should like to thank James Smith, and for drawing the map and plans of pub interiors William Sutherland RIBA. I thank David Gutzke for the copy of his unpublished paper on women publicans. Students on my Drink and Society course at the University of Bradford have offered many useful thoughts on the subject. For commenting on all or part of the work in progress I thank John Chartres, David Fahey, Louise Jackson, Pete Rushton, Dave Russell, George Sheeran and Andrew Whittingham. Any errors or shortcomings in the book are of course entirely my responsibility. Thanks also to Sophie Bradshaw and Lisa Mitchell at Tempus.

Harrogate, February 2007

I

Introduction:
What is a Pub?

What is a pub? For George Orwell the perfect pub, embodied in
the mythical Moon Under Water, was a place whose 'whole architecture and fittings are uncompromisingly Victorian'. As he evoked
it: 'The grained woodwork, the ornamental mirrors behind the
bar, the cast-iron fireplaces, the florid ceiling stained dark yellow
by tobacco-smoke, the stuffed bull's head over the mantelpiece –
everything has the solid comfortable ugliness of the nineteenth century.'[1] The essence of the pub was similarly located in the Victorian
period in a trio of books published either side of the Second World
War: Maurice Gorham's *The Local* and *Back to the Local* and, written
with H. McG. Dunnett, *Inside the Pub*. In the latter work it became
the 'English pub tradition', having evolved through the centuries to
be a living art form. It comprised both the 'plain interior with modest embellishments' in the pubs of villages and country towns and
the 'fantastic, exotic scene' of the urban saloon or gin palace.[2] To
the question – what is a pub – this became a common response
in the post-war years, as the country experienced the quickening
changes of a more affluent society. For architectural historian Mark
Girouard, writing in the early 1970s, Victorian pubs had 'been much
and rightly admired' and it was their 'splendours' which he wished
to document before the 'tiny fragment' which survived was itself lost.
Christopher Hutt, later national chairman of the Campaign for Real

Ale, fearing at that time the death of the English pub, looked more to the plainer interior in bemoaning the impact of modernisation. For him: 'Luxurious soft furnishings replace the wooden seats, wall-to-wall carpeting covers those worn-out old tiles, the ornate mirror and the dart-board make way for a set of tasteful hunting prints.'[3] For all these writers the Victorian pub was a thing to treasure: it *was* the pub.

Yet for other writers, like Thomas Burke, with several works on the subject in the 1920s and 1930s, this pub was an 'uncouth thing', as pub was an 'uncouth word'. For him the gin palace was a 'flaring, roaring, gilt-and-plate glass abomination', a standardised thing, devoid of individuality. For him, as for many others, it was the inn and the old-fashioned tavern, as they had developed into the early nineteenth century, which were the true geniuses of the public house. Thus for A.E. Richardson, who published in 1934 *The Old Inns of England*, Victoria's reign, far from being the quintessence of the pub, witnessed 'a long eclipse of the tradition of innkeeping in this country, and wherever the germ of the new industrialism developed, the old houses were generally replaced by the reeking, flaring gin-palaces of the nineteenth century'. Theirs is a Dickensian vision, as it greeted Pickwick at the Saracen's Head in the old innkeeping town of Towcester:

> The candles were brought, the fire was stirred up, and a fresh log of wood thrown on. In ten minutes' time a waiter was laying the cloth for dinner, the curtains were drawn, the fire was blazing brightly, and every thing looked (as every thing always does in all decent English inns) as if the travellers had been expected and their comforts prepared, for days beforehand.[4]

It was this ideal of the hospitality of the traditional inn, which drew those from the end of the nineteenth century and through the inter-war years who wished to 'improve' the pub's Victorian debasement. Architect Basil Oliver in this way looked to the *Renaissance of the*

English Public House transforming 'the blatant vulgarity of the declining Gin Palace' or the 'evil-smelling fly-infested Victorian "pub"' into 'their clean wholesome successors of today'.[5]

Whether writing of the inn or the pub, three shared themes stand out in works such as these. One is of a sense of loss. The Victorians felt it, surveying the massive changes of their times, and the old inns and the coaching days were a favourite subject of local antiquarians. A typical example is William Scruton, devoting to it a chapter of his characteristically titled *Pen and Pencil Pictures of Old Bradford*, published in 1890. As he put it: 'In contrasting the old hostelries of Bradford of fifty years ago, with the dramshops of to-day, it is impossible to resist a feeling of regret at the change which has been brought about.' It was not in the gin palace that 'good-fellowship' was to be found, or rest and refreshment for the traveller. As he put it: 'Truly, the "march of civilisation" has not in this respect, brought with it an improvement on the past.'[6] The equally marked changes of the twentieth century evoked a similar response. As Maurice Gorham expressed it in his aptly titled chapter 'Obituary' as he went *Back to the Local* in 1949: 'For those of us who feel sad whenever a pub vanishes, this is a sad life. Progress, reconstruction, town-planning, war, all have one thing in common: the pubs go down before them like poppies under the scythe.' He even experienced his own Dickensian moment:

> I grieved particularly for the White Hart in Lexington Street, for it was a little quiet neglected house, with the door swinging on a strap and a step down to the bar, where I always felt that Bill Sikes might at any moment spring up from the deal tables with his white dog at his heels.[7]

As urban redevelopment really got under way from the late 1950s, similar sentiments were expressed. When the Victorian Society's Birmingham Group surveyed the city's Victorian pubs in the mid-1970s, for example, it found that the highway engineers and the planners had between them destroyed 'many good pubs'. And what they had missed, interior designers were then transforming out of all recognition. Looking back at the survey and subsequent developments in a 1983 publication by SAVE Britain's Heritage and the Campaign for Real Ale, Alan Crawford put it: 'The Victorians had a secret of good pub design which has somehow got lost.'[8]

To the theme of loss we may add that of Englishness. Thomas Burke began his volume by declaring that: 'To write of the English inn is almost to write of England itself ... as familiar in the national consciousness as the oak and the ash and the village green and the church spire.' Expressing unchanged sentiments half a century later, a popular portrait of *The English Pub* observed: 'The pub is an institution unique to England, and there is nothing more English.'[9] But just as the inn was linked to that Englishness felt to be embodied in the past and the rural, so here the urban pub was also seen as expressive of the national genius. Thus a 1928 essay on the London public house found its Englishness in the domesticity of its welcome, the solidity of its architecture and the happiness and contentment of its customers. But the pub was more than just an expression of those qualities, it was 'the true temple of the English genius' – the poetic spirit so essentially a part of the English character.[10]

The third theme has been the idea of the pub as the hub of the community – the local. Although pubs had served this function for centuries, as an idea this too was articulated during the inter-war years as a variety of social, cultural and economic changes affected the pub. It was confirmed by the vital role which the pub played as a social centre during the Second World War. But in the post-war period it has remained central to ideas of what the pub is. This is true for those who fear the pub's decline. Thus the CAMRA newspaper *What's Brewing* headlined its 'Pub in 2000' conference as: 'The battle is on to save Britain's locals.' But it is shared too by the industry. Pub company Punch Taverns, with over 9,200 pubs across the United Kingdom by 2006, categorised this 'portfolio' under nine headings, four of which used the term as in basic, mid market, city and upmarket locals.[11] And of course with the Rovers Return, the

Queen Victoria and the Woolpack, the nation's popular soap operas have placed a local at their very centre.

The public house has thus occupied a central place in the nation's imagination, expressing its very identity. It is worth exploring its history for that reason alone. But clearly not everyone has had in mind the same thing. This in turn reflects the reality that we are looking at an extremely heterogeneous institution. For when we speak of the 'pub', we are speaking of something which only became generally known by that name quite late in the nineteenth century. Into its creation went a great variety of drinking places – inns, taverns, alehouses, gin shops, beerhouses and others. And even as 'pub' became finally commonly applied to them, it still covered an astonishing variety of establishments, from big city gin palaces to basic back-street boozers, from railway hotels to rural inns. And more than that, it is possible to see each pub as possessing its own individuality, formed from its architecture and interior design, the types of drink and sometimes food on offer, the publican and his staff and the varied mix of customers and their favoured pursuits. As Mass Observation replied at the end of the 1930s, in its detailed and invaluable study of the pub, in answer to the question – what is a pub – no typical pub in fact existed.[12]

Charting the history of the pub then is a complex task. It is an institution which has always been evolving. Moreover, it has done so in response to changes in the wider society and its development cannot be understood without reference to them. The subject demands to be approached from a variety of perspectives: economic, social, cultural, political, legal and architectural. Further, its study is inseparable from the history of the consumption of alcohol, upon which other perspectives have also been utilised, such as those from anthropology and psychology. In my approach to the subject I have tried to learn from all of them. I have also been mindful of attempts to present more overarching interpretations of drinking or of drinking places. In relation to the latter, one strand of explanation has been to link the modern drinking establishment to the emergence of capitalist society in, for example, its increasing demarcation of the dividing line between the worlds of work and play inherent in the capitalist work ethic.[13] Another has been to bring a feminist perspective 'to construct a view of the gender relations of pubs' and portray it as a 'male domain of recreational public drinking', enjoyed at the expense of women. As Germaine Greer expressed it in *The Female Eunuch*: 'Women don't nip down to the local.'[14]

My approach has also been informed by looking at the experience of other countries. If the pub is so English, what is it about English society which has produced it and the way people use it, in contrast to say the French café or the American saloon? Within the British Isles too Ireland and Scotland have had contrasting drink histories and their pubs were quite distinct from their English counterparts.[15] Whilst I focus on the English experience, I am also mindful of the importance of local and regional variation within the country. This is true, for example, of the very basic question of the numbers of pubs in relation to population, with marked differences between towns, or of the nature of pubs in so many differing communities: rural, dockland, mining and so on.

In writing this history I am drawing upon the work of many scholars. But it is also the product of my own researches in a wide range of sources, some of which were written up in my earlier case study of the pub in the northern industrial city of Bradford.[16] It is also, inevitably, provisional. There are many questions which merit further study and I hope at least that I have provided a helpful framework for future work on the subject. The book's succeeding chapters are structured as follows. Beginning in the late seventeenth century, when the term 'public house' comes into use, I chart in chapters two to five the evolution of England's varied drinking places up to the 1860s. It is at this point that the 'pub' as a recognised entity emerges. Chapters six to nine then focus on the pub in what we might loosely think of as its Victorian heyday. They look at the institution itself in all its aspects – buildings, publicans and customers, at the question of how society sought to police it and at how it was subject to a variety of political pressures. The next two chapters then take in the important effects of the First World War, the story of the pub in the inter-war years and the experience of another war. The final chapter concludes with a survey of later twentieth-century develop-ments and an assessment of the place of the pub in the contemporary national life.

2

The Evolution of the Public House 1700–1830

Historically, there were three main types of establishment for the sale of alcoholic drink: the inn, tavern and alehouse. All three dated back to the medieval period and were the designations used in a government survey of 1577, which provides the first detailed information we have on drinking places.[1] The term 'public house' only came into general use in the late seventeenth century. Its precise origin is unclear, but it seems likely that it derived simply from a contraction of 'public ale-house', as this form was also employed.[2] The use of public house was, however, not confined to alehouses. Celia Fiennes, touring the country in 1697, was disappointed not to find accommodation – an essential inn service – at a 'Publick house' at Brandesburton in the East Riding of Yorkshire, 'it being a sad poore thatch'd place and only 2 or 3 sorry Ale-houses'.[3] The term was also used at this time in a statute requiring standard measures for the sale of ale and beer addressed to innkeepers, alehouse keepers, victuallers and keepers of any 'publick house'.[4] Similarly, in the 1720s Daniel Defoe distinguished 'inns and publick-houses', but also paired 'inns, and ale-houses' under a more general description of 'publick houses of any sort'.[5] The term, it would seem, was thus used in an overlapping way for inns and more substantial ale-houses, and in an inclusive way to cover all types of establishment.

The use of public house in those ways certainly increased over the course of the eighteenth century. This is clear, for example, from the numerous references in newspapers, the production of which expanded greatly in this period. It is also possible to chart its usage over time in the published proceedings of trials at the Old Bailey, which contain hundreds of references to drinking places.[6] Whilst both sources show public house coming into general use, the older forms continued to be employed. The diaries of John Byng (later Viscount Torrington), which record his travels throughout England and Wales in the 1780s and 1790s, clearly illustrate both this and the overlapping nature of usage. He refers to the same establishment alternately as an inn or public house, but he also does the same with alehouse in describing, for example, the George at Market Harborough as an 'alehouse inn'. Although this might seem on the face of it to be terminologically confusing, in Byng's mind it clearly corresponds to a hierarchy of establishments. Thus, in his typically acerbic way, he opines that 'the best Cambridge inn wou'd form but a bad Oxford alehouse', or that at Stafford: 'All the inns … are merely alehouses.'[7] To begin our survey then, it makes sense to introduce the three original types: inn, tavern and alehouse, before examining in more detail the nature of this hierarchy.

The inn was defined, both in everyday practice and in law, by its primary purpose: the service of travellers. For this reason inns were not included in the legislation of 1552 which required alehouses to be licensed by magistrates. The fact, however, that they too sold ale led to its being extended to them.[8] This did not remove the distinction between the two types. The position was summed up in the following way by the authoritative guide for eighteenth-century magistrates: 'Every inn is not an alehouse, nor every alehouse an inn: but if an inn uses common selling of ale, it is then also an alehouse; and if an alehouse lodges and entertains travellers, it is also an inn.'[9] Upon innkeepers the law placed obligations to receive travellers and to safeguard their goods; failure so to do made them liable for damages.[10] Performing these functions, inns developed during the later Middle Ages, gradually replacing the hospitality provided for the growing numbers of travellers at monasteries or in the houses of the nobility. By 1577, an estimate based on the survey of that year suggests there were around 3,600 inns. This total in turn may more or less have doubled, to between 6,000 and 7,000 inns, by the close of the seventeenth century.[11] At that date, for the nineteenth-century historian Thomas Babington Macaulay in his famous survey of the social scene, 'England abounded with excellent inns of every rank'.[12] A more mixed picture is conveyed by travellers' tales, as they will. Samuel Pepys, for example, at the George, Salisbury, on the way to Bristol in June 1668, enjoyed the 'silk bed and very good diet', but complained about the horses provided and later bemoaned 'the reckoning which was so exorbitant'. Later on the journey, at a little inn at Chitterne, he reports the beds were good but 'we lousy'.[13] Although standards clearly might vary, there is no doubt that inns were essential for travellers.

The tavern also dated back to the Middle Ages as a specialist establishment for the sale of wine.[14] Its distinctive role was recognised in statute in 1553 when the sale of wine was restricted to a permitted number of taverns in specified towns. Although this law appears to have been limited in its effect, since the survey of 1577 reported more than the permitted numbers, the separate administration of wine licensing was maintained: they were either granted by the Crown or enjoyed as a right by freemen of the London Vintners' Company.[15] At the close of the seventeenth century they retained their specialised function as generally rather more upmarket purveyors of wine and food. Pepys was a great frequenter of taverns. In April 1663 we find him enjoying 'Ho Bryan' at the Royal Oak Tavern in Lombard Street, and in February 1668 at the Bear Tavern in Drury Lane, 'an excellent ordinary after the French manner', that is with the courses served separately. Once again, however, standards varied. At the Three Cranes Tavern, Old Bailey, in January 1662, in the 'best' room of the house, a wedding party found itself crammed, according to Pepys, 'in such a narrow dogghole … that it made me loathe my company and victuals; and a sorry poor dinner it was too'.[16] The Three Cranes was a tavern of long standing, deriving its name, it has been suggested, from the three lifting cranes which unloaded casks of wine from boats into the warehouse of the Vintners' Company above London Bridge. It was usually represented pictorially on its sign by the feathered variety.[17] Although it is not possible to give a national figure for taverns, London, with its far greater concentration of people and wealth, undoubtedly had the most. A survey by William Maitland in the 1730s gave a figure of 447 taverns, compared with 207 inns.[18]

Vastly outnumbering inns and taverns were the alehouses. They were common by the early fourteenth century in town and country. Based on the survey of 1577, estimates of between 20,000 and 24,000 alehouses for the country as a whole have been made.[19] From 1552 they required a licence from the magistracy. This also extended to what were called tipling (or tippling) houses. Although the Act itself does not clarify what distinguished the two, and in practice they may have been synonymous, it seems likely that tiplers simply sold drink. In 1594 the tiplers of York were reminded by the city's corporation that they were not allowed to brew. Similarly, at a licensing session in the West Riding of Yorkshire in 1723 the tiplers were distinguished from the brewsters. In any event, except in the archaic language of the licensing system, where it was still in use, for example, in 1786 in the East Riding, the term as applied to a drinking place had largely disappeared by the beginning of the eighteenth century. It did continue to be used to denote prolonged or habitual drinking, again to be found in statute, and for much longer of course as 'tipple' – a generic term for strong drink.[20]

Arriving at a total of alehouses at the close of the seventeenth century is not easy. Contemporary estimates exist, but the only precise figures we have are Excise statistics of those victuallers who brewed their own beer, which includes innkeepers and of course excludes all those supplied by common brewers, brewing that is for general sale. Over the period 1700 to 1704, there were on average per year nearly 44,000 brewing victuallers. Based on an estimate that one-third of the alehouse keepers did not brew their own beer, Peter Clark suggests a total figure of as many as 58,000 alehouses. This works out at one for every 90 of the country's inhabitants, which is comparable with the figure Maitland gave for the capital in the 1730s of 5,975 alehouses, or one for every 100 of its citizens.[21] These thousands of alehouses had developed as the basic, everyday social drinking place of the lower orders. By the later seventeenth century, however, many of them were aspiring to greater respectability and in this way making the transition to public house.[22] Thus we find Pepys also frequenting alehouses, for example with his wife, or with companions enjoying music from harp and violin. But there were clearly for him degrees of alehouse. He noted of the Gridiron in September 1661: 'the little blind alehouse in Shoe Lane ... a place I am ashamed to be seen to go into.' And the previous November necessity clearly drove him: 'being very much troubled with a sudden loosenesse, I went into a little alehouse at the end of Ratcliffe and did give a groat for a pot of ale and there I did shit.'[23]

We thus return to my suggestion of a hierarchy of drinking places. There were distinct types, but there was also overlap between those types and differentiation within them. Further, the types themselves, the element of overlap and the differentiation were all in turn subject to change through the eighteenth and into the nineteenth centuries. At the top of this hierarchy were the great inns of England's major towns, whose dominating presence and imposing exteriors were often remarked upon by contemporaries. Defoe noted that Doncaster, on the Great North Road, was 'very full of great Inns', or that the George at Northampton looked 'more like a Palace than an Inn'. Based on this and similar comments, and on the evidence of the building and rebuilding of inns, Peter Borsay characterised them as 'the true palazzi of the English Augustan town', key features of an urban Renaissance.[24] Building and rebuilding went on throughout the seventeenth and eighteenth centuries. Although it is impossible to give precise overall figures for the process, numerous individual examples might be given. I will take just two from Yorkshire, early and later in the period. In Ripon, a cathedral and market town boasting, Defoe thought, 'the finest and most beautiful square that is to be seen of its kind in England', the Unicorn, which dated back at least to the early seventeenth century, was rebuilt and extended to the rear in the mid-1740s. In the town's Georgian transformation a number of other inns were also opened or rebuilt. At Beverley, the county town of the East Riding, the Blue Bell was rebuilt in 1794, raising it from two to three storeys, adorned with portico and balcony and renamed more grandly the Beverley Arms.[25]

The Beverley Arms later also adopted the title of 'hotel'. The use of that term would seem to date from the late 1760s, adopting for added distinction a French word that covered mansions as well as inns. The huge York House Hotel was built at Bath at this time and became its premier establishment. The first landlord of the Hotel at Exeter, which opened in about 1770, Peter Berlon, was himself of French origin. Of the 'new hotel' in Birmingham, John Byng expressed himself 'much pleased with our entertainment', contrasting it with 'the bad inns in the old town'. A nice example, finally, of the overlapping and changing use of names comes from Margate, with an advertisement of 1775 for the New Inn, Tavern and Hotel.[26] The use of hotel to designate larger establishments particularly devoted to the provision of accommodation gradually became more common. In the Yorkshire spa town of Harrogate, as in other watering or seaside places, we find by the 1820s its adoption by older inns, like the Crown, Dragon, Granby, Queen's Head or White Hart Hotels, and its use with the proprietor's name, as at Gascoigne's or Hattersley's Hotels. Even as late as this it perhaps retained some novelty, as one still finds places called simply the Hotel, like the one kept by Sarah Greaves in Briggate, Leeds, although the commercial directory which listed it did so under a heading of Hotels, Inns, Taverns and Public Houses.[27]

In addition to this process of building new inns and rebuilding or improving old ones, alehouses were also being upgraded to perform more inn functions. One estimate puts the number of such upgrades over this period at perhaps seven to ten thousand.[28] Licensing magistrates began to insist on the provision of stabling and suitable lodgings, and more generally the improvement in housing and the rising expectations of customers worked to effect this change. Evidence from a sample of probate inventories covering Kent, London and Leicestershire from 1660 to 1750 suggests a significant advance in the number of rooms compared with the first half of the seventeenth century. The valuations of properties after fires provide further support for this. Eight alehouses destroyed at Blandford Forum, Dorset in 1731 were valued at £134 each. Whilst some were small, like the little thatched house just four-and-a-half yards square worth £36, the majority were more substantial. The Black Horse, part thatched and part tiled, with a ground area of ten square yards plus stable and brewhouse, was worth in all £205.[29] Later evidence confirms alike the improvement and the hierarchy of establishments. Looking at the West Riding market and textile town of Bradford, a rate book of 1805 lists twenty-six inns and public houses, of which the seven principal inns were of an annual value of £40 or over, forming one quarter of all property in the town so valued. Over half had a value of £20 or above, with just five smaller houses valued at between £5 and £9. A much larger database of policy values for 2,295 publicans from the 1770s and 1780s, derived from the Sun and Royal Exchange insurance companies, shows an enormous range of values. Around half of the businesses lay in the range £100–500, but 20 per cent reached £1,000 or more. Those in the top quartile ranked alongside medium-sized cotton or worsted spinning mills. This, according to John Chartres, who compiled the database, placed 'innkeeping pretty high in the business hierarchy of the later eighteenth century'.[30]

We can see the hierarchy too when we look at the design and internal layout of inns and public houses. Looking at the larger inns first, two types of plan have been identified, both in use from its medieval origins. There was the courtyard plan in which the central yard was enclosed by two or more storeys of public and private rooms, sometimes galleried to give independent access to them. This plan was dominant in London, economising as it did on space on the major thoroughfares, with great inns like the Bull and Mouth (Figure 1) or the Belle Sauvage striking exemplars, but was found too in provincial towns, as at the New Inn at Gloucester.[31] More numerous, however, was the block, or gatehouse, plan in which the main rooms were to the front facing the street and the yard was to the rear, often accessed from a lane behind the inn in addition to the entrance from the street. The innkeeping town of Stony Stratford, on the London to Chester road in Buckinghamshire, had several designed this way along its High Street, with long yards to the parallel back lane.[32]

Apart from the distinctive galleried inns, however, there was little to distinguish the inn or public house from ordinary houses of similar size (Figure 2). One thing that did was their sign, and indeed the phrase – 'the sign of the … ' – was commonly used to refer to them. Medieval legal requirements for the display of signs would appear to have lapsed by this time, as magistrates were advised that one was 'not essential to an inn', but an 'evidence of it'.[33] Naturally though, one was almost universally displayed. They took four basic forms. Most simply, the name of the house was painted on a wooden board fixed to the wall. This might be accompanied, or replaced, by its pictorial representation. Pepys drank at the Mother Redcap in Holloway, whose sign showed 'a woman with Cakes in one hand and a pot of ale in the other'. These signs might be the work of journeyman painters, like the Mayfield, Sussex schoolmaster Walter Gale, who painted them along with other odd jobs, but artists like John Crome, William Hogarth and George Morland also turned their hands to them. More elaborate were projecting signs, some spectacularly so. The German Carl Moritz, visiting in 1782, was 'much astonished' on the Dartford to London road 'at the great signboards hanging on beams across the street, from one house to another'. Fourth, the name of the house might be given three-dimensional representation, as the carved signs for the Three Kings and the Three Crowns in London's Lambeth Hill, or most notably the massive sign for the Bull and Mouth.[34]

Whilst the signs might be reduced to four essential types, the immense variety of public-house names defies easy categorisation, although Larwood and Hotten's classic nineteenth-century work on the subject came up with fifteen, and the reader is referred to that and other works on the subject.[35] Many were in widespread use: the familiar Angels, King's Heads, Red Lions, Rose and Crowns, Royal Oaks and others. Patriotism was a common inspiration, not only in numerous allusions to royalty, but also in the commemoration of military and naval heroes, from the now less well-known Granby, Wolfe or Rodney to the universal Nelson and Wellington. Those emblems of national pride – horse and cattle flesh – provided a further dimension of patriotism. The celebrated Yorkshire Bay, for example, gave its name to no fewer than seven York public houses by the 1820s, or the Durham Ox, which for six years from 1801 toured England and Scotland in a specially designed carriage drawing crowds of admirers.[36] It is those with local significance which are perhaps the most interesting. In the 1820s Sheffield thus had its Cutler's Inn and Cutlers' Arms and the Old Grindstone; Whitby its Fishing Smack and the Greenland Fishery; Hull the Baltic Tavern and the rather charming Jack on a Cruise and Jack's Return; and on the opposite coast, Liverpool had its New York Tavern, five Livers and no fewer than twenty Ships.[37]

The interiors of inns and public houses naturally also varied with the scale of the establishment. The grandest had rooms to match their status. The principal house in Exeter, the New Inn, was rebuilt after the Restoration and embellished with its famous Apollo Room. Its elaborate ceiling displayed the royal arms and those of the See of Exeter and important county families. The George at Northampton at this time boasted forty-one rooms. Most of them were distinguished with individual names: the King's and Queen's Heads, Globe, Mermaid, Mitre and Rose rooms among them. At Lancaster, the King's Arms, the most important of the town's inns, had in the late 1680s fourteen bedrooms plus special rooms for permanent residents. Their names included the Fox, Greyhound, Half Moon, Mermaid, Swan and Sun. Seventeenth-century Hertfordshire inns had for public rooms a hall and/or parlours, plus named bedrooms. As premises became

more substantial through the eighteenth century, this practice seems
to have become common. In Kendal, the Royal Oak in 1743 had
Green and Red rooms, Far, Middle and First parlours, and in addition
a 'Coffy House' and 'Billyard Room'.[38] Many alehouses, however,
remained small, with probably just two drinking rooms in most town
houses by the mid-eighteenth century. This is the pattern commonly
met with in London when they feature in the Old Bailey proceedings: a parlour/private room and a tap room, or just kitchen and tap
room. This was the arrangement, for example, at the Two Brewers
in Vine Street on Saffron Hill in 1764, where a woman was served
in the kitchen by the fire. The domestic nature of many establishments may also be seen at the Bull and Butcher in Smithfield in 1767,
with the landlady on washday hanging wet washing on the horse in
the tap room.[39] But even the largest houses had their tap room, or tap,
which was sometimes run separately from the main establishment, as
we find John Clarkson, for example, in 1755 looking after the tap at
the Four Swans, a coaching inn in Bishopsgate Street. This arrangement was also referred to as a tap house, as at the Saracen's Head, an
inn in Friday Street, in 1735. And, further, tap house was also used
for those premises attached to breweries, like the Angel tap house in
Whitechapel, where we find the brewery staff drinking in 1745. This
term too seems to have developed a more general application. The
working-class radical Samuel Bamford, on his way from Macclesfield
to Leek in 1820, had breakfast at a 'neat little tap-house'. And in a
nice example of yet more variety of terms, he also described it as
a 'pleasant little hostel', evoking a medieval alternative to inn.[40]

Whatever the scale of the establishment, another common feature
was the bar. This had been in use for some time. An inventory of
1627 records one at the King's Head Tavern in Leadenhall Street, and
Pepys noted the 'barr' at the Dolphin Tavern in Tower Street in 1660.
At this time it was a separate office and store for drinks and valu-
ables, although it is sometimes described as in the tap room. This was
the case, for example, at the Rising Sun in Covent Garden in 1765,
where a silver cup which was used to mix rum and water was kept

in a cupboard in the bar.[41] Its modern form, where the customer is served across a counter, developed with the growth of specialist spirit shops from the 1780s, to be examined below. Another feature of the bar, in both its old and new forms, which became common from the turn of the century, was the beer engine. Patented by Joseph Bramah in 1797, its use, though not under his patent, quickly spread. In busy town public houses it was quick and efficient and did away with the need to bring beer up from the cellar. They were advertised in Leeds, for example, by 1801, but within four years we find one installed in a rural Hertfordshire alehouse, the Rose and Crown at Tewin.[42] The prominent pump handles of the beer engine were thus quickly established as a characteristic feature of the public-house interior.

Other fixtures and fittings also varied with the establishment. The grandest inns could be luxurious. In the mid-eighteenth century many of the rooms at the Red Lion at Northampton were lined with hangings and pictures and in three of its principal ones there were nearly ninety yards of tapestry. Furniture included Japanese tea tables and Virginia chairs.[43] But most public- and alehouses were becoming more or less comfortably furnished. In the tap room were chairs, or benches, and settles and deal tables on a bare, sanded floor. Some rooms had boxes, or booths to sit in, like the original taverns. We find this, for example, in 1752 at a London public house, the Coach and Horses in Swan Alley, Coleman Street, which also had a settle and table before the fire. In parlours there were perhaps carpets and, as in the 1780s at another London house, the King's Arms in Arundel Street off the Strand, stuffed leather benches fixed to the walls and mahogany tables, in what was described as 'a very superior public house parlour'. Decorative features like mirrors, pictures, clocks and barometers were increasingly found.[44] Nevertheless, there was a huge range of comfort, and there continued to exist fairly basic establishments. Thus, for example, a traveller to the Lake District in 1821 enjoyed the 'delightfully situated' Lowwood Hotel overlooking Windermere, with its 'elegant upper room' furnished with piano and organ. But he also enjoyed an overnight stay in an inn 'of the old school' in the remote Kentmere valley. There, the floor of the main room was 'bespread with tubs, pans, chairs, tables, piggins, dishes, tins and other equipage of a farmer's kitchen', and wash-hand basin or a looking glass 'seemed luxuries unknown to the unsophisticated natives'. Similarly, in the country near South Cave in the East Riding of Yorkshire, Robert Sharp, a local teacher, called in March 1829 at the Malt Shovel, 'a real hedge Alehouse'. In its one room the fire-place had no chimney piece, and the fixtures included a tin can 'used for airing the Ale of such customers who chose that indulgence' and 'a collection of old black tobacco pipes', which the landlady assured him were 'superior to clean ones'.[45]

Here, with the hedge alehouse, we reach the base of our hierar-chy, where we also find places referred to as pot houses. Although an early reference of 1724 is to a Hermitage pot house in London, described as 'large and well accustomed', it clearly was used gen-erally for a small, basic alehouse. In Leeds, in December 1772, the landlord of what the newspaper described as a little pot house fell down the cellar steps going to get a pint of ale. Edward Jackson, the vicar of Colton, north of Ulverston, had to make do with a 'paltry pot house' in Langdale in June of 1775. Rather less sniffily, another clergyman, Parson Woodforde, enjoyed porter with his brother and 'some jolly Tars' at a 'Pot-House on the Quay' at Yarmouth in May 1790. But these too could be comfortable enough. Towards the end of our period here, Samuel Bamford found excellent lodgings 'at a respectable-looking little pot-house' in Leicester, and at Redbourn in Bedfordshire, a 'delicious repast' at a 'very humble pot-house'.[46] Later usage seems to have become more self-consciously literary and archaic. Both Dickens in *Barnaby Rudge* and Thomas Hardy in the *Mayor of Casterbridge* use it in this way, to describe respectively a man 'reeking of pot-house odours', and an old woman behaving badly against the church wall, in a constable's words, 'as if 'twere no more than a pot-house!'[47]

The variety of drinking establishments is not yet exhausted, how-ever, and we must return first to the tavern, which we saw Pepys frequenting as a specialised place for the sale of wine and food. As a distinct type they continued to trade well into the eighteenth century. Samuel Johnson and James Boswell used the Mitre Tavern in Fleet Street, which the latter described in 1763 as 'an orthodox tavern'. Johnson himself, in his famous encomium, confirms that: 'No, Sir; there is nothing which has yet been contrived by man, by which so much happiness is produced as by a good tavern or inn.' At Bath in 1769, the Old Queen's Head Tavern and Eating House advertised its daily 'genteel ordinary' at two o'clock.[48] Outside the capital, however, their numbers remained small. At Norwich, for example, a commercial directory of 1783 listed just four taverns separately from the inns, including the Three Cranes, the derivation of whose name we saw earlier.[49] It was of course open to the keepers of inns, or indeed alehouses, to take out wine licences, and in this way the distinction might become blurred. Defoe noted the vintner who kept the King's Arms Inn at Dorking in Surrey, but at Bramber in Sussex, where the chief house was described by him as a tavern, he wrote of the proprietor as 'the vintner, or ale-house-keeper rather, for he hardly deserv'd the name of vintner'. Similarly, in London in 1740, the Black Boy in Saint Catherine's was described by its proprietor as 'both a Tavern and an Alehouse'.[50]

Thus the tavern began on the one hand to lose its distinctive status, and on the other, the fact that they were not subject to the requirement of a justices' licence contributed to their association with vice. This was not entirely new. Pepys had used taverns for sexual encounters on several occasions, enjoying, for example, claret and a 'tumble' with Doll Lane at the Swan in Westminster in November 1666. Boswell too might relish the intellectual cut and thrust with Johnson and others at the Mitre, but he also tells us of having sex with two women whom he paid with a bottle of sherry in a private room at the Shakespeare's Head, a tavern in Covent Garden.[51] Within a few years of this transaction, magistrate Sir John Fielding was inveighing against the 'brothels and irregular taverns', for which Covent Garden was a prime location. Prostitutes, he alleged, appeared 'at the windows of such taverns in an indecent manner for lewd purposes'. Nor was this confined to the capital: in dockyard towns like Chatham, Plymouth and Portsmouth the proprietors traded under wine licences. The parliamentary committee to which Fielding gave this evidence resolved that their grant be restrained. This was not effected until 1792, however, when the sale of wine was placed under the jurisdiction of the justices.[52] This did not wholly resolve the problem. It was claimed in 1816 by the chief magistrate of Bow Street, Sir Nathaniel Conant, that some old wine licences were still being renewed to houses he described as 'a higher kind of hotels, kept for the reception of men and women, for purposes which one cannot be blind to'. Furthermore, the rights of the Vintners' Company had been preserved in 1792 and premises continued to trade under its authority throughout the century.[53] Their numbers were, however, insignificant and the word 'tavern', rather belying this notoriety, was used generally as another term for, or as part of the name of, an ordinary public house. Commercial directories in their listings distinguished inns from taverns and public houses, but also classified together hotels, inns and taverns, or hotels, inns, taverns and public houses. Within the lists, as at Liverpool in 1824, for example, we find (appropriately) the Irish, New York and North Wales Taverns.[54]

The coffee house should be noted here, as they occupied a similar social position to that of the tavern in the earlier phase of its existence. They were of course specialist establishments for the sale of coffee, which dated from the middle of the seventeenth century. They were important meeting places for professional, commercial, literary and scientific men. The most famous coffee house is probably that kept by Edward Lloyd, whose City premises, with its booths like those of taverns, was used by marine underwriters and who began to publish his shipping list as early as 1692.[55] Maitland's survey counted 551 coffee houses in London in the 1730s, where their greatest concentration was to be found.[56] They adopted names like taverns or inns, above all the Turk's Head, from the origins of the habit, and they also performed other inn/tavern functions, including the sale of drink.

Boswell noted coffee houses selling alcohol, as in April 1763 'at the great Piazza Coffee-house, where we had some negus and solaced our existences'. Parson Woodforde, on a visit to the capital in April 1775, ate and slept at the best-known Turk's Head Coffee House in the Strand.[57] By the later eighteenth century the distinctive nature of the coffee house was thus being subsumed into those of the inn or public house. In the Norwich directory of 1783, of three coffee houses listed one was in fact an inn – the Angel in the Market Place. Commercial directories generally listed them with inns and public houses. Those of Baines for Lancashire and Yorkshire did so in the large towns like Hull, York or Liverpool. Inns and public houses also incorporated coffee rooms in their premises, as we saw at the Royal Oak in Kendal by 1743. The coffee house was also fragmenting socially upwards into the private world of the gentlemen's club, and downwards to a more working-class clientele as coffee became cheaper.[58] All-night coffee shops illegally selling spirits and resorted to by people of the 'worst description of both sexes' were described to the parliamentary committees looking at the policing of the capital in the mid-1810s. But there were respectable coffee-shop keepers who provided food, particularly breakfast, and also supplied newspapers and magazines. They were as yet few in number, however, and much greater expansion followed further price reduction in the budget of 1825. By 1840 there were nearly 1,800 coffee shops in London.[59]

The growth in the consumption of spirits caused our final change to the drinking scene. Spirits had been available for public drinking certainly by the mid-seventeenth century. Pepys in March 1660 was taken to an unspecified place in Drury Lane 'where we drank a great deal of strong water', and in September 1667 called at the Old Swan 'for a glass of strong water'.[60] The market for spirits remained small, however, until the last quarter of the century, and prior to 1689, when war intervened, consisted mostly of imported French brandy. But from this time onwards British spirits, in effect gin, became: 'the principal dynamic element in the home market for drink'.[61]

After 1689 the amount of officially imported spirits (other than smuggled that is) collapsed, and did not exceed the late 1680s figure until the 1760s. In contrast, British spirits excised for sale rose from just over half a million gallons on average per year in 1684–9 to almost three times that by the first decade of the new century, and continued to grow overall to the 1740s, reaching an annual average of over seven million gallons. The estimated share of the drink market taken by spirits rose from 5 per cent in 1700 to over a fifth in 1745.[62] For this remarkable growth Parliament was partly responsible by opening up both the distilling trade and the retail sale of spirits. Although sale had in fact at first been limited to those houses licensed by the justices, this had been almost immediately repealed for proving a hindrance to another of Parliament's aims – the support of agriculture.[63]

The existing drink establishments naturally took to selling spirits. Surveys of London in 1726 and 1736 showed that about half the spirit retailers were established publicans.[64] They were very popular made into punch (mixed with hot water or milk and flavoured with sugar, lemons and spices), and both coffee houses and specialised punch houses sold it from about the turn of the century. Ned Ward, the 'London Spy', records the company drinking punch at a coffee house at this time and in 1763 Boswell drank three, three-penny bowls at Ashley's punch house. The proceedings of the Old Bailey make frequent reference to the drinking of punch.[65] But much the most common in the early eighteenth century were distinct places for the sale of spirits. Maitland in his survey of London recorded no fewer than 8,659 brandy shops (a little confusingly the term brandy was for a time used as a generic one for spirits) over half the total establishments selling drink in the capital. They could be found in all parts of the city, but more especially in the poorer districts in the East End and south of the river. In turn, many were located in the poorest back lanes, courtyards and alleys. They included some of London's most infamous neighbourhoods, like Cock Lane in the East End, known appropriately enough for prostitution, with at least fifteen retailers; or Rosemary Lane, with twenty-one, some of which disorderly 'Geneva Shops', as they were called from the Dutch word for the juniper berries with which the pure malt spirit was redistilled, were singled out by a grand jury in 1728 for harbouring and entertaining thieves and street robbers.[66] Many of the spirit shops were also chandlers' shops, general stores selling kitchen necessities in small quantities. A survey of gin sellers in Westminster in 1725 identified over two-thirds as chandlers; another of the mid-1730s, mostly in the East End, found over two-fifths.[67] Women constituted a significant minority in the trade, particularly at its poorer end, comprising almost a quarter of spirit sellers in the Middlesex surveys of the mid-1720s and -1730s. They were probably more prominent among the ranks of petty hawkers of gin in the streets, like an elderly woman called Chapman, sent to prison in January 1737 'for selling Spirituous Liquors on the Footway to Chelsea', or those selling from stalls, or even wheelbarrows. In 1736 in Whitechapel there were at least thirty-nine of these roadside vendors and another twenty-seven along the Mile End Road. Watermen on the Thames sold gin, it was available in prisons and workhouses and hawked wherever large crowds gathered, notably at public executions and their grisly aftermath of the gibbeted corpse.[68]

Selling gin was clearly a heterogeneous trade, from the premises of respectable publicans and coffee-house keepers, through those of shopkeepers and small one-room spirit shops to hawking by individuals in the streets. A succession of statutes from 1729 sought to confine its sale to the first of these by requiring once again a justices' licence and prohibiting hawking, but without success. Further Acts of 1743 and 1744 again limited the sale of spirits to those places licensed by the justices and they in turn were not to be run by distillers, grocers, chandlers or solely as spirit shops. This seems to have been effective, as statistics of those taking out licences commence in the latter year. It was temporarily blunted by the exemption of London distillers in 1747. This, however, was swiftly rescinded in 1751 by yet another Act, which reiterated the provisions of those of 1743 and 1744 and introduced for London a minimum rating qualification of £10 for establishments retailing spirits (raised to £12 in 1753). Further provisions forbade sale in prisons and workhouses and sought to restrict credit and prevent payment by pledging goods.[69] In 1744 licences for the sale of spirits were issued for 22,821 premises throughout the country, roughly half of the total public houses.[70] Spirits were clearly widely available. Already at the end of the seventeenth century a big London distiller had warehouses in Exeter and York, and evidence shows gin being drunk in places like Bristol, Manchester, Norwich and Portsmouth. Nor was it confined to the larger towns. In Liskeard, Cornwall, we find a man accused in 1749 of 'frequenting Gin-shops on Sundays during Divine Service', although smuggled brandy was there the more usual drink.[71] Spirits had clearly become an integral part of the public-house world.

It was the capital's excesses, however, which gave rise to the idea of a gin epidemic, immortalised in Hogarth's depiction of Gin Lane of 1751, regarded by one historian as conveying the era's 'essential truth'.[72] Whether or not epidemic or craze are apposite terms, the period of high consumption came to an end in the succeeding decade. This was due partly to the legislation of 1751, but also to a combination of competition from the new drink of porter and periodic government bans on distilling in the face of bad harvests and grain shortages.[73] But the later eighteenth century saw a resurgence of consumption and the development of a new generation of gin shops.[74] Possibly more so than in the earlier period of high consumption, these gin-or dram shops became common in provincial towns. A diarist in Hull observed one Storm's dram shop there in 1784: 'Several of the poor people came into his shop ... called for a Dram which they paid for and drank of immediately and that is the manner of which his trade runs.' By 1787 dram shops had become 'numerous' in Sheffield as the authorities first tried to restrict and then to suppress them. The increase in spirit drinking was noted in Leeds in 1790, with a threat from the town clerk to refuse the licences of retailers selling drams on Sunday. In Manchester in 1789 there were said then to be 193 retailers of spirits. In Plymouth Thomas Trotter, then a surgeon in the navy, who was to develop the idea of heavy drinking as a disease, claimed to have got 200 gin shops closed down on the conclusion of peace with France in 1802.[75]

As the Sheffield example illustrates, this new generation of gin shops soon became a cause of concern for the authorities. This was particularly the case in London. Patrick Colquhoun, who began to act as a licensing justice in Tower Hamlets in 1792, claimed within two years to have suppressed 87 gin shops of the total 1,100 public houses.[76] Attempts to eliminate them focused on the statutes of 1743 and 1744, which had restricted the sale of spirits to public houses licensed by the justices. As Sir Nathaniel Conant put it, the aim of the licensing magistracy was 'to prevent any gin-shop, not being an alehouse, to be kept open'.[77] In February 1803 all the licensed houses in Southwark and the East Half Hundred of Brixton were informed that in future the law would in this way be strictly enforced. Five varieties of establishment were identified: spirit shops with no tap room or beer trade; shops like this, but which pretended to sell a little beer; the same, but selling beer for home consumption; bona fide public houses with a tap room and beer trade, but with a separate spirit shop usually at the front; and public houses where the tap room was to the front and the spirit bars were accessed by side doors. Legal opinion was sought, which affirmed the right of magistrates to refuse licences, but cautioned against causing financial injury to businesses that had been tolerated for some years. It was, however, certainly an 'evil', and thus desirable that in future their numbers should be reduced if it could be done without 'oppression'.[78]

Magisterial efforts certainly continued, focusing on the provision of a tap room and the discouragement of separate doors to the spirit shop.[79] This seems to have had little effect. In 1825 the duty on spirits was reduced significantly and consumption rose further, although much of this was probably due to a transfer of supply from illegal to legal channels. The number of publicans taking out a spirit licence increased sharply, from 38,472 in 1825 to 42,599 the following year and reached 45,675 in 1830.[80] By that year at least magistrates were calling them 'flaring and glaring gin palaces', according to the land-lord of the Macclesfield Arms in the City Road, contrasting them with his own 'beer house', dependent, that is, totally on its beer trade. In the parish of Saint Luke, Old Street, he claimed, 27 of the 113 public houses were exclusively gin shops.[81] Similarly, in Manchester one study at this time claimed that three-quarters of the 430 licensed taverns and inns had gin shops attached to them, and that in addition there were a further 322 (by implication illegal) gin shops, which abounded 'in the poorest and most destitute districts'.[82]

We will return to illicit sale, the gin palace and a new kind of beerhouse. Here I will briefly sum up the position in the 1820s. There were then still inns, with many now affecting the title of hotel. The great mass of drinking places, although they differed greatly of course in scale, had largely come to be termed public houses. Taverns had been subsumed into their ranks. Alehouse was applied to the most basic town or village establishment, although its use was retained in the language of the licensing system. More and more public houses sold spirits, and for a growing number it was a key, or sole, part of the business.

3

The Public House and Society 1700–1830

In the eighteenth and early nineteenth centuries inns and public houses played a central role in the economic and social life of the country. Indeed, this importance was enhanced as the economy grew over the long term and the country became increasingly urbanised. But by the close of the period this central role was beginning to contract, although the degree and pace of the process was locally varied. This chapter examines this economic and social role, before going on to look at how society regulated its drinking places and the impact, in particular, this had on their numbers.

Inns were a key element in the country's growing transport network. They provided services for travellers and their horses at regular intervals along the road. This can be demonstrated for the beginning of our period from data provided by a War Office survey of 1686 of available 'guest' beds and stabling for the military. Looking at a key route – the Great North Road to Scotland – accommodation was available on average every ten to fifteen miles, with greater provision in the main towns: Huntingdon, Stamford, Grantham, Newark, Doncaster, York, Durham, Newcastle, Morpeth and Berwick. In those towns the number of available beds ranged from the latter's 142 to York's 483, where stabling for 800 horses was also offered. Demand from transport growth increased the number of inns, which was effected, as we saw, by a process of new building and upgrading of alehouses. Extrapolating from figures of 1756 covering northern and eastern Wiltshire, western Berkshire and Oxfordshire and part of Gloucestershire, John Chartres suggested a figure of between 19,000 and 20,000 inns nationally by mid-century, roughly three times the figure for 1700.[1] The largest number naturally was in London, with over 200 inns according to Maitland's survey of the 1730s. But smaller towns on important routes had high concentrations: on the Great North Road, Wetherby, with a population of around 900 in the mid-1770s, offered travellers nine inns on its High Street alone. Such places became in effect innkeeping towns, like Towcester or Stony Stratford on the London to Chester road, or Sittingbourne at the mid-point on the London to Dover road.[2]

In the movement of people and goods inns performed a number of functions. Of course, as we saw with Pepys, they offered food and lodging, catered for travellers' horses, or provided their own for hire. From about the middle of the eighteenth century this latter service was enhanced with the provision of the post-chaise. By 1754 there were 2,308 chaises for hire paying Excise, more than two-thirds of them in London. Innkeepers cooperated in providing the service. For example, on the London to Oxford road via Henley at this time at least fifteen inns provided chaises to cover the sixty-mile journey, sharing advertising in up to five partnership arrangements. Typical newspaper advertisements of 1809 show similarly a competing trio of innkeepers offering chaises on the trans-Pennine route from the West Riding to Manchester, cutting their rates to 1s 3d per mile for each pair of horses.[3] Travelling post was thus expensive, but gave people greater control over their journey. It was also of course more exclusive, as William and Dorothy Wordsworth found, journeying by post-chaise to the Three Tuns at Thirsk in the summer of 1802. The landlady there treated them well, but on learning that they intended to continue their journey on foot, leaving their luggage behind, as Dorothy noted: 'threw out some saucy words in our hearing'.[4]

The more public form of transport was the stagecoach, with services first linking London to provincial towns. In 1706, for example, a coach was advertised from the Black Swan in Holborn to its namesake in Coney Street, York, taking four days 'if God permits'.[5] The number of services expanded enormously over the period. By 1835 there were some 700 mail- and 3,300 stage-coaches in regular service in Great Britain. A combination of better roads, improved coaches and more efficient organisation of services had reduced journey times dramatically, with London to Leeds now covered in less than a day.[6] Innkeepers and their inns were essential to that organisation. In the capital Edward Sherman presided at the Bull and Mouth in St Martin's le Grand, which as it specialised in the London to Scotland route has been aptly dubbed 'the Euston of the era of road travel', with over fifty mail- and stage-coaches leaving every twenty-four hours (Figure 1). Greatest of all the proprietor was William Chaplin, who at the height of his career owned several City inns and operated a West End booking office dealing with some 200 coaches.[7] As with the provision of post-chaises, innkeepers cooperated. John Bradford and William Green, of Bradford and Leeds respectively, for example, formed one such coaching partnership, and John himself was one of a team of drivers for their Highflyer coach from York to Liverpool, which commenced running in 1807.[8]

Of the experience of travel and the comfort, or lack thereof, of inns along the way we have a wealth of travellers' tales upon which to draw. Even allowing for the apparent grumpiness of the traveller committing him- or herself to paper, of whom John Byng is a notable example, they present a varied picture. Celia Fiennes in Yorkshire praised the civil treatment of their 'Land Lady' at Knaresborough, but up the road in Ripon found 'some of the Inns are very dear to Strangers that they can impose on', a common enough travellers' complaint in itself. Near Sheffield the 'poor sorry Inn' offered 'just one good bed for us Gentlewomen'.[9] Sharing beds in this way was actually quite common. It could be problematic, as John Cannon recorded of his night at the Hart Inn, Stockbridge, Hampshire, in 1726, when his bedfellow 'in his sleep grasp'd me & cry'd out, Ah my

dear Peggy, thinking he had been in bed with his wife, but I soon
made him sensible of ye mistake by awaking him'.[10] Sharing probably
remained a possibility for the poorer guest, although it is likely that
it declined as inns were improved. But when not actually sharing,
the experience might not be far removed, as the Halifax gentle-
woman Anne Lister found at a Malton inn in September 1818. The
chambermaid found the first room to be occupied, but on entering
instead a small back room: 'the bed was literally smoking from some
gentleman who had just left it'. Anne was too sleepy to mind, and the
sheets were clean.[11] For an aristocratic Prussian traveller in the 1820s,
Pückler-Muskau, in contrast, the beds at inns were excellent, and
he praised generally the standard of service for travellers, although
he did note that this deteriorated with distance from the capital,
whilst conversely the expense increased.[12] For another thoughtful
foreign visitor, Gustave d'Eichtal, journeying north in 1828, rooms
were poorly furnished and dirty, and the staff 'dirtier still'. But the
food he thought 'the best feature of English inns', with on offer 'one
or more portions of good meat, potatoes, some vegetables and a good
wedge of cheese'. At York and Durham he also found his rooms provided with bibles.[13]

In London inns d'Eichtal thought guests were treated with indif-
ference, and this lack of civility is a common complaint, as we saw
with the Wordsworths. Samuel Bamford too found this as a foot
traveller when he was refused drink and breakfast at the Bedford
Arms, Woburn, in 1820. He told the landlady he had a mind to bring
a complaint to a magistrate, or to the Duke himself, for refusing
to entertain a traveller without sufficient cause. As he recollected
the incident:

> I wonder whether the people of the Duke's Arms are yet in business?
> And if they are, whether, like scores of their arrogant brotherhood,
> they have not been so far humbled by those great levellers, the railways,
> that if a wayfaring man now enters their house, he can have a cup of ale
> for money?[14]

The Liverpool to Manchester line opened in 1830, and as the network developed so the coaching trade was superseded, with consequences for the inn that we will examine in due course.

Inns were also important bases for the carriage of goods, with their yards where carts could load and unload, warehouses where goods could be stored and rooms where carrier and customer could meet, sometimes designated as the 'Carriers Parlour', like the one recorded in the inventory of a Rotherham inn in the 1720s.[15] For long-distance carriers they also offered accommodation. By the 1630s we find carriers from Lancashire and Staffordshire to London lodging at the 'Two-necked Swan' in Lad Lane. Such was the amount of trade to the capital that local groups of inns provided support services to carriers from specific regions.[16] Some inns combined coaching and carrying functions, whilst others concentrated on a particular service. Although to some extent replaced by the development of specialised warehouses, carrying remained an important service of inns throughout this period and to the end of the nineteenth century. Commercial directories provide detailed evidence for this, as they gave their users information on the inns and public houses used by particular carriers. Leeds at the beginning of the 1820s had 140 carrier services so based, beginning its list with carriers for Aberford from the Boy and Barrel and the Harewood Arms, departing Tuesdays and every second Friday. At the port of Hull, market boats, steam ships and sailing packets also could be booked at inns.[17]

In addition to this vital role in the transport of people and goods, inns and public houses provided a base for a wide variety of trading activities. They functioned as markets for agricultural produce and manufactured goods. In late seventeenth-century Croydon, then a market town, inns had largely supplanted the market place for the sale of corn, with a 'cornroom' at the Three Tuns and the King's Arms and an 'oatroom' at the Ship. The inns of Southwark and Canterbury became the chief hop markets of the country. In Northampton the horse and leather trades were centred on inns. In the West Riding textile districts inns held markets for the sale of cloth, and even after the provision of dedicated cloth-, or piece-, halls, manufacturers continued to base themselves at public houses. In Bradford in the early 1820s, 313 manufacturers made use of 33 public houses in this way, with 63 using the Nag's Head, directly opposite the Piece Hall itself. Similarly in Manchester at this time, whilst most of the almost 500 manufacturers had a designated warehouse, they used public houses extensively for the purchase and sale of goods.[18] The yards of inns were the location for a wide range of trades, such as blacksmiths, wheelwrights or butchers, and varieties of travelling salesmen. Inns also provided a convenient base for the itinerant providers of an enormous range of services: dentists, opticians, all kinds of quack, truss-makers, vets, portraitists, tailors or tutors, among many others. They similarly provided venues for a range of travelling shows, of such as waxworks, wild animals and other 'natural curiosities', like O'Brien the Irish Giant, appearing, for example, at the King's Head in Norwich in 1797. Business more or less routinely conducted at public houses included banking, the settlement of accounts, sealing of deals, payment of rents, the leasing of property, creditors' meetings, job interviews and the auction of all manner of property.[19]

Inns and public houses also provided accommodation for much of the administrative business of the period. Quarter and petty sessions, manorial courts, licensing sessions, courts of requests for the recovery of small debts, courts martial and coroners' courts were all convened there. After the assassination of the Prime Minister, Spencer Perceval, in May 1812, although in this instance the jury viewed the body at Number Ten, they reached their verdict at a public house on the corner of Downing Street.[20] Local government bodies and the agents of central government, such as the Excise or Post Office, also used them. They provided convenient places for the meetings of turnpike trustees or shareholders, like those of the Leeds and Liverpool Canal Company from its originating meeting at the Sun in Bradford in July 1766.[21] The use of public houses in this way (and space precludes a complete listing of such bodies) continued throughout the period, and in some instances, as with coroners' courts, well beyond it.

But one can also see the activities increasingly being moved elsewhere, to town halls or court houses, as at Bradford at the very end of the period here, with its Grecian court building of 1832.[22]

One of the most contentious uses of the public house was by the military. Billeting soldiers was a legal obligation, and although their keep was subsidised, its cost was very much resented by otherwise patriotic publicans. In 1741, in Lancaster, it was claimed that troops quartered there were costing innkeepers £20 a week for hay alone, and nearly as much again for meat and drink. Croydon publicans in 1759 (the country's *Annus Mirabilis* of victories) petitioned the government for troops not to be billeted there during the fair, as it took up much needed accommodation. And during the American war it was complained from Guildford, on the road from London to Portsmouth, that so many troops had been quartered there during the preceding three years that more publicans had gone out of business than in the previous thirty.[23] Nor were other customers always well-disposed. John Byng at the Beaufort Arms in Monmouth in 1781 found it a 'plague' to be at an inn with troops.[24] Public houses were also used for recruiting, either by volunteers or through impressment. In 1758 we find Thomas Turner, a Sussex overseer and churchwarden, with a fellow parishioner going round the local alehouses unsuccessfully looking for likely 'disorderly fellows' to fulfil their recruitment quota.[25] Publicans disliked the press gangs. One was based at the King's Arms, off the Strand, when Francis Place's father took it over in 1780, although he managed to get rid of them, and the gang removed appropriately to the nearby Waterman's Arms. They were supposed to inform landlords of their intention to search and, if requested, show a warrant. Proprieties, however, were not always observed. In 1744 a Bermondsey publican was assaulted and coughed blood for days after remonstrating with a zealous lieutenant on the hunt for deserters. Others collaborated, like the Plymouth publicans acting as crimps, as the entrappers were called, through their use of credit for customers.[26]

Universally welcomed by publicans, in contrast, was the role of drink and the public house in the country's political life. Throughout this period, and well into the nineteenth century, candidates used inns as committee rooms and spent freely there on food and drink for voter and non-voter alike. As a Gloucester diarist commented at election time in 1675: 'every Belly in town is a little vessel of ale.' The sums involved could be prodigious. In the 1790 election at Exeter the cash book of just one of the three candidates shows some £12,000 distributed through the town's publicans.[27] A key figure in Hogarth's election series was thus the landlady counting the takings (Figure 3).

In many of the above situations, be it as voters or travellers, shareholders or local officials, we find the well-to-do in society frequent customers of inns and public houses. They also catered, in a wide variety of ways, for their social needs, in what has been described as 'the growth of polite leisure'.[28] They provided the venues for theatres, musical events, dancing assemblies and dinners for an enormous variety of celebratory occasions. Royal births and coronations, military and naval successes, among others, were the occasion of feasts at inns. The mayor of Leicester, for example, Joseph Cradock, kept the Angel in Cheapside and in 1688 celebrated there the birth of the Prince of Wales. The following year diners were lauding the coronation of his usurpers.[29] The annual dinner was also a feature of the great range of clubs and societies which met at inns. Their historian has counted over 130 types in the eighteenth century and estimated that inns hosted nine out of ten of their meetings. They included lodges of freemasons, friendly societies, trade clubs, county societies and clubs for what were later to be termed hobbies, like floral societies or the entrants in the canary show held at the Black Lion in York in 1784.[30] Perhaps exemplifying this social world were those centres of the polite, leisured life – the spa towns. Inns and innkeepers were of central importance in their growth, particularly in the northern spas of Harrogate, Scarborough, Buxton and Matlock. Landlords acted as promoters of the resorts and their inns were the centres of communal life.[31] But whilst inns continued to provide accommodation for this great range of social activity, alternative, purpose-built premises also began to be developed. Established provincial centres were increasingly embellished with theatres and assembly rooms. By the late 1820s an industrialising town like Bradford could also boast its 'Public Rooms', a building comprising a ballroom plus separate library, news- and billiard rooms. Significantly too, its name was later altered to the Exchange as the merchants, manufacturers and trades-men attending the Piece Hall also found a new home there.[32]

Publicans also promoted sports. They were important, for exam-ple, in the development of prize-fighting, cricket and horse-racing. Thomas Thornton of the Talbot Inn organised the first Leeds race meeting on the town's Chapeltown Moor in 1709. Entries had to be made at the inn a fortnight before and bets could also be laid there. Thornton also promoted cockfights, as publicans frequently did; they provided the pit, pens for the birds, and of course refresh-ments, in an activity as organised and commercialised as the races.[33] Other blood sports were badger-baiting, such as at the Sergeant in Horstead, Norfolk, in March 1777, and bull-baiting, as at Berkshire public houses, for example, in the 1770s and 1780s.[34] By this time the fighting and baiting of animals was beginning to fall out of favour with those in authority. The Ripon justices, for example, announced in 1774 that they intended to refuse licences to publicans permitting 'cock-matches, plays or any interludes.'[35] It would be some time yet, however, before they were made illegal, and, as we shall see, they did not then altogether disappear from the world of the public house. The inn long remained, however, as a gathering place for pursuers of those blood sports which retained their legality.

Sufficient has been said, I hope, to suggest the huge variety of activity centred on inns and public houses, which flourished over the eighteenth century. We have also seen how in some ways towards the end of the period that range of activity was beginning to contract, although the process was locally varied in its timing and extent. That contraction was also beginning to sever the connection between the middling and upper groups in society and the world of the public house. In this way public houses were becoming more exclusively social centres for those who had always formed the great mass of their customers – the lower orders in society. We will return to those customers and their world, but for the second part of this chapter I want to look at a subject in which they played a considerable, if unwilling, part – the regulation of drinking places.

Liquor licensing, as the regulation of drink and drinking places has usually been called, is a complex subject. A nineteenth-century Lord Chief Justice fittingly described it as 'a labyrinth of chaotic legislation', and it remains a daunting field, as the sheer bulk of the standard reference work on the subject testifies.[36] Nevertheless, some understanding of the origins and development of the system of licensing is essential to any study of public drinking places.

Precedents for later regulation can be found in the medieval period. Rules covered the right to trade and the number of drinking places; the location, designation and construction of premises; permitted opening times; the character and conduct of the retailer; the behaviour of customers; and the supply, cost and quality of the drink. Some of this regulation applied to the whole country, like the thirteenth-century Assize of Ale, which governed its cost. More typically it was localised, like the mid-fourteenth-century order to Bristol ale sellers to display a sign, or a Nottingham requirement of 1463 that they close at 9 p.m.[37] Local initiatives such as these continued to be taken, but over the course of the sixteenth and the first half of the seventeenth centuries a national legal and administrative framework of liquor licensing was put together in a long series of statutes, royal proclamations and government orders. Driving this process was the hostility of the upper ranks in society to the growing number of alehouses. They were seen as a source of disorder. Religious concerns focused on the drunkenness and immorality alleged to abound there, and the threat they posed as an alternative social centre to the church. Wider contemporary concerns over the perceived growing ranks of the poor naturally found a focus on the alehouse. The process was also driven by the desire of the central administration to exert its authority in the localities and to raise revenue. Government taxation of drink and of those who traded in it became a key element in the administrative framework in the form of the Excise.[38]

What then were the key features of the system? Authority over the retail sale of drink lay with the justices of the peace. A statute of 1495 concerned with 'vagabonds and beggars' gave them the power to suppress alehouses and to take surety of alehouse keepers for good behaviour. But it was the 'intolerable Hurts and Troubles to the Commonwealth of this realm' caused by 'common Alehouses and other Houses called Tipling houses', according to its preamble, which prompted what is generally taken to be the first licensing act of 1552. Henceforth alehouses had to be licensed by the justices.[39] The authority thus given was from the first discretionary. As an early guide for justices put it: 'they may allow and discharge Alehouse-keepers as they thinke meet.' During the later Tudor and early Stuart period the government enjoined magistrates to curb unnecessary or disorderly alehouses and to pay heed to the character of the person licensed and the location of the house. As their guide again put it: 'all persons are not fit to be allowed for Alehouse-keepers, neither are all places meet for an Alehouse.'[40] Nevertheless, and more particularly with the waning of attempts at central direction after the Restoration, this discretionary power was maintained. It was confirmed, for example, in a judgement of 1758 on an information brought by a Wiltshire innkeeper against justices who had refused him a licence. The legislature, it ruled, had made the justices the sole judges, as from their local residence they were best able to know its circumstances and the character of applicants. Nor were they obliged to give reasons for their decisions. Only if they had been 'partially, maliciously, or corruptly influenced' in the exercise of that discretion could they be prosecuted.[41] Such cases were rare, however, typically involving political partiality by justices refusing licences to those supporting opposing candidates. This may have been the tip of a more substantial iceberg. In the notorious Oxfordshire election of 1754, for example, both sides accused each other of using the licensing power to secure support. In Nottingham, in the same year, the borough magistrates were similarly accused of suspending licences for political reasons.[42] Clearly the exercise of that discretion could be controversial and was to remain so as long as magistrates possessed it.

Licensing was at first confined to alehouses and tipling houses. But as inns also served beer to the public, and were made subject to laws designed to curb excessive drinking, it was established fairly quickly that they too should be licensed.[43] The sale of spirits and later wine were, as we also saw, eventually brought under the authority of the justices. The exercise of that authority evolved in two ways: licensing became confined to specific divisions within counties and the grant of licences was limited to special sessions for the purpose. This had in fact become common practice before the law in 1729 (amended in 1753) required it.[44] The licensing, or brewster, sessions were thus an important annual event. Publicans had to attend in person, and the day thus provided an opportunity for conviviality, especially as they were often held at inns. After the sessions at Beverley in 1827, Robert Sharp recounts how one of the landlords going home to South Cave, 'a good deal hellevated', fell off his horse and asked the beast not to strike him while he was down. The sessions themselves were pretty informal. The magistrates of the Holborn division of Middlesex, for example, at this time deliberated in a room at the Freemasons' Tavern in Great Queen Street, Lincoln's Inn Fields, where their refreshments of tea, coffee, wine and cold meat also awaited them.[45]

In their study of licensing Sidney and Beatrice Webb characterised the eighteenth century as 'a period of extreme laxness' on the part of the justices, during which the number of alehouses multiplied. This period was brought to an end, in their view, in the mid-1780s by 'the most remarkable episode in the whole history of public-house licensing in England, the sudden and almost universal adoption by county and borough benches of a policy of restriction and regulation'.[46] Other than those for the number of spirit licences, however, the Webbs did not have the statistics to test those assertions. Rather, they relied on the opinions of contemporary commentators and the reported actions of magistrates. Our first task, therefore, is to look at the numerical evidence which we now have. This exists particularly for the years after the 1753 Act, which required clerks to the justices to keep registers of licence holders (who had also to enter into recognizances for their conduct of the premises) and their sureties. Unfortunately, none of this evidence produced a national total of licences. But from 1810 we have such statistics, as from 1808 publicans had also to obtain an Excise licence to sell beer, which it seems likely virtually all would do. In that year, a little over 49,000 did so. Our estimates for 1700 gave 6,000 to 7,000 inns and as many as 58,000 alehouses. They came from two sources, with probably some overlap between the two categories. But if we take an approximate figure for all public houses of 60,000, which both sources accept, then we can see that the total in fact fell over the century by more than 10,000 and the ratio of premises to population declined from 1 to 87 to 1 to 207. That figure then remained virtually stationary, with only slight fluctuations, before rising by 1829 to 50,442 licences, or around 1 for every 276 inhabitants.[47]

Within the total there were local variations. In the older provincial towns there was some expansion in the 1730s and 1740s, but later in the century numbers were either static or falling. In Bristol the number of public houses peaked in 1760, fell to an annual average of 481 in the early 1770s and to below 400 in the new century. In York the peak year was earlier, in 1683, with 263 licences. This total fell through the eighteenth century to a low of 164 in 1795, before rising slightly to reach 173 in 1822.[48] There was a similar overall trend, with local variation, in smaller towns. Also in Yorkshire, the number of Richmond's public houses rose slightly from 40 in 1724 to 44 in 1752 before falling to 31 in 1774 and remaining virtually static thereafter. Ripon saw a rise from 36 in 1773 to 54 in 1785, before too falling away to 41 in 1801 and again to 36 in 1826.[49] In contrast, the newer industrialising towns, with much greater population growth than the older centres, saw a rise in numbers, but one which markedly failed to keep pace with that growth. In Manchester township, for example, licences rose from 164 in 1773 to 223 in 1802 and to 436 in 1828–9, but the ratio to inhabitants declined from 1 to 134, to 1 to 326 over the same period. The same was true of other Lancashire towns like Bury or Bolton. In Bradford, the fastest growing industrial town of all, whilst the number of public houses in the half century from 1781 rose by 50 per cent, the population soared by over 410 per cent.[50] In rural areas, finally, the overall picture is one of contraction. In the six counties of Kent, Essex, Shropshire, Oxfordshire, Northamptonshire and Cambridgeshire the trend from the mid-eighteenth century was downwards, only reversed towards the very end of the period, for example in Kent. This general picture was true also of rural north Lancashire, and the East and North Ridings of Yorkshire.[51]

The statistical picture then is not one to suggest 'extreme laxness'. Given the importance of inns and public houses to economic and social life, it was necessary to grant a limited number of new licences to more substantial premises to meet increased demand. But it was limited, and in rural areas and older centres an actual reduction was effected. The whole process reflected a growing anxiety over the course of the century with the drinking habits of the lower orders. In London the gin 'craze' of the early eighteenth century had acted as a focus for a range of concerns. These included the threat posed by excessive drinking to the health and thus the utility of the poor as workers, soldiers or mothers; the perceived links between drunkenness and crime and a general disrespect for authority; the luxury and conspicuous consumption of the poor; and the undermining of home and family life.[52] Articles and pamphlets through the century continually echoed those fears. A piece in the *Gentleman's Magazine* in September 1736, for example, claimed that no fewer than 120,000 public houses were corrupting and debauching the nation, ruining 'honest labourers' and fostering crime. Another essay three years later linked disturbances in the Wiltshire textile trade to the proliferation of alehouses. This and other commentators blamed the problem on failure to enforce the law. The magazine in 1754 featured a farce wherein justices renewed a licence to a disorderly house 'because we have often been entertained there with much pleasure'. A reviewer of another 1759 pamphlet by a Kent clergyman on the 'pernicious' effects of alehouses wished that the magistrates had less discretion. A further concern, which was also to grow, was voiced in another piece of 1773. Its author again blamed the alehouse for undermining industry and increasing the burden of the poor, and castigated brewers and distillers who 'buy up paltry houses and settle retailers in every little parish, as well as in every town and city'.[53]

The concerns of reviewers and pamphleteers can be found reflected in the actions of the authorities, which cumulatively worked to reduce the number of alehouses. From the beginning of the period, for example, the Gloucestershire Quarter Sessions in 1706, and again in 1713, recommended to local justices that they limit the number of alehouses and suppress those deemed to be superfluous.[54] Local clergymen also acted. In 1766 the rector of Newport Pagnell, informed of the habit of his younger parishioners of frequenting 'Ale-Houses & Places of Ill Fame', personally intervened with the justices to stop their licences.[55] Landowners too were active in this way. At Terling in Essex in 1768 the squire was complimented by another local gentleman on the 'prudent and necessary regulations' observed in its last remaining alehouse. Also at this time at Kirkleatham, close to the Yorkshire coast near Guisborough, landowner and magistrate Charles Turner replaced 'a collection of little blackguard alehouses, which not only encouraged idleness and drunkenness among all the villagers, but were constant receptacles of smugglers', with two 'handsome inns': one in the village and one for his new bathing resort.[56]

This concern to reform the behaviour of the lower orders, to replace drunkenness and vice with sobriety and industry, seems to have quickened in the 1770s. A clerical justice in Lincolnshire addressed his fellows on this theme in a pamphlet of 1776, calling for greater 'circumspection' in licensing public houses.[57] It flowed in the mid-1780s into the movement for the reformation of manners. Another clerical justice, Henry Zouch, published in 1786 at the request of the West Riding Quarter Sessions his *Hints Respecting the Public Police*, which brought together all these concerns. For him public houses were:

Licensed receptacles for rogues, vagabonds, night-poachers, and dangerous persons of all kinds. It is here that the scanty earnings of the manufacturer and labourer, which ought to be applied to the maintenance of their families at home, are improvidently squandered away. Nor doth anything contribute so much to encrease the poor rates, as such places ...[58]

It was at the urging of one of the movement's most influential exponents, Zouch's fellow evangelical William Wilberforce, that George III issued in the following year his Royal Proclamation against 'vice, profaneness and immorality'. Although such proclamations had been issued before, it was this one which produced for the Webbs the 'remarkable episode' in the history of licensing. Certainly the rhetorical effect was considerable, as they documented in detail, with magisterial benches throughout the land resolving to enforce the relevant laws more diligently. Further, they began to adopt tighter regulations regarding closing times and Sunday opening, instituted closer scrutiny of existing houses and were prepared to withdraw licences from those which were badly conducted.[59] The Webbs, however, were keen to make a point of relevance to their own licensing concerns at the beginning of the twentieth century. The reality would seem to have been less dramatic. The statistical evidence does not support a significant shift in policy, rather a continuation of existing trends. Nor, as we shall see, does the evidence of prosecutions suggest much translation of rhetoric into action. But more broadly, the concern may be seen as helping to prepare the ground for the later temperance movement.

Before then, however, two concerns which were foreshadowed during the eighteenth century came to prominence in the early nineteenth, with rather more significant results. These were the issues of the alleged abuse of magisterial discretion and of the growth of brewers' control of public houses. Both were linked in the agitation to free the licensing system, which was connected in turn with a wider movement for free trade.[60] To a large extent they were focused on London. There the number of drinking places had also contracted.

The Maitland survey of the 1730s had produced an astonishing total of 15,839 establishments, if one includes the coffee houses, which also sold drink. More than half this figure was made up of the more or less transitory gin retailers. Even excluding them gives a ratio of drinking establishments to population of 1 to 84. Although it is difficult to compare like-for-like geographical areas, the figures we have all show a contraction. In the county of Middlesex licences fell from 3,467 in 1732 to 2,913 in 1759 and to 2,738 in 1813, before picking up to 2,774 in 1827. At the very end of the period, in 1831, the recently formed metropolitan police district contained 4,073 public houses, or 1 for every 371 inhabitants.[61]

Clearly the number of licences was being outstripped by the constant growth of the capital's population. This no doubt contributed to the growing number of complaints about the arbitrary use of magisterial power. In 1807 about a thousand publicans lobbied Parliament in protest at it.[62] A notable campaigner in this cause was J.T.B. Beaumont, a Middlesex magistrate who had unsuccessfully applied for licences for houses he had built in developing suburbs. He put his views strongly to the parliamentary committee of 1816 looking at the policing of the metropolis, castigating the justices' 'despotic power' and accusing them of collusion with brewers and gin sellers. Such views, and revelations of the closeness of magistrates to brewers in the East End, plus a petitioning campaign, led to the committee setting up a special investigation the following year into licensing in the capital. Its report was critical of both magistrates and brewers. It found 'strong evidence' of 'improper prejudice' in the minds of some of the one, and that the monopoly of the other over public houses was 'very prejudicial to the community at large'. Beaumont also gave evidence to a further committee set up in response to petitions complaining of the high price and inferior quality of beer. Although its report exonerated the brewers of profiteering and adulteration, it too deplored the trend towards monopoly in the growth of brewery control of public houses.[63] But despite all this, and a continuing and vigorous campaign, the immediate legislative results were meagre.

Two moves by the government to open up the beer trade had little effect. In 1823 a new 'intermediate' grade of beer, between 'strong' and 'table', was introduced and its off-sale only permitted. In the following year, brewers were allowed to sell beer for consumption off the premises without a magistrates' licence. In the year to July 1826 there were just fourteen intermediate brewers licensed and 773 retail brewers. Although the number of the latter did rise to 1,269 by 1829, their share of beer brewed was negligible.[64]

Where the campaign did finally have an effect was on the consolidation of the existing licensing laws in an act of 1828. Earlier measures proposed by Henry Grey Bennet, who had chaired the London police committees, which embodied the hostility to magistrates' abuses and brewers' collusion with them, had failed. An amending measure of 1822 acknowledged that existing law was 'defective and insufficient', but was limited in scope and in any case temporary.[65] The new measure was sponsored by the Tory MP for Oxford University, Thomas Estcourt, and usually bears his name. Whilst the essential discretion of magistrates was maintained, their authority was also limited in a number of what in some cases were to prove uncertain ways. The licence holder no longer had to enter into recognizances and to find sureties. The licence itself, 'granted for One whole Year and no longer', was subject to the conditions specified on it: that there should be no adulteration, no drunkenness or disorder on the premises, no bad characters assembling, no unlawful games and no use of illegal measures. Houses had to close during church services on Sundays, Christmas Day and Good Friday, except to receive travellers. Provision was made for special sessions for the transfer of licences, rather than at any petty sessions, for greater openness. Finally, a right of appeal lay from the licensing justices to quarter sessions. The Act repealed a mass of previous legislation and remained the basis of licensing law until 1910.[66] Although the principle of free trade had been discussed at the Bill's committee stage, the Act as passed made relatively modest reforms. Within two years there followed the much more dramatic innovation of free trade in beer.

4
Free Trade in Beer
1830–1869

From 1830 to 1869 the retail drink trade was divided into two distinct sectors. One comprised those houses licensed by magistrates under the terms of the Act of 1828. The other consisted of beerhouses, whose proprietors obtained their licence to trade direct from the Excise under the provisions of the Beer Act of 1830. This legislation has received an 'appalling press', both from contemporaries and historians. [1] As the Reverend Thomas Page of Virginia Water Parsonage, Egham, Surrey put it in 1846: 'if Satan himself had had a seat in the counsels of the nation, the Beer Act was the very kind of measure which the great enemy of mankind would have suggested.' And to Thomas Beaumont, a temperance campaigner of Bradford, speaking in 1849, it was 'one of the most mischievous Acts that ever passed the British legislature'. [2] For the Webbs seldom had 'so instantaneous and dramatic a transformation … been effected by any Act of Parliament'. The temperance historian George Wilson colourfully likened the country when the Act came into force to 'a proclaimed American territory … thrown open to the drink adventurers'. Their perspectives shaped the views of later historians. To S.G. Checkland, for example, in a survey of public policy making from the eighteenth to the twentieth centuries, the Act was emphatically 'a disastrous step'. [3]

There is no doubt that the consequences of the Act were indeed dramatic, if not as baleful as the above suggests. But our first task is to try and answer the question posed by another contemporary: 'how the deuce this Beer Act ever passed'?[4] Its long-term genesis lay in the movement for free licensing and, more broadly, free trade. The two were brought together in an 1826 review by the Whig wit Sydney Smith of an article critical of the arbitrary conduct of licensing magistrates. He castigated those 'little clumps of squires and parsons gathered together', who decided 'whether the Three Pigeons shall be shut up, and the Shoulder of Mutton be opened'. Forcefully he went on to argue: 'If the trade in public houses were free, there would be precisely the number wanted; for no man would sell liquor to his ruin.' Subject to the safeguards of character certificates and penalties for abuses, 'the trade in hospitality [should be] as open as the trade in sugar'.[5] In the event the apparent rise in spirit consumption following the reduction in duty in 1825 (ironically, itself favoured by free traders seeking to equalise the rate with that in Scotland), and the associated growth of gin shops, contributed to a focus on the freeing of the beer trade. Beer was regarded as the more wholesome and temperate beverage. That the measure subsequently passed was the result of other, short-term, considerations of the years 1829 and 1830, demonstrating the 'reactive pragmatism', as it has been styled, of the Duke of Wellington's administration. It would assuage the government's unpopularity, help agriculture gripped by a severe depression and produce the happy political results of dividing its opponents and showing that an unreformed parliament could be no less responsive to the people's grievances.[6]

The Chancellor of the Exchequer, Henry Goulburn, appointed a parliamentary committee to look at the issue in early March 1830, which questioned twenty-nine witnesses on seven days, including brewers from London and the provinces, others in the drink and related trades and officials from the Excise. As was common with such committees it began with its conclusions already formed. Its basic premise was that the duty on beer would be repealed to compensate for the introduction of free trade, which Goulburn duly announced in his budget speech while the committee was sitting. The revenue thereby lost would be recouped by growth in that from the malt duty as beer production rose, together with an increase in the spirit duty. The committee duly recommended freeing the trade in beer, by which time the government had already published its Bill, which in turn was introduced on 8 April. As Goulburn put it, he wanted a 'free trade in Beer', without restriction of sale as to on or off the premises. Support for the Bill rehearsed all the arguments about the justices' arbitrary use of their powers, the evil of the brewers' monopoly and the beneficial effects of competition. Both Goulburn and Wellington claimed it would benefit the labouring classes, upon whom the high price of beer fell particularly hard.[7]

How did the drink trades view the measure? Three of London's major brewers, all MPs, gave evidence to the committee. Although they broadly accepted that it must pass, they voiced their opposition and sought to limit its impact by, for example, confining it to off-sales. Charles Barclay, the most important of the three, thought the plan 'utterly fallacious': it would ruin thousands and transfer the beer trade from victuallers to chandlers, who would adulterate and spoil it. But asking rhetorically who was to supply the new beer-shops, he answered: 'the persons who can sell the cheapest and the best, and we say we can sell cheaper and better than others. We are power-loom brewers, if I may so speak.' The anticipated increase of consumption would provide plenty of trade for everyone.[8] Brewers elsewhere, and publicans everywhere, were less sanguine. The latter were most solidly opposed to the threat to their interests posed by the competition of beerhouses. There was a widespread petitioning campaign against the measure. The licensed victuallers of Leeds, for example, sent two petitions with a deputation to the capital signed by them and over 1,500 fellow townspeople. Towards the end of the Bill's passage over 4,000 of London's publicans had signed a petition against it. Altogether 228 hostile petitions were presented. It was to no avail. As their newspaper, the *Morning Advertiser*, put it, the licensed victuallers 'consider themselves to have been SOLD'.[9]

More broadly, opposition to the measure focused on the threat to public order posed by the new drinking places. These fears found alarmist expression during the debates, with one member prophesying 'scenes of drunkenness and debauchery … from one end of the Kingdom to the other'.[10] Rural interests were particularly apprehensive (although they were of course meant to benefit, and liked the lower taxes), as in fact they had been in the discussions about free trade at the time of Estcourt's measure. As Charles Barclay had reminded the 1830 committee, they did not mind free trade in London or in other big towns but 'cannot have it in our own neighbourhood; there would be a public house stuck up in such a village and such a hamlet …'[11] But concern was not confined to rural districts. Lord Stanley voiced, for example, Lancashire's 'considerable degree of alarm and apprehension'. In the West Riding one W.J. warned the readers of the *Leeds Mercury* of a catalogue of evils that would be the 'Probable Results of the Proposed Throwing Open of the Beer Trade'. These included riots, drunkenness, increased crime and political subversion.[12]

The government countered every argument and fended off all amendments. Proposed restrictions similar to those for existing public houses would preserve the peace. Publicans would still enjoy their monopoly of the sale of wines and spirits. Their superior accommodation would give them the edge in competition. The abolition of the duty on beer would increase sales all round.[13] The Bill, 'to permit the general Sale of Beer and Cyder by Retail', passed on the 23 July 1830 to take effect, along with the repeal of the duties, on 10 October.[14] The Act certainly introduced free trade in beer by removing the requirement of a justices' licence, but the restrictions which the government included angered some free traders. As the Radical MP Joseph Hume complained: 'The Bill was called a Bill for the Free Sale of Beer, and every clause was a restriction on those who might desire to engage in the trade.'[15] In the first place an applicant for the new licence had to occupy property assessed to the poor rate. He also had to provide surety of £20 for offences against the Act, a condition removed for publicans in 1828. The licence itself was obtained direct from the Excise, cost two guineas (one if only for the sale of cider or perry), and was valid for twelve months. The conditions were the same as for those houses licensed by the justices. Opening hours, however, were more restricted: the new beerhouses could not open before 4 a.m. and had to close at 10 p.m. On Sundays, Good Friday and Christmas Day the hours were from 10 a.m., with afternoon closing also from 3 p.m. to 5 p.m. These restrictions were stricter than those of the 1828 Act and were to be a great source of complaint from the beersellers, both for commercial reasons and the greater likelihood they brought of prosecution. They also had the perhaps not totally unpredictable consequence that customers at closing time simply adjourned to the public houses. A small element of magisterial discretion was introduced in 1834, but in 1840 closing time was fixed at 12 p.m. for London, 11 for places with a population over 2,500 and 10 elsewhere.[16] Finally, they had to display a sign bearing their name and the words 'Licensed to sell Beer by Retail'. This also was a new requirement for drink retailers.

Neither of the terms 'beerhouse' and 'beershop' was used in the Act itself, but both were current and were therefore applied to them. Boswell had recorded a visit to a 'beer-house' back in 1765, and, as we saw, the term was used to distinguish houses with a predominantly beer trade from the gin shops.[17] The proprietors of the new houses were thus variously known as beerhouse and beershop keepers, but also as beersellers or retailers of beer. All of those terms were used by the compilers of commercial directories. They also acquired a range of nicknames. The most common was 'tom and jerry', or simply 'jerry', shop, although here too its use predated the Act: it had been used in London, for example, for unlicensed drinking places. Corinthian Tom and Jerry Hawthorn were a pair of Regency bloods in Pierce Egan's 1821 bestseller *Life in London*, which was dramatised and toured the country as *Tom and Jerry*. It has also been suggested that it derived from the use as in 'jerry' built. Whatever the origin, and having two roots is possible, they were used all over the country.[18] Other names were more regionally specific, like 'tiddlywinks' or 'kidleywinks' in the Midlands and West Country.[19] What the new beersellers did do, naturally enough, was to adopt the sorts of names used for existing public houses, although some simply traded under the landlord's name, and with the sudden surge in numbers opened up a whole new chapter in the enormous diversity of pub names.[20]

Within a little under three months a total of 26,291 licences had been issued by the Excise. In 1831, the first full year of its operation, 31,937 were issued, trading alongside 50,547 publicans. These figures, it should be noted, do not correspond precisely to premises. The beer licence was not transferable and thus in a given year two or more licences might be granted to proprietors of a single house. In Manchester and Salford in the years 1836 to 1838 such cases amounted to 4.7, 11.1 and 10.6 per cent respectively of the total licences granted. With this in mind it was still the case that more than one in three drink retailers were now the new beersellers. Further, their introduction arrested the falling ratio of drinking places to population. Without them there would have been one house for around every 275 of the inhabitants of England and Wales. With them that now rose to one for every 168.[21] They opened throughout the country, but their incidence was broadly relative to the existing provision of public houses. In that sense free trade was achieved. In rural areas, with often few or no public houses, the result might indeed be startling. Twenty-two Somerset parishes with the same number of public houses, for example, now had ninety-one beershops between them. At Rottingdean, near Brighton, where the inhabitants had been restricted to just one public house, they now had four new beershops. In both cases a low ratio of one drinking place for over 800 inhabitants was raised to the national average. In the East Riding, similarly, the villagers of Ellerker, near South Cave, having been without a public house now had two new beerhouses. South Cave itself showed that even where provision was comparatively generous men were tempted into the beerhouse trade: within four years six publicans were joined by three beersellers.[22] The same was true of larger established towns, like Liverpool, Newcastle, Nottingham or Plymouth. All saw the creation of impressive numbers of new beerhouses, but in all of them the existing public houses remained in the majority.[23] In London the picture was broadly similar. The 4,073 public houses of the metro-politan police area represented a comparatively low level of provision at one for every 371 inhabitants. Whilst 1,182 beerhouses were now opened, reducing the ratio to one for every 288, they formed only about one in five drinking places.[24] The greatest effect was seen in those towns where population growth had markedly outstripped the supply of drinking places, particularly the new industrial centres. In Birmingham, Bradford, Leeds, Manchester and Salford the number of beerhouses within just a few years exceeded that of licensed public houses[25] (Figure 5).

Contemporaries almost immediately noted the drunkenness pro-duced by the change. Most often quoted in this respect is free-trade advocate Sydney Smith in a letter of 24 October: 'Everybody is drunk. Those who are not singing are sprawling.' This may have been hyperbole, but much the same was heard around the country. The previous day the *Leeds Mercury* had noted: 'We receive from many quarters grievous complaints of the demoralizing effects of this Act …' And in the following month, the *Royal Cornwall Gazette* was similarly reporting from the Camborne district of the mischief done by 'drunken frequenters of cheap beer shops'.[26] Faced with this vol-ume of complaint, the government was compelled to acknowledge, as Goulburn put it in June 1831, that 'inconveniences … had been felt, particularly in some of the agricultural districts', which went beyond what had been anticipated. Although it was not prepared to abandon the principle of the legislation, it did concede that enquiry was necessary.[27]

Two years later a parliamentary select committee duly concluded that 'considerable evils' had arisen from the management and conduct of beerhouses. Witnesses came disproportionately from rural south-ern and eastern England, which had been affected by the widespread and serious disturbances known as the Swing riots. This undoubt-edly coloured their evidence. The very first witness, the Reverend Robert Wright, a magistrate of Itchen Abbas near Winchester, placed the new beershops firmly at the centre of the trouble as 'the focus for the meeting of the different parties, and there all the mischief commenced'. More dramatically William Holmes, a former mayor of Arundel and justices' clerk of thirty-one years, saw from his own house in Lyminster that 'the three first fires were set alight by people who came from beershops'.[28] Historians have dismissed the connection, noting biases in the evidence itself and making the obvious points that the riots predated the introduction of the Act and beerhouses were a national, and the riots a regional, phenomenon. As Brian Harrison put it: 'It was absurd, though convenient, to assume that drink or drinksellers had actually inspired the riots.'[29] For contemporaries nevertheless this connection with subversion and riot clearly helped to damn the beerhouses. It was aired again during the 1830s and 1840s about the Chartist movement. In South Wales, for example, the *Cardiff and Merthyr Guardian* was convinced that beerhouses were a major cause of the promotion of Chartist activity. Or, as the magistrates in the West Riding reported: 'Our police are always looking for information but cannot get into the small parties who generally assemble at the Beer House, keeping out any but their own party.'[30]

The concern was linked to the class exclusivity of beerhouses and the lack of control which the authorities felt they had over them. Both customers and proprietors, it was claimed, lacked the respectability of the licensed victuallers. As the Reverend Wright put it: 'I do not think a respectable character ever enters them.' Similarly, John Weyland, the chairman of the Norfolk Quarter Sessions, claimed that a respectable alehouse keeper would not tolerate on his premises such persons as the rioters were drawn from. Beerhouses by definition were not subject to the same magisterial control as licensed houses and, further, were often in out-of-the-way locations.[31] All this in turn was linked with what undoubtedly were the greatest concerns voiced about the new houses – their connection with drunkenness, immorality and crime. The 1833 committee heard plenty of evidence on this score. William Holmes testified that the beerhouse at Lyminster had repeatedly been complained of for allowing cock-fighting, badger-baiting and a four-corner alley. Ten times the beer, he claimed, was consumed there than at the old public house. The head police officer at Warwick, Thomas Bellerby, blamed the twenty-four new beerhouses for an increase of crime, noting that three of their proprietors had been transported. They were frequented by prostitutes, thieves and boys, and two were even kept by unmarried couples, a domestic arrangement which the licensing magistrates would never countenance.[32]

Such complaints recur throughout the period of their existence independent of magistrates' authority, and little is to be gained from simply amassing examples. But it is not the whole story. The 1833 committee itself heard evidence which belied its overall conclusion. The MP for Totnes, Jasper Parrott, lauded the Act as 'one of the greatest boons ever given to the landed interest and to the consumers of beer'. He characterised the new beersellers as decent labourers and reported no complaints of them or their houses. A number of beersellers, naturally enough, gave positive evidence. George Bush of Westminster Bridge Road, for example, catered for respectable skilled workmen. There was also a customer, of the Globe beershop in Clerkenwell, watchmaker Joseph Hogan, who went there in the morning for a glass and a look at the paper, and sometimes too in the afternoon if he was 'dry'.[33] Elsewhere positive voices are also heard. Robert Sharp in South Cave wrote in April 1834: 'What a deal of trouble several people seem to give themselves, on the immorality of Beer Shops ... I do not believe one word of the *general* bad effects which are said to arise ...' Rather more pithily, from Clayton near Bradford, a correspondent to the local paper wrote in May 1837: 'I contend that the working classes are indebted to them [Peel and Wellington] for that act which allows others besides Magistrates' favourites and dependents to sell beer.'[34] Similar positive evidence can be found in two further parliamentary investigations. The first, a committee of the House of Lords of 1849 to 1850, looked specifically at the Act's operation. The second made its enquiries as part of a much more wide-ranging investigation of the licensing system, and reported in 1854. In their conclusions, however, both were critical. The first had 'no hesitation in stating, that the expectations of those who proposed the existing system had not been realized'. The second, which was actually favourable to free-trade ideas, put it succinctly: 'The beershop system has proved a failure.'[35]

It was the negative view which became the more widely held, at least among the respectable and governing classes. What is perhaps surprising in view of the extent of condemnation is how little change was made to the essentials of the system for so long. The legislation of 1834 and 1840 mostly enacted resolutions which the 1833 committee had made to bring about improvement. Some of them had in fact been put forward in the debates on the original Bill. That of 1834 required prospective beersellers to obtain a certificate of good character signed by six rated inhabitants of the parish, who must not be connected to the drink trade, and certified by one of the overseers. The committee of the House of Lords reporting in 1850 found that this was inefficient and did not prevent undesirables from obtaining licences, an allegation which had in fact led to the removal of the same requirement for licensed houses in the legislation of 1828.[36] A distinction was created, for the first time, between on- and off-licences. The latter did not require a character certificate and cost just one guinea. The cost of an on-licence was raised to three. Its impact also was not dramatic. Numbers of off-licences peaked in 1839 at almost 6,000, or just over 13 per cent of beer licences issued, before falling away again to fewer than one in ten in 1846, and fewer than 7 per cent for the whole period 1856 to 1869.[37]

In a further effort to improve the standard of beerhouse premises, the qualifying rateable value was raised. The 1833 committee had heard evidence as to their low value and minimal public rooms. The Reverend Wright described them as 'mere cottages', with seldom more than two rooms and an average value of just 50s. Similarly, in the area around Battle in Sussex, they were described by the magistrates' clerk as usually two- or three-roomed cottages, with values beginning at just £1. The highest rated was £11 in the centre of Battle itself. From a larger town, Leeds, evidence was slightly differing, but houses were generally in the range of £5 to £10 value, substantially less than public houses.[38] The 1834 Act provided for a £10 annual value for places where the population was over 5,000; that of 1840 introduced a sliding scale, also based on population, from £8 in rural areas, £11 in places over 2,500 people, up to a minimum of £15 for towns and cities of 10,000 or more. Allegations of evasion of this provision were made, either by overseers falsifying the rating certificate it was their duty to provide or by proprietors joining together two or more properties for the purposes of the valuation whilst trading from just one of them.[39] It is difficult to isolate the effect of this change from the improvement of beerhouse property for commercial reasons and the related desire to obtain a full publican's licence, but the value of premises certainly did rise. A parliamentary return of 1839 showed that 43 per cent of beerhouses were rated at under £10, including 10.1 per cent under £5, and 23.8 per cemt at over £15. By 1853 whereas 21.1 per cent were now rated at under £10, 54.7 per cent were now at or above £15.[40] The 1833 committee evidence shows that initially, many beerhouses were simply opened in private premises. This continued. Alternatively, a shop might be converted. In Portsmouth, for example, the Ivy House was for almost twenty years the Ivy Dairy before its change of use. Shopkeepers, or craftsmen, also sold beer alongside their other business (Figure 4). But from the first they were also purpose-built, often as part of a larger housing development. Bradford builder Thomas Wadsworth erected eight houses on a plot of land he had purchased in Bowling Old Lane, three of which formed the Bridge Tavern in 1850. Many beerhouses were thus little distinguished, except by their sign, from the houses which surrounded them. Internally they followed the arrangements of existing small publics, as at the Bridge, with bar, tap room and parlour[41] (Figure 7).

After 1840 there were no more regulatory changes to beerhouses, but a further measure of free-trade for the sale of wine was extended to them. This was the work of Gladstone as Chancellor, who wished to promote the sale of wine by extending its social reach, as he put it, to 'the whole middle classes – of the lowest order of the middle classes, and even of the better portion of the working classes –' through 'new, and cleaner channels for consumption'. It was also envisaged in part as a temperance measure, promoting the sale of light wine in favour of strong spirits and linking the habit of drinking more closely with eating. Accordingly, duty was reduced, and in his Refreshment Houses and Wine Licences Act of 1860 the trade was opened up in two ways. Shopkeepers were permitted the off-sale of wine, and Refreshment Houses, that is places open for 'public refreshment, resort and entertainment', which also sold food, could now offer their customers wine. To clear up any doubts the facility was explicitly extended the following year to the beerhouses.[42] The overall impact was limited, with just 3,237 refreshment house wine on-licences in 1870, and take-up by beersellers was also low. Wine consumption did rise, but so did that of beer and spirits, and wine benefited more than the others only during the 1860s.[43]

There is, finally, one minor aspect of free trade in beer to consider, that in table beer. This had originally been introduced as an intermediate level of strength between strong and small beer. In 1802 small and table were merged to the single category of table as the weaker brew traditionally for children, women and servants. In 1830, shortly after the Beer Act came into effect, a Treasury Order interpreted the 1802 statute to the effect that table beer could be sold without any kind of licence – justices' or Excise – if for not more than $1\frac{1}{2}d$ a quart.[44] For this reason it is difficult to get a clear picture of the trade. As the Webbs put it, deploring this for them extreme example of free trade, such 'swankey shops', as they were widely named, were 'unenumerated, untaxed, unlicensed, and unrestricted'.[45] A Birmingham brewery agent claimed in 1833 that the trade was unprofitable, as it was not possible to brew a pleasing article at such a price. It is probably significant that the main evidence of their existence comes from the economically troubled 'hungry forties'. In Somerset houses for its sale were known as 'Tib Shops'.[46] They seem to have been common in the West Riding. Several were reported to have opened in the neighbourhood of Holmfirth in August 1843. Around Bradford many houses, not infrequently kept by women, sold what was locally known as 'stiff shackle', 'brewer's washings' according to the report. The constables of Horton sent a memorial to the Home Secretary describing them as fitted up like regular licensed premises and voicing concerns about the low character of the customers, after-hours drinking and their use by thieves. The law was brought to bear on them. In September 1848 seven table-beer retailers were charged with selling their beer for more than the law allowed. And in the following year again, when a retailer charged with keeping a disorderly house maintained that it was impossible for any man or woman to get drunk on beer at that price. The justices at Halifax, at the end of 1849, decided that the beer could not be sold in quantities of less than four and a half gallons. Sale was still reported around Wakefield in 1850, and its use as a cover for the sale of stronger beer elsewhere attracted comment, although the Excise office itself claimed that overall there were not many complaints.[47] In 1861 Gladstone brought in a requirement for an Excise licence and confined it to off-sale. The number of licences issued peaked at 2,170 in 1866.[48] They still aroused comment. The table-beer retailers of Burton upon Trent were reported as selling 'bumclink' – bad ale which had been returned – for up to 6d a quart.[49] But the number of licences issued continued to decline, and plummeted when they were returned to magistrates' control in 1869.

Before we examine the legislation of 1869, we must chart the trends in the number of beerhouses to that year. An initial peak of licences issued of 40,102 was reached in 1837. Numbers then fell away into the 1840s to a low in 1843 of 31,227. They then rose, but slowly, and the 1837 figure was not again reached until 1853. As the trend in beerhouse numbers mirrored that for beer consumption, economic considerations were clearly paramount. To give one local example: in Bradford the closure of twenty beerhouses in the previous six months was attributed in February 1841 to the poverty of the people. The national total then stayed fairly level until a surge from the mid-1860s took it to 49,130 by 1869, again mirroring the trend of beer consumption and the wider growth of the economy. The local and regional distribution of beerhouses remained broadly the same as in the first years of their introduction, but it was influenced in particular places, as we shall see, by the policies of local licensing justices on the grant of full-licences.[50]

The Act of 1840 had not been the end of legislative efforts against the beerhouses. Several proposals were brought forward over these years, including a Bill of 1857, which would have put them under the control of the magistrates. None was successful, however, despite the widespread and continuing condemnation.[51] But by the late 1860s enthusiasm for free licensing had definitely waned, and was dealt a further blow by the ending in 1866 of a brief experiment in its use in Liverpool. In contrast, the star of the magistracy had risen since the years of widespread criticism. Thus in 1869 a Conservative private member, Henry Selwin-Ibbetson, succeeded in getting 'an unresisting parliament' to require beersellers in future to obtain a justices' licence.[52]

The Wine and Beerhouse Act took effect on 15 July 1869.[53] A justices' certificate was now required for both on- and off-sale of beer. It provided just four grounds for its refusal, thus limiting the justices' discretion over what came to be termed 'ante-69' beerhouses. These were:

that the applicant failed to produce satisfactory evidence of good character;

that the house, or adjacent house owned or occupied by the applicant, was of a disorderly character, or frequented by thieves, prostitutes or persons of bad character;

that the applicant had previously forfeited a licence for misconduct;
that the house or the applicant was not duly qualified by law [its rateable value, for example].

The law was in place in time for the brewster sessions and gave licensing benches the opportunity to get rid of the kind of house that had been for so long the subject of complaint. Throughout the country magistrates did so. In rural Bedfordshire, for example, 18 of the existing 70 beerhouses were refused a licence, of which 13 were for harbouring thieves and bad characters and receiving stolen goods, with three having insufficient rateable value and two failing to give the required notice of application. Up in Cumberland, 35 were refused from 169 beerhouses, based on previous convictions or other police evidence of misconduct. The same was true of towns. In Liverpool 156 were refused for reasons of the character of the applicant; in Blackburn 73.[54] In Bradford 60 beerhouses, about 13 per cent of the existing total, were now refused. Almost without exception they were in the slum districts adjoining the centre of the town. In one notorious street, Southgate, licences were refused to William Brook, who kept the Brick House, because of thieves and disorderly characters; John Crabtree of the British Queen, because of prostitutes and thieves; Mary Gould of the Uncle Tom's Cabin, for having prostitutes in four adjoining houses; and Samuel Woodrow of the Sportsman Inn, whose housekeeper was said to be a prostitute. Objections to refusal were not entertained where, for example, a large sum of money was said to have been invested in the house, or the applicant had not actually been convicted of an offence, or where the disorderly conduct was laid at the door of a previous tenant. Whilst expressing sympathy with such cases, the editor of the local paper praised the bench for carrying out the Act 'in its spirit and intent'.[55]

This was typical. The Act met with general approval. It was renewed, and its provisions made permanent in 1872. As the House of Lords Committee on Intemperance concluded in its report of 1879, praising its effects: 'The process of weeding out the most disorderly beerhouses has been carried on throughout the country.'[56] By 1871 the total number of beerhouses had fallen by 6,540 to 42,590. This represented just over 13 per cent of those in existence prior to the Act.[57] Whilst this reduction was not wholly due to the disorderly nature of the house, clearly it was the reason in a substantial proportion of cases. But clearly too, disorder was a long way from the whole of the beerhouse story. I return first, however, to those houses which had remained licensed by the justices.

5

The Licensed Trade
1830–1869

The opening of thousands of beerhouses was bound to have an impact on the existing publicans, who continued to be licensed by the magistracy. They certainly feared that it would, as we saw. An analysis of their position during the period of free trade in beer will inevitably also be concerned with the relationship between the two sectors. In this chapter I shall examine the policies pursued by the licensing justices and their impact on numbers. I then go on to look at changes within the licensed trade, focusing in particular upon the development of the gin- or dram shop, or as it came to be known – the gin palace.

Let us look at numbers first. The statistics refer to full on-licences. As these were required by any establishment wanting to sell wine or spirits as well as beer for consumption on the premises they include not only public houses but also hotels, restaurants, railway refreshment rooms and concert halls. The proportion within the total of all those places rose, although it is not possible to give a precise overall figure. In the year to 5 January 1830 there were 50,442 such full on-licences. Over the almost forty years of free trade in beer the number rose by a little under 19,000 to 69,369 in the year to September 1869, an increase of 37.5 per cent.[1] The number of beerhouses in those years of course had risen from none to over 49,000. That growth, in contrast to the beerhouses, was fairly even across the period. This modest expansion, which contrasts with the long preceding period of contraction, continued the small upward trend of the 1820s.

This overall growth once again masks considerable local variation. Mapping those variations is no simple task, however, as the 1828 Act no longer required local clerks to the justices to keep registers of licence holders. Some continued to do so, but many apparently did not. The picture has to be drawn from a variety of sources: parliamentary inquiries, commercial directories, which from the 1820s are generally pretty reliable guides, and the newspaper reports of brewster sessions, which become increasingly detailed from the 1830s. In some places the number remained unchanged or actually fell. This was particularly the case in rural areas and older towns. In the East Riding South Cave's six public houses of 1828 dropped to four by the mid-1870s. At Chester around 170 in the early 1830s fell slightly to 163 by 1872. But the same was true of the industrial giant of Manchester, where the number of licences fell from 502 at the beginning of the 1840s to 479 in 1869. Elsewhere there were varying degrees of growth. In Norwich, another old provincial capital, where the number of beerhouses was negligible, full-licences rose by 18.6 per cent from 501 to 594 by 1876. This was slightly less than the industrial city of Birmingham where, in contrast, the number of beerhouses almost doubled between the late 1830s and 1869. Finally, some towns experienced marked growth, like Derby or Newcastle, where the number of public houses more than doubled.[2]

It was the policies pursued by individual benches of licensing magistrates which were the means to producing those differences. They clearly varied between places, but also changed at different times at the same place. They covered the entire range of options, from granting them to all eligible applicants to complete restriction. Of the small number of free-licensing benches the most important was Liverpool, due to its size and corresponding prominence in national debate on the subject. There the number of full-licences had risen by almost a quarter from 1,169 in 1830–31 to 1,452 by 1848. During those years the number of beerhouses had doubled the

501 taken out within a year of the Act's operation. The comparatively modest growth of full-licences represented, however, but a small proportion of those applying for one. In the seven years 1846 to 1852 the number of applications averaged over 200 a year, of which fewer than one in ten were granted. The justices based their decisions, as indeed did many up and down the country, on police reports and personal inspection of the premises. They brought to bear three criteria: the suitability of the applicant and the premises and the needs of the locality. The latter was the main reason for refusal. Before the parliamentary committee which examined the regulation of all types of place of public entertainment during 1852 and 1853, the clerk to the Liverpool justices, John Wybergh, deplored the lack of any guiding principle behind the decisions, which ultimately came down to the 'varying temper' of the bench. In this he was supported by some of its members, who blamed the lack of clarity in their powers. One of them, Robertson Gladstone, brother of the future prime minister, felt with Wybergh that the operation of supply and demand would regulate matters satisfactorily. He also rehearsed another familiar argument in seeking to curb the influence of brewers on the licensing process. A meeting of the bench had in fact narrowly chosen, on the mayor's casting vote, to adopt such a policy, but opposition from some members, and the fact that not all the magistrates had been present, meant that it was taken no further at that time.[3]

With a change in the feeling of the bench the policy was subsequently adopted, but by a narrow majority and only briefly between 1862 and 1865. A total of 370 licences were granted in those years. A further shift in the composition of the bench led to the policy then being rescinded. Edward Lawrence, a magistrate who joined the bench in 1866 and helped to bring this about, argued simply that more drinking places meant more intemperance.[4] The Liverpool 'experiment' was not widely followed. Where it was adopted, as at Prescot and St Helens, and also in Norwich, its pursuit was either limited or short-lived. In the former, justices looked at both the character of the applicant and the quality of the premises before grant, whilst at the latter they pursued the policy only spasmodically towards respectable applicants whenever the minority of free-trade justices managed to press their case.[5] Overall, the fading of free licensing as a viable policy option could only help to strengthen the wider feeling against free trade in beer, which ultimately produced the Act of 1869.

Whilst in the above cases older concerns about free licensing or the brewers' power seem to have been the main driving force, elsewhere the advent of the beerhouse was crucial. Some benches deliberately granted full-licences to prevent their establishment, as at Dartmouth, where the number of public houses was doubled.[6] Others saw the grant of a full-licence to a beerhouse as a means to raise their general character, by holding out its expectation to deserving applicants for well-built premises, and by the greater control which they then would have over them. The Leeds bench early adopted this approach. Where a public house was deemed desirable, preference was given to a respectable beershop keeper.[7] Bradford's licensing justices also pursued this strategy from the late 1840s, granting some forty new licences, including eleven in a single year. The policy was not sustained, however, and by 1859 the bench was firmly setting its face against any additional licences so long as the 'beerhouse system' continued.[8] In Portsmouth justices pursued the same strategy, but the timing differed. There, for thirty years after the Beer Act, almost no new licences were granted. In the twelve years to 1853, for example, the only successful applications were for two hotels and the East Hampshire Cricket Club. Those from beerhouse keepers almost invariably failed. But from the late 1850s the justices began to feel that this policy had succeeded only in removing the incentive for beerhouse proprietors to improve their premises. Reversing it saw the number of full on-licences rise from 238 in 1858 to 332 by 1870. All but three of those granted were to existing beerhouses. These had to be substantial premises. Where structural alterations had been carried out to meet with the justices' approval, these cost typically above £1,000. This meant in fact that many more beerhouses were refused than were granted a full-licence, with inevitable, and familiar, complaints about the process and its consistency.[9] Finally, there was in some places a consistent policy of complete restriction. This was most dramatic in Manchester where, as we saw, the number of full-licences actually fell. The result was a huge growth of beerhouses, reaching 2,143 by 1869. As at Bradford this growth in itself was seen as justifying the restrictive policy, which had been pursued since the bench was first constituted in 1839.[10]

The disappointed beerseller became a common figure. Many who entered the trade clearly had aspirations to what they saw as the more lucrative and prestigious sector. Certainly where they had an opportunity to raise that status relatively simply, as in their census return, some took it. Getting on for one in five of the beerhouse keepers in the 1851 census of Bradford were actually recorded as 'innkeeper' or 'publican'.[11] The select committee sitting in 1852 and 1853 heard a lot of evidence from, and on behalf of, aggrieved beersellers, including the familiar allegations of magistrates' partiality and the influence of brewers. It thus concluded in 1854: 'Beer-house keeping requires but little capital; many are attracted to it and overstock the trade by the hope that it will lead to a license, and though disappointed and unsuccessful, continue in the business.'[12] Complainants came particularly from London, including individual beerhouse keepers and trade representatives like the solicitor to the Metropolitan Beersellers' Society, who described the licensing system as a 'lottery'.[13] Although particular allegations of partiality were strongly denied, there is no doubt that licensing policy overall in the capital was comparatively restrictive, and that there was considerable variation between licensing divisions. Statistics for the first half of the 1850s show that 20.6 per cent of 2,448 applications in the capital as a whole were successful, but this included one in three in Croydon, for example, but in Southwark only one in ten.[14] Over the whole period of free trade the number of full-licences in the metropolitan district rose from 4,285 to 6,549 (in 1868) or 52.8 per cent, whilst the number of beerhouses almost doubled. Within the overall total of drinking places the proportion of beerhouses rose from about a quarter to over 40 per cent.[15]

When they were first created some magistrates took the view that it was not Parliament's intention that they should be 'stepping-stones' to a full-licence, and consequently refused all applications.[16] But in general, as elsewhere, the beerhouse became the natural route into the trade. By the early 1850s Robert Tubbs, the chairman of the Kensington bench, covering Kensington itself, Fulham, Chelsea, Hammersmith, Chiswick, Ealing, Acton and Willesden, professed to regard the well-conducted beerhouse as an asset. Most new applicants were indeed beer retailers, although once again only a minority was successful, just 80 of 449 applications in the years 1844 to 1856.[17] But of course the unsuccessful applicants could still trade as beerhouses.

Such policies worked to improve the stock of licensed premises. Wherever justices granted licences, even in those areas of free or relatively liberal licensing, it was only to substantial premises, as we saw in Portsmouth. There, a successful beerhouse like the Briton, licensed in 1862, had a bar, bar parlour, smoking room, tap room and club room, a range of rooms which was now quite typical (Figure 7). Others offered accommodation, like the Victoria Arms the following year, with seven bedrooms plus stabling for eighteen horses. This latter provision was often insisted upon. The Leeds bench, for example, in 1840 granted full-licences to two beerhouses only on condition that six or eight stands for horses should be erected.[18] In restrictive Manchester the stock of full-licences was not static. The demolition of some older parts of the town for improvements, such as along Deansgate, naturally included public houses, and the justices were willing to redistribute some at least of their licences to newly developing districts.[19] The redevelopment of central areas in this way worked particularly to remove older licensed houses, including small, old-fashioned publics, to which the grant of a new licence would no longer be contemplated. Thus, negatively too, the overall stock of licensed premises was improved.

Redevelopment, however, also claimed many of the substantial old inns. In Leeds, for example, the Rose and Crown and the Talbot in Briggate both made way for shopping arcades, for which their long narrow plots made them ideally suited. This shape also made the yards of inns useful central locations for houses as the populations of towns expanded. This was the case in Leeds and York, for example. In the latter, in once prosperous Walmgate, among several publics developed in this way, in an extreme case the yard of the Britannia enclosed sixteen two-roomed cottages, which at the census of 1851 housed no fewer than 171 persons.[20] Demotion, or demolition, was thus the common fate of an institution many of whose functions, as we saw, were being lost by 1830. For the coaching trade the arrival of the railway invariably signalled the end. Wherever a line was opened, the immediate result was the cessation of coach services, which could not compete for speed, comfort, cost or capacity, although there was a transitional period when feeder coaches took passengers to the nearest railway connection. Bradford, for example, not reached by the railway until 1846, offered by 1834 the Perseverance coach from the Bowling Green Inn to Manchester to connect with the Liverpool train and the Railway coach from the Sun Inn to Leeds for trains to Selby and the steam packets to Hull.[21] In the provision of accommodation for travellers, inns now faced competition from new, purpose-built hotels. Of course existing premises were rebuilt, like the Bull and Mouth as the Queen Hotel in 1830. In a spa town like Harrogate, similarly, older inns were extended or rebuilt, like the White Hart Hotel in 1846. But visitors could also there put up at a growing number of lodging houses and new hotels.[22] The railway of course also brought the railway hotel, such as the Midland at Derby in 1840, enriching the urban scene around the country. Hotels like these, the growing number of private gentlemen's clubs and from the 1860s in particular the proliferation of restaurants, also provided alternative venues for the Victorian diner, whether formal or informal.[23] And, as noted, with the exception of private clubs all those premises required a justices' on-licence and thus represented a growing proportion of the total licences issued.

In other ways the use of inns and public houses was declining. For commercial purposes it further contracted with the continued growth of specialist accommodation in warehouses, exchanges, auction rooms and solicitors' offices. But there was, as ever, local variation. In rural east Kent pubs were used by auctioneers, dealers and commercial travellers into the twentieth century.[24] This was true also of administrative business. In the early 1860s, for example, the chief constable of Cornwall noted that petty sessions in six places were still held at public houses, and in rural areas particularly coroners' inquests continued to be convened at them throughout the century. The Liverpool coroner reported this in outlying districts in the 1890s.[25] Nevertheless, their use in general for such purposes had become increasingly unusual before the law was brought to bear on the subject, prohibiting the use of licensed premises for public administration in 1882, 1894 and, coroners' courts finally, in 1902. Even then it was permissible if no other premises were available, and in Edwardian rural East Anglia they were still convened, and parish councils sometimes met, in public houses.[26]

Political life was in this respect something of an exception. The growth in the number of contested elections increased the centrality of public houses during the campaign – as committee rooms, for treating voters and general alcoholic celebration, although this encompassed beerhouses too. The spirit of eighteenth century elections thus lived on well into the next century, as much in the new industrial constituencies as in the old counties and pocket boroughs. As the *Bradford Observer* commented, looking back on the town's elections from the calm and order of that of 1874 to a time 'when every public house was a political rendezvous and beer was to be had ad lib'.[27] The expansion of the electorate after the Reform Act of 1867 and the introduction in 1872 of the secret ballot, and with it the ending of nomination day and the hourly announcement of the progress of the poll, contributed to its decline. Legislation in 1883 and 1884, which included a ban on committee rooms in licensed premises in parliamentary and then municipal elections, effectively ended the connection.[28]

Both this diminution of functions and the competition posed by the new beerhouses stimulated the further growth of the gin palace.

As we saw, gin- or dram shops had been opened from the 1780s in larger towns, and particularly London, either by spirit dealers or by publicans converting the whole, or part, of their premises. At the end of November 1829 the Middlesex Quarter Sessions had issued a broadside condemning the 'alarming increase of gin-shops ... by the conversion of what used to be quiet respectable public-houses, where the labouring population could find the accommodation of a tap-room or parlour, into flaming dram-shops, having no accommodation for persons to sit down, and where the only allurement held out was the promise of "Cheap Gin"'.[29] By 1834 London police magistrate Robert Broughton was likening the number of such conversions to a 'torrent', and his colleague in Southwark, Robert Chambers, specifically linked the conversion of 'old victualling houses' into 'splendid gin-shops' to the Beer Act.[30] The Select Committee on Drunkenness, which heard this evidence, also was treated to a description of the process at a public house nearly opposite him by George Wilson, a grocer of Tothill Street, not far from Westminster Abbey:

> ... it was converted into the very opposite of what it had been, a low dirty public-house, with only one doorway, into a splendid edifice, the front ornamented with pilasters, supporting a handsome cornice and entablature, and ballustrades, and the whole elevation remarkably striking and handsome; the doorways were increased in number from one, and that a small one only three or four feet wide, to three, and each one of these eight to 10 feet wide; the floor was sunk so as to be level with the street; and the doors and windows glazed with very large single squares of plate glass, and the gas fittings of the most costly description; the whole excited the surprise of the neighbourhood.[31]

The gin palace thus incorporated features that were transforming retailing generally. Plate glass and gas-lighting enabled the creation of distinctive, conspicuous and enticing shop fronts. Significantly, the designer of what is sometimes claimed to be the first gin palace, Thompson and Fearon's wine and spirit stores on Holborn Hill, was a pioneer of improved shop fronts.[32] Dickens, in a sketch of gin shops which appeared in early 1835, described how this retail revolution had spread like an epidemic through London's trades until it 'burst forth with tenfold violence among the publicans and keepers of "wine vaults" ... knocking down all the old public-houses, and depositing splendid mansions, stone balustrades, rose-wood fittings, immense lamps, and illuminated clocks, at the corner of every street'. He went on to note the interior, 'even gayer than the exterior', beginning with its 'bar of French-polished mahogany, elegantly carved, [which] extends the whole width of the place.'[33] Serving over the counter in this way was another important innovation of the gin shop, and probably dates back to their late eighteenth-century development. The bar ceased to be the private office of the publican and became instead the centrepiece of the establishment. The transition is captured in an architectural guide, which included the design of public houses, first published in 1833. This differentiated between the office and store type of bar of an inn and the bar and counter of a public house where many customers would drink standing up, or had come for off-sales. And just as the beer engine had made more efficient the dispensing of beer, so taps and cocks connected by tubes to casks speeded up the service of spirits.[34] This was clearly an advantage in a busy urban public house with a large passing trade and many customers purchasing for home consumption. Thompson and Fearon reckoned that about a third of their customers and a good deal more than a third of their takings came from off-sales.[35]

By this time gin shops had been established in towns throughout the country. For Manchester two witnesses to the 1834 committee gave contrasting figures and descriptions. One claimed that two-thirds of the public houses had opened dram shops, none as splendid as those in London, but 'improving in splendour', whilst the other counted 130 dram shops with separate doors to the vault, and of these 'gin palaces', or 'gin-temples', 50 were 'of the most splendid description'. In Leeds the number of spirit shops had grown in the last five years and the premises had increased in size. A witness from Bristol noted little public houses fitted up for the sale of spirits, and from Preston there were no gin palaces, just a parlour used for a spirit shop.[36] They continued thus to develop, with minor variations on the basic theme. A French observer in Manchester, Leon Faucher, wrote in 1844 of earlier, primitive dram shops, with just 'a candle placed behind the window', now transformed when 'the dim lights have been replaced by the dazzling gas; the doors have been enlarged; the pot-house has become a gin-shop; and the gin-shop a species of palace'.[37] Bolton at the close of that decade had vaults where spirits were sold over the counter, but which, it was claimed, 'were not very splendid'.[38] By 1865 across the Pennines in Bradford, there were said to be fifty spirit vaults, or dram shops, more than a third of the total licensed premises in the town. Among them were the Commercial dram shop in Tyrrel Street with its 'bright, pewter-topped counter', or that in a cellar at the Spotted Ox in Ivegate, 'brilliantly lighted, adorned with gorgeously painted barrels and shining taps, and fitted up in the most expensive style'.[39]

Much of what we know of the gin palace or dram shop is through disapproving, if sometimes fascinated, eyes (Figure 6). That disapproval was based upon a number of concerns. First was their attraction to a particularly low class of customer. This was especially notable where the gin shop had been opened at existing licensed premises. As the mayor of Leeds put it to the town's licensing sessions of 1837, in expressing his 'sorrow' that dram shops had been attached to the premises of 'highly respectable innkeepers' for the inducement of the 'least respectable class of customers'.[40] Second was the fact of their apparent appeal to women and children. Grocer Wilson, observing the gin shop opposite his home, had been particularly agitated by this, describing the customers surrounding the place at 7 a.m. on Sunday, including the Hogarthian image of a woman 'almost in a state of nudity' with an infant at the breast, plied with gin. Reinforcing the point in its eyes, the committee heard impressive statistical evidence from observation of fourteen 'leading gin-shops' around London. In one week, 40.3 per cent of customers entering were women and 6.8 per cent children. Or, on average each day, nearly 1,300 women and children were entering each house.[41] Third was the animosity felt towards the rapid consumption which it was believed they encouraged by providing no, or minimal, seating and thus forcing customers to drink standing up. As the chief constable of Newcastle described it: 'the long bar or rapid spirit-drinking system.'[42] Fourth was an amalgam of familiar complaints, including rising crime and equally rising poor rates and the deleterious effects of excessive spirit consumption on the nation's workforce.[43]

As London had from the late eighteenth century, provincial authorities too sought to curb the spread of the gin shop, with equally limited success. In Manchester the new borough bench from 1839 had set its face against conversions to gin palaces by insisting that a house be run as when it was first licensed and by getting new applicants to promise not to convert. But as the clerk to the justices, Thomas Higson, explained, after ten or so years of the policy's successful application the bench had been advised that they had in fact no power to interfere in this way with the layout of premises and it was rescinded. The result was that by the mid-1870s over 80 per cent of the town's licensed premises, according to a then member of the bench, were 'mere dram shops'.[44] The licensing justices in Bradford faced the same problem. Efforts to halt dram-shop conversions were made from the 1830s onwards, but were unavailing, with, as we saw, over a third of the town's public houses so converted by 1865. In that year the chief constable presented a report to the licensing justices outlining alterations at several public houses since the previous year, which had either created a dram shop or enlarged an existing one. In one case, that of the Nag's Head in Kirkgate, where a dram shop had been reopened despite earlier warnings as to its conduct, the licence was refused on the grounds that it was no longer a proper inn capable of performing those functions. A new landlord, Samuel Roberts, had in fact spent £2,000 on the place, extending the dram shop into two further rooms and the kitchen and raising the ceiling by removing an upstairs room. Roberts successfully appealed to the quarter sessions, which judged that there was no evidence of misconduct against him or that the alterations made it ineligible to be an inn. This would seem finally to have settled the matter, as the justices took no further action except in cases of misconduct. In this way the bench was finally able to remove the licence of the Nag's Head in 1882 and that of another dram shop two years later.[45] However much some urban benches might then disapprove of the gin palace, in practice they faced limits to their powers. Over alterations it had been shown that they had no legal authority. This was finally granted by the Licensing Act of 1874, but only in respect of new premises, which was not in turn extended to all alterations until the 1902 Licensing Act.

With these developments, however, we are getting ahead of ourselves. What made the gin palace possible then and what is its significance in the history of the pub? It was an urban phenomenon and thus flourished as a result of the huge growth of towns and cities in Victorian England. It was based too on a high level of spirit consumption, which was to peak in the mid-1870s, as we shall see. Although it represented an escape from poverty for many of its customers, it was in the end based on their ability to pay for its services, which was clearly increasing. This was a market opportunity, and one which for many existing publicans was made all the more attractive by the decline of many of the older functions of inns and the arrival of the new beerhouses on the drinking scene. It represented also innovation in the retailing of alcoholic drink. This was in the manner of its service, with the development of the bar counter for the more rapid turnover of a fluctuating urban scene and in its setting, with all that the epithet 'palace' conveyed.

These developments had a much wider impact on the pub scene. We must remember also that many gin shops were in fact one part of premises which also retained other drinking spaces – their parlours and tap rooms and so on (Figure 7). But the gin-palace style, so to speak, fed widely into public-house decoration. This is true, for example, of a 'first class tavern' like the Clarendon Hotel in London, built in 1846. It had a parlour, private parlour, bar parlour, tap room and bar on the ground floor. There was traditional public-house furniture, like the deal tables, wooden forms and wooden settles around the walls in the tap room, or in the parlour, where the settles were of mahogany not deal and the seats had horsehair stuffing. But the bar was fitted up in palatial style with a 'painted and panelled' counter with a metal top and twelve brass spirit taps plus a seven-motion beer engine with ivory pulls. Above the bar were shelves for the spirit casks. The 'fine plate chimney-glass' in a mahogany frame was matched by the plate-glass lining of the Spanish mahogany door leading from the bar to the bar parlour.[46] These in fact became common features in many pubs.

In the later nineteenth century the gin palace came to be thus rather one style of pub than a particular type of establishment. Pubs still had rooms described as dram shops. They were noted, for example, in a survey of York pubs in 1902. But it seems likely that publicans by then generally wished to get away from the rather sordid overtones of the 'dram'. George Wolstenholme's Dram Shop in High Petergate, York, which opened in about 1869, had by 1887 become Haigh's Vaults.[47] But the gin-palace style was also to reach its greatest magnificence at the close of the century.

6

Running a Pub

In the mid–Victorian public house there were a number of influences working towards homogeneity, but it remained at the same time an extremely heterogeneous institution. We have seen the decline of the coaching inn and the merging of the tavern into the generality of public houses. Allied to those trends was the disappearance, to a large extent, of the middle and upper classes from the world of the public house. There were also a number of influences which had the effect of making premises as a whole more substantial. These included growing urban demand and the associated development of the gin palace, the desire of beerhouse proprietors to obtain a full-licence and the imposition of legal requirements for a minimum rateable value. The spread of the gin-palace style to public houses generally may also be seen in this light. A further influence came from the growth of opposition to drink, not only from the temperance movement but also more widely in society. As the respectable classes ceased to use public houses, and as drink came to be identified as a major social problem, it was natural to conflate the problem as 'drink and the public house'. But despite this, it remained a varied institution, ranging in scale from the back-street or rural beerhouse to the large urban gin palace, from the basic little publics of Ellerker to the comforts and splendour of London's Clarendon Hotel.

It is from these years – the 1850s and 1860s – that one can begin to think of an institution called the 'pub', subsuming under that name the various types of drinking place, just as the term public house had earlier come to cover the different eighteenth-century establishments. It is, however, perhaps oddly, difficult to be precise on the origin of the use of the term. On the face of it, it is a fairly obvious contraction of public house and one which surely must have been used. Indeed, a diarist recording a journey in 1812 found 'so many handy pubs all the Way'. The Old Bailey proceedings, which include hundreds of references to drinking places, have only two which use it, both in the form 'pub-house', in 1825 and 1830.[1] But an 1859 dictionary of slang terms in 'every-day use and employed by thousands' in London (and apparently the Universities of Oxford and Cambridge) cites its use for a 'public' or 'public house'. Ancient usages, such as 'booze' or 'boozing ken' are also listed, along with the newer 'jerry' for a beerhouse, together with others which do not appear to have gained wide circulation like 'suck-casse', 'panny' or 'lush-crib' for a public house and 'sluicery' for a gin shop.[2] Part of the difficulty in pinning down the use of pub is that so much of our knowledge comes via the literate and respectable in society in sources such as parliamentary inquiries or newspapers. Either 'public house' or 'beerhouse' are given in full, or the establishment is named, even when, for example, witnesses in court cases are apparently being quoted. Certainly in my detailed examination of a local Bradford paper the term pub was not used until the late 1880s in a report of the 'Ideal Pub' proposed by the Bishop of Chester.[3] Other newspaper studies may turn up earlier references. By this time, however, it was becoming common usage. Jack London, for example, delving into the abyss of the East End in 1902, certainly used pub.[4] Although it is thus impossible to assign a precise point in time when it became the generic term, from the middle decades of Victoria's reign one is nevertheless looking at an institution that we can call the pub.

In this and succeeding chapters I shall then speak of the pub, but it will be necessary to keep in mind the institution's protean nature and to range back again to its origins. I will begin with the men and women who presided over the institution and go on to examine what was involved in running a pub. It is beyond the scope of my space here to seek to answer those questions both chronologically and by type of establishment, but the questions are common to all, and the answers too, whilst of course differing in many ways, often have common themes. Accordingly, I will address myself to my period as a whole.

The designations of the proprietors were naturally as varied as the establishments: innkeeper, alehouse keeper, tavern keeper and so on. For the former there was also the term 'innholder', which was that used by the London company which replaced the more ancient 'hostelers'. It was, however, in less everyday use than innkeeper and one finds it more particularly in legal documents. After the great 1723 fire at Wetherby, insurance policies, for example, were then taken out by several of the town's innholders.[5] A victualler, strictly speaking, sold provisions, and victualling houses were designated separately in legislation. However, it is equally clear that the term became synonymous with publican, as it was clearly used in this way by the Excise from the late seventeenth century in its records of brewing victuallers. Licensed victualler thus came commonly to be used. It has, one might suggest, both a self-important and an archaic or traditional ring to it. It was used by a Friendly Society of Licensed Victuallers formed in London in 1794, and by successor organisations of publicans. The latter term developed of course with public house and it too became general. Publications aimed at the trade, for example, addressed themselves to them, like *The Publican Protected* of 1800.[6] More colloquially, proprietors throughout the period were known as landlord or landlady, as Celia Fiennes had noted the civility of the 'Land Lady at the Inn' at Knaresborough.[7] Other designations similarly followed the fortunes of the institution: the dram-shop keeper and the beerseller came on the scene, whilst the alehouse keeper disappeared. By the late nineteenth century publican or licensed victualler, according to context, were common.[8]

How did men and women get into the trade of publican? One way was from the trade itself. Clearly there was always movement to new and/or better premises. Of 107 recruits to innkeeping in London and the west of England in the period 1650 to 1760, 41 had moved from another inn. Beerhouse keepers, as we saw, often aspired to become publicans, and from 1830 the beer trade became the main route into the fully-licensed sector. Others aspired from a position of service within the trade. 10 of those 107 were inn servants, and this remained a common route, like John Rushforth, applying for a licence in Richmond in 1822, having worked 16 years as a 'Boot Boy'. Others made the transition from household service. Another 9 of the 107 did so, or men like John Day of the Three Tuns in Northampton, who had formerly been a servant or groom in two noble households. James Farren, a London brewer and beer retailer, claimed that former publicans, waiters and general servants with a little capital comprised the second largest category of entrants to his trade. Another branch of the retail trade was the starting point for others. Keepers of chandlers' shops formerly selling table beer, were, according to Farren, the largest single group entering the beerhouse trade in the capital, echoing their earlier role in the sale of gin.[9]

To many more in quite unrelated occupations the new beer trade in particular represented a business opportunity. The ranks of labourers and artisans provided many recruits. This is clearly shown in the report of the 1833 Select Committee on the Sale of Beer, although the Webbs used some of its evidence to paint a much blacker picture of the poor, idle and criminal flocking into it. For Samuel Lucas, farmer and assistant overseer of Tilehurst in Berkshire, two of the twelve beerhouses there were kept by the 'better class of labourers', the remainder by 'labouring people'. To MP Jasper Parrott in Devon they were 'decent kind of labourers'. Former magistrates' clerk George Wells thought the great majority of Sheffield beerhouses were kept by labourers and workmen, including, naturally enough, grinders and cutlers. And in Lewes in Sussex an attorney noted blacksmiths and carpenters among the entrants.[10] Their evidence is supported by other sources. The six men who took out beer licences within the first month at Hedon in the East Riding were respectively mariner, horse breaker, baker, tailor, shoemaker and labourer.[11] Finally, turning to the fully-licensed trade, of twenty-four new applicants in Southampton in 1852 the majority were beer retailers or in some other way in the trade, but the remainder were in unrelated occupations: auctioneer, carpenter, carver and gilder, house decorator and two in the coal business.[12]

Another occupation was carried on alongside the sale of drink by many. Farming was particularly common. It comprised almost a third of the 31 different by-employments of 139 inn- and alehouse keepers identified in the period 1650 to 1777. At the census of 1851, 3,434 publicans or beersellers in England and Wales were also farmers. But a wide variety of trades were carried on. Of the 139 the next largest group comprised a range of craftsmen, retailers and dealers. At the turn of the eighteenth and nineteenth centuries Peter Stubs, the landlord of the White Bear Inn at Warrington, was also a file manufacturer. As a maltster and brewer too, he used the malt dust and the dregs of the beer barrels to make the paste which protected the files from damage.[13] In the beer trade dual occupations were particularly common. In Leeds, for example, at the close of the 1830s just over half of the 235 beerhouse keepers in the central wards of the borough carried on another trade on the same premises. In Manchester, a decade later, it was claimed that almost half of the more than 1,100 beersellers had another day job away from the beerhouse.[14] Dual occupations remained common in rural areas. In the Yorkshire market town of Easingwold the 1891 census showed that seven of sixteen publicans had them, including two farmers, a saddler, groom, shoemaker, labourer and a blacksmith, appropriately at the Horse Shoe Inn. Similarly in Edwardian east Kent other trades included blacksmith, carter, carrier and even undertaker.[15] But in urban areas its incidence generally declined; its prevalence in Edwardian Norwich was considered unusual. More typical was Bradford, as demonstrated by a comparison of the census returns for 1851 and 1891. At the latter date only 3 of some 160 publicans did so: a butcher, horse dealer and an overlooker, Richard Pearson of the Farmyard Inn, who went out to work while his wife Mary ran the pub, describing herself as the landlady. Around 15 per ceny of the nearly 300 beerhouse keepers did so, just under half of them grocers.[16] The licensing magistrates came to view this combination with distaste, linking as it did everyday shopping, generally a woman's task, and drink. In 1917 they objected to it at the five remaining pubs which did so. Three were already scheduled for closure, but the licences of the other two were only renewed on condition that the grocery business was given up. In addition some brewer owners of pubs, as Hammonds in Bradford, made it a condition of the tenancy.[17] What had once been common had thus become unusual by the twentieth century.

One other route into the trade finally was from occupations which had a limited life span – in sport, the military and later the police. The sporting landlord in particular was a common figure. There were ex-prize fighters in the eighteenth and early nineteenth centuries, like Tom Belcher and Tom Spring, successive hosts at the Castle Tavern, Holborn, and later ex-professional boxers, like French Canadian Tommy Burns, a former world heavyweight boxing champion, who kept the Beeswing at Felling near Gateshead in the 1920s.[18] Former cricketers, footballers and rugby players were also always well represented in the publicans' ranks. England rugby captain Dicky Lockwood took the Queen at Heckmondwike, although his great fame in the north of England did not keep him from bankruptcy in 1897. A number of footballers kept pubs while still players: several of the first generation of Lancashire professionals did so. But making the transition on retirement was more usual: it was one of four most frequently mentioned post-football employments.[19] Of ex-military men examples are Alfred Savigear who left the army as a sergeant-major in 1877, at the age of thirty-nine, to become a publican in London. Having been a riding instructor in the army he developed at the same time a riding school. Or winner of the Victoria Cross in the Crimean War, Matthew Hughes, who after twenty-one years in the army eventually took the Gardeners' Arms, a Bradford beerhouse, in 1874. His earlier heroism failed to impress the licensing bench, however, when he applied for a full-licence the following year.[20] Finally, was the ex-policeman. Before the advent of professional forces, beginning with London's in 1829, the part-time post of constable was often filled by a publican, despite many attempts to prevent the practice. Thereafter retirement prompted the move, although disability might hasten it, as with Owen Lamb, who took Bradford's Ashley Hotel in 1894, but who was reunited with his former colleagues when he was prosecuted four years later for allowing betting on the premises.[21]

Where the publican pursued another occupation it was his wife naturally who ran the pub. But in general they were essential business partners. Marrying a woman with experience in the trade was a good move. David Tillotson was a spinning overlooker before taking a Bradford beerhouse in 1877, but he and his wife soon crossed the road to assist in her father's fully-licensed house, to which they in due course succeeded.[22] Whilst the typical hosts were a couple, women on their own always constituted a significant minority of licensees, usually widows or related in some other way. In the Agbrigg division of the West Riding in 1771, 55 (14.2 per cent) were women, a proportion which was typical, and all but three of them had been widowed into it.[23] A study of Chelmsford, Margate and London St Pancras over the period 1840 to 1939 similarly found that slightly more than one of every ten publicans was a single woman or widow, with the latter continuing to predominate. Where they were single they assumed control of a pub previously held by a male relative, be it father or brother. In the three places examined they ran the pub for roughly the same length of time as men. They had the experience and it made good sense for the owner, increasingly a brewery company, to permit them to continue. It was easier than installing a temporary tenant and she also could be given the opportunity to prove herself. Married women were, it was claimed in the 1890s, in some places granted licences in their own right. This might be

where there was an objection to the husband's character, or a disqualification by reason of his job, such as county court bailiff, or
where local conditions merited, as at Bristol, where many husbands
were at sea. But it is difficult to see it as common given the foregoing local evidence.[24] They were certainly seen as good at it. As the
author of a guide to the trade in the 1920s put it, whilst still however
favouring couples: 'almost all the qualities necessary for successful
innkeeping are natural to some women', and in particular 'they find
much more work for idle hands to do than men, and enjoy doing it'.
Their ability to deal with difficult customers was often noted, and in
some instances they attained a quasi-legendary status. Women like
Pal Hammond who kept the Old Black Horse Inn, Little Horton
near Bradford in the early nineteenth century: 'who when the orgies
of her customers were at their height often asserted her authority in
a manner to astonish even the rough collier lads.' Perhaps, as Thomas
Burke noted, 'men in fractious mood will more often take notice of
a woman's orders than a man's'[25] (Figure 8).

It was very much a family trade. Children or other relatives worked
too, particularly where the licensee was alone. The Chelmsford,
Margate and St Pancras widows and single women typically relied on
teenage, or young adult, sons and daughters, less frequently sisters, for
assistance. Mary Swain, for example, who kept the Coach and Horses
in Chelmsford between 1852 and 1867, received help from two sons in
succession. But over one-fifth of all the female publicans ran the pub
with an exclusively female staff. It was a family trade too in sometimes
descending the generations. Studies have in this way identified innkeeping 'dynasties', like those of Hanoverian Northampton. In some
instances the degree of continuity was remarkable: in Hertfordshire
the Jackson family kept the Sword in Hand at Westmill from 1800
to 1956 and the Clares the Compasses at Radwell for some 200 years
to the 1950s. But it was not uncommon generally in the pub trade for
it to descend at least one generation.[26]

If the trade was a family one it was also dependent upon staff. Larger
houses might employ several live-in servants. The Beverley Arms, for

example, in 1841 had the landlady's sister and niece, but also four male and three female servants, living there. Similarly, from the census returns for the whole of Bradford, in both 1851 and 1891 they were employed at around three-quarters of the licensed houses, but at only around a third of the beerhouses. Noticeable was the decline in the number of male servants at the former, largely attributable to a reduction in the number of ostlers. Beerhouse servants were always mostly young and female, like servants generally. For female pub servants duties would encompass normal household chores as well as waiting on customers and clearing up after them. Hannah Cullwick, aged twelve or thirteen, worked at the Red Lion, Shifnal, Shropshire in the 1840s for 1s a week, cleaning floors and tables and waiting 'on the farmers dinner of a market day'. Tasks might be more varied where the landlord carried on another trade. Lucy Luck, thirteen, worked at a St Albans beerhouse in the early 1860s where they kept a cow, and she made butter and delivered milk as well as serving in the tap room. Later, at a pub in Luton where the trade was combined with that of straw hat-making, she helped with finishing the hats in addition to the housework and serving in the bar.[27]

The specific jobs of barmaid and barman were distinguished separately in the later census reports, that of 1901, for example, returning 28,625 barmen and 27,707 barmaids nationally. In the case of the barmaids especially this is certainly an underestimate. The licensed trade itself gave a figure of 100,000 for the middle years of that decade.[28] Many would escape the census report by simply being recorded as 'servant' in the returns. Others would of course be part-time, and into the twentieth century it is likely that their proportion increased. The term barmaid may originally have indicated a higher status post. An advertisement of 1817 in the *Leeds Mercury* sought 'a young woman of irreproachable character, who writes a good hand, and has a competent knowledge of accounts for such a situation'. But the exact origin remains obscure. Attention from historians has focused on the London barmaid. There her appearance, in both senses, has been linked to the gin palace, where she can be found from the 1820s at least working behind the new counter 'as a further item of allure-ment among its mirrors and mahogany, its brass ware and coloured tile'. At the same time the counter kept her physically out of reach of the customers and also acted like a stage, making her 'conspicuous and seductive'. However alluring, she certainly worked hard, with 70 to 80 hours common and even up to 100 in some instances, for a basic wage of from 8s to 10s a week by 1900. No wonder the trade press carried advertisements for bunions, flat feet and varicose veins. She was the object of successive campaigns to improve her lot and to abolish her altogether, neither of which had any effect. She remained an essential element of the pub scene.[29]

What were our publicans like? They were predominantly mid-dle-aged. At the censuses of 1851 and 1891 those of Bradford were on average in their forties, which was true also of Nottingham's pub-licans at the latter date.[30] As to character, Francis Place has left us a vivid portrait of his publican father Simon, who entered the trade in 1780. He was 'a very bony muscular man about five feet six or seven inches in height dark complexion and very strong for his height'. He excelled in 'Drinking, Whoring, Gaming, Fishing and Fighting'. But he was much respected; people 'placed the utmost reliance on his word' and could depend upon him in an emergency. His sociability is evidenced by his 'abundance of friends' and in the way he looked after the locals in the parlour, with his own reserved seat.[31] It seems like a caricature, but all its facets may be glimpsed in the evidence we have from among the tens of thousands of publicans who at one time carried on the trade. Although the source perhaps biases it towards the type, the short biographies in the *Licensed Victuallers' Gazette* and *Licensing World* for the 1890s of new and popular publicans reveal him as 'a race-course, big-cigar, loud-checks type'. Men like Bob Prudhoe of the Norfolk Arms off the Strand, with his 'showy dog-cart, with high-stepper, silver-mounted harness and crest and motto', his keen business sense and glamorous reputation of being an illegit-imate son of the Duke of Norfolk. The notices in the local Bradford trade press provide many similar examples, like Tom Cullen, retiring from the Station Hotel, Clayton Lane in 1913, 'a well-known figure in the local boxing world'. Or finally, epitomising landlordly sociability, was Willie Hardcastle, who kept the Albert Hotel in Huddersfield for twenty-three years from 1908. He was an officer in the Royal Antediluvian Order of Buffaloes, a music hall artists' agent, chairman of Huddersfield Town football club and a noted raconteur.[32]

One drawback to sociability, and arising from the very nature of the business, was a fondness for drink. Many paid the price in their health and life. In the period 1880 to 1882 mortality from alcoholism among publicans was five times the general rate for males and from diseases of the liver six times greater. Victoria Cross winner Matthew Hughes, who succumbed to liver cirrhosis and exhaustion when only in his late fifties, was not untypical. Alcoholism also correlated with mental illness and suicide, with the rate for the latter almost double the male average. Nor were women immune, like Ann Field of Firth's Hotel, Bradford, who drowned herself in 1858, having for a long time past 'been addicted to intemperate habits', and who had been drunk every day of the week preceding her death.[33]

Turning now to the business itself, the single most significant change over the period was the growth of brewery control of public houses. At the beginning of the eighteenth century roughly speaking over two-thirds of publicans brewed their own beer.[34] The great exception to this was London where common, that is wholesale, brewers already dominated production. A mere 0.6 per cent of strong beer was brewed by victuallers. The capital provided a huge, concentrated market for an industry that was in the vanguard of industrialisation, and over the course of the eighteenth century a small number of major brewers came to dominate production. Along with this came the development of the so called tie, whereby a publican agreed to take the product of a particular firm. This was not at first a deliberate strategy, but arose out of commitments made as an ordinary condition of trade. The publican might become indebted to the brewer, or an aspirant to the trade without sufficient capital might seek financial help from him. The rising value of land in London, the increasing cost of equipping a public house and the higher premium put on the lease as the number of licences was restricted, all made it more costly to get into the business. It was natural for the brewers to offer credit, since the incentive was to secure the supply of beer. Further incentives to the tie lay in the ability of the brewer to estimate sales, the reduction of delivery costs achieved by supplying more beer to fewer houses and the maintenance of quality. The more restrictive licensing climate led to competition among brewers to secure available outlets. In the decade after 1800 around eight out of ten houses were tied to the large brewers, although the proportion thereafter did fall. One result of the tie was in the way brewers now exploited their own brand name by displaying it on the outside of the public house: Meux Reid, for example, produced signboards for most of their publicans.[35]

This trend towards brewery supply and control is evident in other parts of the country. By the turn of the century the proportion of publicans nationally brewing their own beer had fallen to under a half, and by 1822, when it is possible to be more precise, 42.8 per cent did so.[36] There had developed a zone of 'intense tieing' in counties near the capital like Bedfordshire, Berkshire, Hertfordshire, Hampshire or Surrey in response, it has been suggested, to the competition of London brewers.[37] There was, however, considerable local and regional variation, which is not always readily explicable in the current state of knowledge. There was a high level of production and control by common brewers in some urban areas such as Hull, Liverpool, Newcastle or Norwich, but in others, like Birmingham, Manchester, Leeds or Sheffield the publican brewer was predominant. Clearly all were large urban centres, and the presence of ports in the former category suggests the importance of good coastal transport links, but the absence of them did not inhibit the growth of the latter towns. Local conditions may thus have been crucial, like Birmingham's tradition of small artisans.[38]

The hostility engendered by this growth of brewery control was, as we saw, one of the reasons for the Beer Act of 1830. But it did nothing to halt the trend. Although in the year to January 1832, 42.1 per cent of beersellers were brewing, this accounted for only 11 per cent of all the malt consumed. By the end of the free-trade era just one in five were still brewing a mere 7 per cent of malt.[39] Within twenty years of the Act a House of Lords inquiry found that a very large proportion were, like public houses, the actual property of brewers or tied by advances to them. In the capital, where the number of beerhouses rose absolutely and proportionately, they provided an obvious opportunity for brewers in an otherwise limited market. By 1850 mild ale brewers Mann, Grossman and Paulin were supplying 500 from their Albion brewery. But it happened elsewhere. In Yorkshire Henry Bentley from his brewery at Woodlesford 'vigorously attacked the nascent Leeds beer house trade' just six miles distant.[40] Fully-licensed houses also continued to be acquired, free trade having depressed licensed property values. Also driving the process, it has been suggested, were several further influences. The demand for beer was unstable; it actually declined from the later 1830s and again in the mid-1850s. Tied houses helped to insulate brewers from the effect. There was the possibility of speculative rewards if the licensing system were to return to restriction. As Liverpool brewer Peter Walker put it, according to one of the magistrates there, in relation to the town's particular free-trade experiment: 'If the magistrates continue … I shall double the number of my [tied] houses, and if they stop it I shall double the value of the houses I have.' Local rivalries and competitive disadvantages were yet another spur, as in Halifax for example, with both old-established and newer firms acquiring houses.[41]

The trend reached its culmination in the final decades of the century. Several developments drove the process forward. One was the growth of a national beer market, with brewers from Burton, the premier brewing centre, accounting for almost 8 per cent of England's total beer sales in the late 1860s, rising to almost 12 per cent in the 1880s and thus threatening local brewers. The legislation of 1869, which ended free trade and the unlimited expansion of numbers, and the Licensing Act of 1872, which tightened up on offences, heralded a more restrictive licensing climate. Following the peak years of beer consumption in the mid-1870s, a general recession badly affected the industry in the decade after 1876. This in turn fuelled the final development, the growing number of brewer flotations, which brought in cash for purchases, both of individual houses and smaller, less successful firms. The result was a 'scramble for property' which intensified the trend to brewery control.[42] By 1900 there were fewer than 3,000 licensed victuallers brewing and about half that number of beersellers, in each case comprising less than 4 per cent of the total.[43] Most pubs were now owned or leased by brewery companies. Although it is not possible to give a definitive national figure, the cumulative local evidence leaves no doubt. The Royal Commission on Liquor Licensing Laws of 1896 to 1899 offers several examples. In Birmingham, the one-time home of the publican brewer, almost 90 per cent of pubs were now controlled by brewers, according to the clerk to the justices. Similar proportions were reported for Bristol, Hull, Manchester, Newcastle and Sheffield. Although it was once again not uniform. In Leeds, for example, the percentages for both fully-licensed and beerhouses were less than forty.[44] In London the loan tie was rapidly replaced by ownership. Falling beer consumption and rising overheads caused publicans to default on their loans. As the Burton brewers began to enter the London market, local brewers sought to secure their outlets. Massive sums of money changed hands in pub purchases. The Cannon Brewery of Clerkenwell, for example, formerly one of the smaller firms, spent £1,363,010 on buying 125 pubs in the years 1893 to 1898. Bigger firms spent even more.[45] Nationally by 1913 the Brewers' Society was estimating that as many as 95 per cent of houses were tied.[46]

The publican thus went from being independent, or semi-independent if tied by loan, to being dependent on a brewery company, which either owned the house or leased it from another owner. The relationship in turn took two forms. The most common was where the publican was a tenant. The brewery owned not only the house but also its fixtures and fittings. It carried out alterations and repairs, to the cost of which the tenant might have to contribute.

But above all it compelled the tenant to sell more or less exclusively its products. The tenant also agreed to do nothing to endanger the licence, not to sub-let and in some cases, as we saw, not to have any other employment. The principle upon which the rent was fixed varied. It might be lower than the market rate, but goods supplied cost more than to the free trade; or standard prices and market rent were paid. The tenant kept the profits.[47] The other form was where the house was put in charge of a manager, who received a wage and sometimes a commission on sales. Whilst not generally common, it was used in some places, like Birmingham and Newcastle, but particularly in Liverpool, where half the city's publicans were paid managers by the mid-1890s. The firm of Peter Walker & Son operated the great majority of its houses there in this way and exercised tight control over their conduct. Rules they were obliged to follow included prohibitions on smoking with customers or treating one another to drinks. Elsewhere the use of managers was more limited, usually to the more substantial premises. When Hammonds brewery of Bradford rebuilt one of its older central pubs in some style in 1898, renaming it the Empress Hotel, a manager was installed on £3 a week plus a commission of 5 per cent on his weekly takings over £70.[48]

The use of managers was actively opposed by many licensing benches, such as those of Leeds or Manchester, who regarded them as mere servants. Their legality was even questioned, albeit unsuccessfully.[49] But the tied system as a whole provoked a great deal of hostility. Brewers were depicted as ruthless, monopolistic, profiteering businessmen foisting inferior beer on the public at high prices through their bound servants.[50] Not the least amongst the complainants were the tenants, who disliked the onerous nature of the tie and the severity with which the agreement might be enforced within an overall context of increasing impersonality and inflexibility, even ruthlessness, in maximising profits. Tenants obtaining supplies from another source were got rid of, as were those falling foul of the law (so that they should not endanger the licence by further convictions) and those getting into financial difficulties. As bankrupt Fred Holt of the Waggon and Horses, Manchester Road, Bradford succinctly put it in 1907: 'He did pretty well for the brewers, but not for himself.' Having said that, the tenants of Hammonds in 1899 professed themselves satisfied with their 'courteous and considerate treatment' and the conditions of their tenancy.[51] Just how well or not the publican was doing is a question to which we shall return. The obviously potentially difficult relationship between brewer and tenant was to be strained even further in the future.

Brewery money had another important effect on the stock of licensed premises in the closing years of the century as the gin-palace style reached its apotheosis. In London the Cannon Brewery spent £250,000 on rebuilding pubs over six years. Brewery money in the capital was also behind many speculators who made an important contribution to the process. Mark Girouard documented in detail these late Victorian pubs. Their architects 'cheerfully adapted, misused or distorted' a succession of styles, of which in the 1890s High Victorian eclecticism, 'Queen Anne' and Flemish were especially apparent. Whatever the style, the aim was to entice the customer inside by the use of prominent advertising boards, features like corner towers or gables, huge lamps, abundant iron work, elaborate window surrounds and lashings of carving (Figures 9 and 10). The richly decorated glass on the ground floor, lit up from behind at night, was similarly enticing, and the entrance itself, with its lobby lined with decorative tiles or painted glass, beckoned you inside. Once there the rich and varied fittings provided a feast for the eyes. A maximum of glitter was obtained by a range of usually brass light-fittings, of sometimes striking design, like the lion's-head brackets of the Ten Bells in Commercial Street, Spitalfields or the electric lamps supported by bronze nymphs at the Salisbury in St Martin's Lane. The lights were reflected in glass and mirror work, which was decorated using a variety of techniques: embossing, brilliant cutting, gilding, enamelling, painting and staining. Ornamental glass was used on walls and partitions and to line the shelves of the back fittings. Painted tiles were also used in some interiors. The unifying element was the pub's joinery, of which the central feature was the serving-bar. In these late Victorian pubs the bar was sometimes developed as a central island to replace or supplement the back fitting, like that of the Princess Louise in Holborn of 1891 (Figure 19). Completing the overall effect was the plasterwork, or its imitation, for the coves, friezes and ceilings.[52]

Other cities witnessed a similar development. The authors of a study of Birmingham pubs dub the period from 1880 'the great rebuilding', as brewers sought to get the most from their newly purchased properties. Either the ground floor alone was modernised or the whole pub was rebuilt in more splendid style. One of the most striking was the Woodman in Easy Row. Its exterior boasted a statue of the eponymous figure over an undulating frontage of wood and glass and the inside featured stained glass, sumptuous woodwork and tiles painted with scenes of old Birmingham. The city also had a number of pubs utilising tile and terracotta, or the glazed variant of it known as faience, which gave them a distinctive appearance both externally and internally. The ceiling of the public bar at the White Horse in Congreve Street was covered with tiles, and they were used generally in Birmingham pubs, the light bouncing off the highly glazed relief surfaces of the rich majolica[53] (Figure 11). The North East was another area which experienced a pub alteration and building boom at this time, and where the use of faience also gave many pubs a distinctive appearance.[54] Portsmouth again saw a similar process, with the great majority of new pubs being built in the last fifteen years of the century, and two-thirds of them in turn by the town's two biggest brewers. They were substantial structures, which dominated adjacent terraced streets, many built in a half-timbered style like the 1896 Talbot, Goldsmith Avenue, which similarly gave a distinctive aspect to the town's pub profile.[55]

One should not in the end, however, overstate the process. Whilst, as I noted above, pubs generally adopted, and continued to adopt, at least features of the gin-palace style, many remained pretty basic establishments. In the older parts of Portsmouth, in contrast to developing areas like Southsea, properties were allowed to deteriorate; almost half of Old Portsmouth's pubs actually experienced a reduction in their rateable value between 1867 and 1906.[56] Bradford too had its examples of the palatial, like the Empress Hotel noted above, whose frontage boasted granite columns and stained glass windows and the interior all the offerings of the style: including mosaic floor, tiles, glass, mirrors, electroliers, carved and polished Spanish mahogany and decorated walls and ceilings. But such houses there were exceptional, and the town had many old, dilapidated beerhouses. But even these might have echoes of their grander brethren. The Ancient Druids' Inn, in Westgate, demolished in 1896, had a glazed partition to the entrance passage, a plate-glass mirror behind the bar in the tap room and, in the parlour, lit by three fancy gas-brackets, were a racing print in gilt and a spring timepiece.[57]

There was then much that changed in the running of a pub in these years, but there were also continuities. For example, although brewing ceased to be done on the premises, there was still work involved in getting the beer ready for sale and the regular cleaning of the beer engine and the pipes.[58] At whatever point in time we look at the job the hours were long, staff had to be rewarded and supervised, a variety of taxes and duties paid and a complex body of law adhered to. To which, not least, might be added a range of problems caused by the customers: running up debts, petty pilfering or generally behaving badly.[59] Advice to publicans multiplied the even minor details to be considered. The *Licensed Victuallers' Official Annual* offered 'notes on public-house management', which cautioned, for example, against allowing barmen to 'strike the handle of the beer-engine back with a sharp blow', as it harmed the engine and annoyed customers, and warned against banging down change on wet parts of the counter. As for mine host, he 'should be dressed as a gentleman, and never appear behind the bar without his coat'.[60] Was it worth it? Once again a simple question is complicated by the great variety of the pub trade at whatever point we choose to examine it, but we must nevertheless attempt an overview.

Innkeepers in the eighteenth century had often been individuals of some substance. Defoe noted that the landlord at the post-house at Doncaster was mayor, kept a pack of hounds, 'was company for the best gentlemen in the town or in the neighbourhood, and lived as great as any gentleman ordinarily did'. In Northampton similarly innkeepers were among the richest men in the town. Further up the Great North Road at Wetherby the innkeepers as a group in 1785 were assessed for more than one-third of the town's poor rate, with the two principal landlords, of the Angel and the Swan and Talbot, accounting for almost 60 per cent.[61] Erstwhile alehouse keepers also enjoyed growing wealth and respectability. A sample of probate inventories for Kent, Leicestershire and London suggest that by the middle of the eighteenth century most 'could claim a modest degree of prosperity'. For the mid-1820s, fire insurance records show that average personal wealth was 'significantly greater' in real terms than a century earlier.[62] As their wealth and status rose so too did their pretentions. As we saw with Samuel Bamford and the Wordsworths it was a common observation from customers. At the beginning of our period Ned Ward, the 'London Spy', railed against the 'lordliness of the victuallers'. The thousands of readers of *Tom Jones* were no doubt meant to recognise the innkeepers who, making their living from 'people of fashion, contract as much insolence to the rest of man-kind, as if they really belonged to that rank themselves'.[63] In general, Peter Clark concluded that 'for most of the period up to 1830 the substantial, improved public house in a good position was an attrac-tive business proposition, with modest fortunes to be won'.[64]

Of course, as Clark also acknowledged, not all were prosperous. At the margins were those who were unable to make a living any other way. In 1771, for example, the clerk to the licensing justices of the Claro division of the West Riding recorded that of 302 individuals licensed that day, 27 were either lame, 'badly', old, or some combination of those characteristics. Inventories of mid-eighteenth-century London show that whilst most tavern keepers and the better class of innkeeper would be worth at least £1,000, many alehouse keepers would be worth well under £100, with many much poorer than most artisans.[65] Patrick Colquhoun, looking at the trade in London at the close of the century, felt that the sale of beer of a 'considerable proportion' of ale-houses was insufficient to make ends meet, a point he reinforced with statistics of the high turnover of tenants. But in his survey of the social structure of the country as a whole, based on the first census of 1801 and income tax returns, he placed his estimated 50,000 innkeepers and publicans on an average annual income of £100. This located them as a group among the less well-off middling persons like farmers and lesser freeholders, but clearly above shopkeepers, artisans and labourers in manufacturing or building.[66]

To the members of those latter groups especially the Beer Act of 1830 presented a new business opportunity, which thousands took up. For some it must have been a struggle. The fact that so many combined it with another occupation suggests that a good living was not always possible from a small beerhouse by itself. The contrac-tion of numbers in the 1830s and 1840s also supports that. On the other hand, the growth in the numbers of more substantial houses, and the aspiration to a full-licence which many nursed, point to the possibility of greater rewards. Their enhanced sense of respectability is evidenced too by the development of their own trade societies. Thus the Leeds Licensed Beersellers' Association held its anniversary dinner in 1839 at the Crown in Roundhay Road, which was served, according to the newspaper account, 'in a manner which would have reflected credit on a first class hotel'.[67] But even the humblest beerseller was of course a man of business, of property even, which itself entitled him to some standing in the community, an essential fact sometimes lost sight of in the torrents of temperance invective. As the West Riding magistrate Ellis Cunliffe Lister put it in 1838: 'The beersellers who had invested their little all in the trade upon the authority of an Act of Parliament, had as much right to his pro-tection as he had to any farm he had in his possession.'[68] Status and respectability are recurring themes. It was common at brewster ses-sions for the licensed victuallers to be praised, as by the mayor of

Leeds, for example, in 1849, that 'they were entitled to the confidence and respect of the magistrates', filling as they did a situation of 'great importance and responsibility'.[69] Robert Roberts put them in the premier position in his Edwardian Salford slum district, along with shopkeepers and skilled tradesmen, and noted their aspirations to middle-class manners and customs. As the customers spoke of the landlady of the best hotel in the district – 'a proper lady if ever there was one'.[70] *Coronation Street's* Annie Walker was thus not entirely a character of fiction.

Success or failure was to a degree in the publican's own hands. The common phrase was: 'There are houses for men, and men for houses.' As the guide for prospective publicans which quoted it warned: 'The path of the licensed victualler is strewn with wrecks of their own folly.'[71] But in the end of course the living to be made was determined by wider social and economic conditions. The growing prosperity of the 1860s, and the rising drink consumption which accompanied it, together with the centrality of pubs to working-class life, seem to have provided a good living for the majority. In September 1873 some 160 members, representing almost all the town's publicans, of the Bradford Licensed Victuallers' Protection Society took part in the parade for the opening of the new Town Hall. It drew from an observer in the local paper the comment: 'This section of the procession attracted a good deal of notice, the members forming it having an air of jollity and prosperity about them which were the theme of general remark.' With the exception of part of the 1880s, the rewards continued in the latter part of the century. In 1888 a substantial fully-licensed house in the town was averaging per year a net profit of £1,086 on takings of about £50 a week. A little beerhouse averaged £430 a year net profit. To put this into perspective, the top wage of an overlooker at this time, the sort of occupation from which publicans typically came, would amount to just under £80 a year. Little wonder that Hammonds was reporting its ability in 1895 to select its tenants from a large number of applicants.[72] But again this was not the whole story. From Newcastle in the mid-1890s it was reported that fifty pubs, mostly beerhouses, were not doing any real trade, about one in ten of the city's premises.[73] From about the turn of the century, however, a combination of developing long-term changes and more short-run problems began to undermine more generally the publican's trading position. As I shall examine, per capita alcohol consumption was in decline from the late 1870s, and the role of the pub itself began to contract. Wider economic difficulties at times in the years after 1900 (when total beer consumption now also actually fell) also contributed, as did the growing burden of taxation, both central and local. The records relating to the working of the 1904 Licensing Act, which introduced a mechanism for removing pubs deemed to be redundant, illustrate clearly how some publicans were struggling. In 1905 in Southampton, for example, a profit of just 30s a week was described as not as good as it ought to be, but 'improving'. Similarly in north Lancashire four pubs in Hawkshead, Warton and Lancaster had average annual takings of £479 in 1907; in the following year another four in Lancaster, Flookborough and Ulverston had £491. This when takings of £2,661 for a substantial fully-licensed house, Woods' Spirit Vaults in Castle Street, Lancaster, were described as a 'fairly respectable trade'.[74] Such a trade was of course then possible, but gloomier times still for the publican were to come with war.

7

Customers and their World

Who were the pub's customers and what were they doing there? In seeking to answer those questions I shall, as in the previous chapter, range over the whole period up to the First World War. There are, once again, continuities as well as changes, and I shall endeavour to highlight them in addressing my common themes.

Men have always formed the majority of pub customers. As Joseph Lawson wrote of the alehouses in Pudsey, a village to the west of Leeds, at the beginning of the nineteenth century, 'nearly all the male population went there, more or less'. In turn, they have mostly been working-class men. As Robert Roberts put it for his Edwardian Salford: 'To the great mass of manual workers the local public house spelled paradise.'[1] This certainly is the common perception of the pub's clientele in the past. But whilst there is essential truth in it, it is a crude portrait. We need to look more closely at the social class and sex of the customers.

The upper and middling classes in the eighteenth century were often to be found in inns and public houses as travellers, or as participants in the wide range of economic and social activity centred there. Their presence too was not unknown in more humble drinking places, as we saw with John Byng or Parson Woodforde. From the beginning of the new century this was becoming less common as, for example, private clubs developed and the inn began to lose many of its economic and social functions. It proceeded swiftly from the 1830s with the demise of the coaching trade and the growth of concern about drink, which was working to undermine the respectability of the public house. In any case, they were never more than the minority of customers. More numerous were skilled workers, small craftsmen and petty traders. Francis Place noted that almost every public house had a parlour for the 'better sort of customers', which included the 'more dissolute' professional men and tradesmen. Lawson described the Pudsey slubbers, at the time a skilled textile occupation, who regarded themselves as a cut above and forsook the company in the tap room for the spirits and superior ales of the bar. Overall, use of the public house by those groups also diminished during the century. Place felt that from the 1820s the better sort of workers tended more and more to avoid alehouses.[2] Such artisanal respectability, and its growing association with sobriety, encouraged this trend. Nevertheless, they remained a significant element, and contributed to social differentiation within the pub world. By the late nineteenth century London pubs had their saloon bars for lower middle-class patrons, and many had two public bars: one for the superior artisan and one for labourers. One of Charles Booth's police informants noted how publicans desired to separate customers as far as possible into social grades, roughly by ability to pay, with higher priced drinks in the saloon. Similarly in Salford, the premier house in Roberts's district was frequented by shopkeepers and foremen who took up the 'Best Room', whilst the artisans occupied the vault – the Lancashire term for the tap room. All the sixteen pubs in the area had their own particular status, over and above such gradations within the pub itself. The same situation prevailed in rural east Kent. Some pubs relied entirely on tap-room trade, but more common was social distinction within the pub, as the village craftsmen, farmers, farm bailiffs, gardeners and tradesmen retreated into the private or saloon bar.[3]

Having said that, the unskilled and semi-skilled without a doubt formed the largest group of customers. The greatest concentration

of pubs was in poorer working-class neighbourhoods, as demonstrated by the numerous 'drink maps' prepared from the middle
of the nineteenth century by temperance campaigners, and in the
social surveys of London and York by Booth and Rowntree, which
plotted the various types of drinking establishment.[4] Modern studies
of Birmingham and Bradford, for example, show the same pattern.
For the inhabitants of such districts the local pub was very much
that, never more than yards away (Figure 5). The Birmingham
study used newspaper reports of court proceedings, which provide
addresses, to map distances between home and pub and showed that
'to a considerable extent people did visit pubs in their immediate
neighbourhood'. Using the same source, Bradford examples are
illustrative. In the summer of 1880 an incident in the tap room at the
Spinkwell Tavern led to a manslaughter charge. Five customers were
mentioned: a quarryman, stonemason, sawyer and two labourers, of
whom four lived in the immediate vicinity of the pub and the fifth
only a short walk away. In 1919 a gambling case at the Commercial
Hotel in Bingley Street provided information on all but one of fifteen men involved: two woolcombers, a millhand, two labourers, a
fireman, two dyers' labourers, a stoker, a warp dresser, a warehouse-
man, two bricklayers and a decorator. Nine lived either in Bingley
Street itself or in one adjoining and four others within a quarter
of a mile. In both those examples too, the occupations were mostly
of the pub's locality.[5]

Pubs in this way might very much have the 'flavour' of particular
neighbourhoods and occupations. Henry Mayhew noted in mid-
nineteenth-century London the Jewish traders of Houndsditch
market, around which 'even the public houses are of the Hebrew
faith'. Dockland pubs similarly had their individual characters.
In Edwardian Ipswich the Dolphin was used by Norwegian and
Swedish sailors, who liked to 'dance and sing and fight', whilst the
pilots, captains and skippers drank in the Union Jack. Similarly in
London, captains and masters from all over the world gathered at
the Great Eastern Hotel at the corner of the East and West India

docks. London inevitably had a good number of raffish or low-life pubs. East End criminal Arthur Harding remembered a Hoxton pub frequented by prize fighters, racing people and music hall artists on Sundays: 'All the rogues and villains – the three card mob and all that lark.' Or criminal pubs like the Spread Eagle, where the Hoxton mob congregated, as he noted with nice distinction, 'more hooligans than thieves'.[6]

If men formed the majority of customers, women were also in pubs, and in greater numbers than is sometimes believed. The difficulty comes when we try to bring more precision to that statement. One problem is that a lot of our evidence comes from people who viewed their presence in pubs with alarm or distaste, and who were prone to believe that the problem, as they saw it, was getting worse. Thus Patrick Colquhoun in the 1790s thought that the previous twenty to thirty years had seen women overcoming the disgrace which once attached to visiting alehouses. A century later Charles Booth similarly believed that more women were drinking in public houses.[7] The wider issue of women drinking was always a cause of concern, as they were seen as the mothers of the nation's future workers and soldiers. The essential sentiments were the same whether voiced during the gin craze or as part of late Victorian and Edwardian anxiety over the future of the 'race'. Journalist Arthur Shadwell's was something of a lone voice at that time in asserting that 'so far from women having recently taken to frequenting the public-house they have never frequented it less'.[8] Of course women are no more an undifferentiated mass than men, or workers, and we must try to chart their use of pubs not only by social class but also by age and marital status.

In early eighteenth-century London women were major consumers of gin and frequenters of the various locations where it was sold – chandlers' shops, public houses and dram shops. They drank on their own, or in mixed- or same-sex groups. It was especially popular with single working women, enjoying the benefits of rising real wages in the capital, the cheapness of the dram itself and the relative freedom of the metropolis over the rural areas from which many of them had come.[9] When gin-drinking revived in the later eighteenth century, women again formed a significant group among the gin shop's customers. In May 1792, for example, the West Riding Quarter Sessions noted the 'constant succession of customers all too often of women and children' at dram shops there. Gustave d'Eichtal, writing in 1828 of the alehouses around Drury Lane, saw 'large crowds, chiefly composed of women. These women are a sight to be seen as they gulp down their glasses of gin, whisky, toddy and cheap brandy, and some of them smoke pipes.'[10] Statistical evidence is forthcoming with the advent of the popular temperance strategy of counting customers. Thus fourteen 'leading gin-shops' in various parts of London were observed for a week in 1834. Over that period women made up just over 40 per cent of those entering. Similarly, it was reported in 1853 that nearly half of those in spirit vaults in Manchester's Deansgate on a Saturday were women. Deansgate was the site of the vegetable market, so many would no doubt have finished shopping.[11]

Women's presence in rural or small-town public houses at this time may have been more limited. Samuel Bamford remembered it at Middleton at the turn of the century on special occasions like the August wakes, the Whit feast or the White Apron fair after Easter, when women could 'display their finery' accompanying sweetheart or husband to the alehouse.[12] But in larger towns, or where employment provided a degree of financial independence, they used them more regularly and without men. Young women and girls working in the small metal trades around Birmingham, for example, thus relaxed, as noted by an observer bemoaning that very independence: 'They often enter the beer shops, call for their pints, and smoke their pipes like men.'[13] But for young men and women pubs provided opportunities to meet, particularly those providing music and dancing. At St Helens in the mid-1860s an employer of young female labour in a glass works noted the public-house dancing saloons where 'the young fellows take the girls'. Pubs around London's docks had long provided rooms for sailors and young women to dance in.[14]

Henry Mayhew reported that some of those dockland pubs were also brothels. Pubs were certainly used for prostitution, above all in port or garrison towns. In Portsmouth, beerhouses in particular often functioned as brothels, or adjacent premises were used. In the late 1860s, for example, the landlord of the Battle of Inkerman, William Newton, specialised in the provision of young girls, so that the pub became known as the 'Infant School'. In Aldershot at this time prostitutes either rented from the publican a room on the premises, or a nearby or adjacent cottage. Publicans there even employed surgeons to ensure that the women were free from disease.[15] But the connection between pubs and prostitution was by no means confined to those towns. In Bradford the chief constable of the new borough police force produced figures for beerhouses where prostitutes lodged, or which had adjoining properties used for prostitution, showing a peak of twenty-seven of the former in 1856, comprising about 10 per cent of the beerhouses in the town. Houses like the Huddersfield Arms run by Lavinia Kingston, where a private room was available for which customers paid 4d. Her conviction was part of something of a purge, which reduced the number of brothel beerhouses to just four in 1857.[16]

A problem for historians is the tendency of contemporaries to conflate commercial with casual sex. Women engaging in the latter were deemed to be prostitutes.[17] A Bradford committee looking at the 'moral condition' of the town concluded in 1850 that many of the beerhouses were brothels in all but name and that almost all of them afforded 'facilities for dishonourable intercourse between the sexes'. Similarly at this time the town's clerk to the justices told a parliamentary committee of how at a beerhouse 'dice were thrown for a pretty girl of loose character' and the man who had the highest number then 'bedded the girl in full daylight'.[18] Making a distinction between commercial and non-commercial sex, we find that drinking places had also often been used for the latter. London gin retailers in the early eighteenth century provided room or space needed for casual sexual encounters. But courting couples used them too. Rebecca Clements of Chelsea took up with John Coustos in 1746, and they had sex several times at the Angel Inn and also the Cheshire Cheese there.[19] There was also from the beginning of the eighteenth century, we might note here, a homosexual world in London of 'molly houses', clubs or particular public houses where men met, socialised and had sex together. Such were the Royal Oak and Three Tobacco Rolls alehouses in Pall Mall and Drury Lane in the 1720s. A century later the *Times* reported raids on public houses like the Barley Mow, the Rose and Crown and the Bull Inn. But it was not confined to the capital. Thomas Rix, a Manchester artisan hanged for sodomy in 1806, had most of his encounters with other men in the street or in public houses.[20]

The legislation of 1869 and 1872 helped to bring to an end the use of public houses for sex. The former Act, as we saw, allowed local authorities to get rid of beerhouses which were connected with prostitution. The latter Act made brothel-keeping the most serious offence a publican could commit, providing for forfeiture of the licence and permanent disqualification from holding one. It also made it an offence to permit reputed prostitutes, whether or not their purpose was prostitution, to frequent licensed premises except to obtain 'reasonable refreshment'. As we will see in the next chapter, the threat to the increasingly valuable licence now provided a strong incentive not to contravene the law. Prostitutes of course still continued to get their reasonable refreshment, but prostitution itself was becoming less common by the late nineteenth century. It is surely significant that when the licensee of a Manchester pub, the Imperial Wreath, was prosecuted for harbouring prostitutes in 1897, the *Manchester Guardian* opined, 'the time had long passed for a house of this kind to exist in the centre of the city.' Rowntree in York thought that there were not more than a score of professional women, but claimed young women did use pubs to meet men for 'immoral purposes'.[21] For courting and 'immoral purposes' couples thus still used and met in pubs, but the sex itself, if there was to be any, was enjoyed elsewhere.

It would of course be wrong to suggest that women in pubs were there chiefly for sex, commercial or otherwise. For women customers particularly we have a unique source for the mid-Victorian period in the form of a survey of drinking places which actually went inside and recorded details of the patrons. James Scurrah, a house painter, lay preacher and temperance activist, carried out his survey of Bradford pubs in 1875. He found that the beerhouses were very much male preserves. Even on a Saturday women there were few. They were more to be found in the fully-licensed houses and dram shops. In those in the town centre 15 per cent of the customers over three Saturdays were women. In only two instances does Scurrah specifically identify them as prostitutes – the 'gay class' as he put it in contemporary usage. There are sixty-nine references to their being in some way 'loose', which can include in Scurrah's eyes simply being Irish or 'of the locality', as well as sitting on men's knees. But in thirty-eight instances it is the women's respectability which is of note. Overall the women were either with other women in groups, with husband or sweetheart, or coming to market.[22] Other scattered evidence supports this. Bill Williams, a store keeper and clerk at a Forest of Dean colliery, recorded in his diary at this time going to the pub with his sweetheart. He was also then a chapel goer.[23] Scurrah similarly noted seeing Sunday school teachers and a class leader in pubs, suggesting that it would be wrong to think of a complete divide between the worlds of pub and chapel, although Williams himself later did become teetotal. Finally, we find servant Hannah Cullwick happy to share a pint and some bread and cheese with another girl at a pub.[24]

In the late nineteenth century concern over women drinking increased, which in turn greatly expanded the amount of evidence on the subject. Working-class London in particular had a 'considerable women's pub culture'. In the East End Monday was recognised as ladies' day, when women still had a little money left over, and the pubs they used became 'cowsheds', from the local male epithet for women. South of the Balls Pond Road the King's Arms in the High Street was the 'cowshed par excellence', according to Booth's police guide. Late morning or early evening were the favoured times for their favourite tipple of gin. The local butcher helped things along by offering a drink to anyone who bought a joint.[25] Elsewhere in London more 'respectable' women liked a drink too. In a number of West End neighbourhoods larger public houses opened special ladies' bars to accommodate them.[26] In the provinces the evidence is more mixed. The informant on the West End ladies also noted such bars in the hilly districts of South Wales, where they were 'known by a very coarse slang expression which is very well understood among people to mean bars for women'. In Manchester too, Monday was said to be women's day. In Birmingham at the close of the Saturday night market married women would sit in the pubs waiting for the sale of meat to begin. Older married women tended to be the main female group in Birmingham pubs. The rooms where they congregated away from their husbands were nicknamed the Cow Shed in Aston or the Duck Pen in Sparkbrook. In Hull the snug was the place for women, either with men or by themselves, or else they drank in the passageway at the bar window.[27]

In the end, however, many women shunned pubs, either by choice or compulsion. Roberts noted that 'few respectable wives visited public houses' in his Salford slum. Rowntree also found a 'comparatively small amount of public-house drinking done by women in the more respectable working-class districts' of York. A report in a Dewsbury newspaper at this time similarly saw a 'notable absence of women'. This was true of rural areas. In east Kent few women went to the pub unless with their husband on a Saturday night. It again was not thought to be respectable, a view reinforced by the fact that London women down for the hop-picking did.[28] Some publicans would not let women come in, like the landlord of a York pub, whose daughter noted too: 'It would never occur to me to go into a pub.'[29] This was probably a common sentiment. It is supported by the growth over the century of the ideal of the woman's place in the home. Overall it seems likely that Shadwell had the better of the argument. The use of pubs by women declined over the nineteenth century, and those that did were overwhelmingly from the poorer classes in towns and cities.

Their children and babies sometimes came with them. Until the twentieth century there was nothing to prevent them. The law did not interfere with children and drink at all until 1839, when in London the sale of spirits was prohibited for on-consumption to children under sixteen. Other towns followed this lead in local legislation, but it was not made general until 1872. This was extended in 1886 to all forms of alcoholic drink for children under thirteen. In 1901 this was raised to fourteen by legislation which principally sought to deal with the common practice of children buying drink to take home for their parents. In London, for example, a survey of two pubs on a Sunday afternoon in September 1897 had shown 283 infants and children going in with jugs and bottles. Publicans were accused of giving sweets and even cheap cigarettes as inducements. The so called Child Messenger Act then prohibited sale to children except in 'corked' and 'sealed' vessels.[30] But the contemporary concern over the welfare of children was not to be assuaged. In February 1907 London journalist George R. Sims published a series of articles in the *Tribune* titled 'The Cry of the Children'. In emotive and immoderate language he blamed children's exposure to alcohol and the pub for the failure of the infant mortality rate to improve and the threat this posed to the future of the nation. Babes were being 'slowly murdered in the dram shop in their mothers' arms', exposed to the 'reek of tobacco smoke and alcohol' and allowed to crawl around in the spit and sawdust on the floor.[31] Mothers did certainly take infants and children into the pub, as the 1897 survey also showed. But as the chief constable of Leeds conceded in 1908, they were of course too young to be left alone. He was providing evidence to a Home Office inquiry on the subject, claiming that in his city it was not common. His colleagues from Birmingham, Bristol, Manchester, London and Sheffield, however, gave the opposite view. In Liverpool licensees had been pressed to discourage it and many had put up notices to that effect, but women could still sit with the children on the pavement outside, or take it in turns to watch over them.[32] The result of the campaign which Sims had provoked was a section in the 1908 Children Act which banned children under fourteen altogether from the bars of licensed premises. The wider issue was also addressed by sections in the Act which made it an offence to give alcohol to a child under five, except for illness, and provided a penalty for 'over-laying' – the suffocation of a baby in bed by its drunken parent. As to the legislation's effects, J. W. Crombie, who piloted the 1901 Act through Parliament, reported a month later that landlords found not serving young children at all preferable to coping with corking and sealing. The 1908 ban was said in contemporary newspapers to have had a dramatic effect.[33]

Although women did go to pubs, their greater use by men was often a source of tension, as they spent time and money there which could have gone on their families. At the beginning of the nineteenth century popular literature had portrayed this, reviling the rich publicans' wives, in an example of 1800, who 'flourish in their rings, gold chains, lockets, and what not, while we and our children have not bread to eat'[34] (Figure 6). The contrast between the alleged wealth of the publican and his wife and the misery caused by their trade remained a key element of temperance propaganda (Figure 13). In Edwardian London wives were in a 'continuous tug-of-war with pubs' for part of the housekeeping. A variety of stratagems were used to obtain it, from physically dragging the offending husband out of the pub, to arrangements with obliging publicans to limit spending, to going with them, like Ann Jasper of Hoxton, whose local landlord would push the change in her direction. But at the extreme, drink could also fuel violence. As one London magistrate put it: 'If I were to sit here from Monday morning till Saturday to protect women that had got brutal and drunken husbands, I should not get through half of them.'[35]

Until the First World War pubs were open most of the time. Restrictions imposed during the preceding century covered only Sunday and opening during the night. Historically, closing during the hours of divine service was the only limitation. This was formalised, along with Good Friday and Christmas Day, as a condition of the licence in the consolidating Act of 1828. Statutory opening hours were first introduced for the new beerhouses, as we saw, covering night and Sunday. The principle was then extended to all licensed premises in London in 1839, when they were required to stay closed on Sundays until 1 p.m. Other localities did the same, and with evidence of its beneficial effects national legislation followed in 1848, prescribing 12.30 or the end of divine service. Legislation in 1854, the so called Wilson-Patten Act, closing pubs on Sunday for most of the afternoon, proved to be unpopular and was repealed within a year, but a pause from 3 to 5 p.m. was retained. Finally, the Public House Closing Acts of 1864 and 1865 covered London pubs between 1 and 4 a.m., but could be adopted elsewhere, and many places did so. In some of the numerous examples of the endless complication of the licensing laws, railway stations were exempted altogether and magistrates could do so too for those attending markets or any other lawful trade or calling. The Licensing Acts of 1872 and 1874 then codified opening hours for the next four decades, distinguishing London and other places, but essentially restating night-time and Sunday morning and afternoon closing. Only in Scotland and Wales was total Sunday closing enacted respectively in 1853 and 1881.[36]

Although restrictions alone did not shape the pattern of pub use, they were an important contributor to it. Sunday was the only full day of leisure, but the pubs then were increasingly closed. With Saturday the last working day, and for many for much of the period also a full working day, then Saturday night was the great time for the pub and drinking. In the 1834 survey of London gin shops cited earlier nearly one-third of the customers went in on that night alone. As the West Riding magistrate Ellis Cunliffe Lister put it, also to that 1834 committee: Saturday was pay night and thus working people congregated 'in large quantities, and by that means excite each other to get drunk'. This could make for some unpleasant scenes. The *Leeds Mercury* in 1824, for example, reported gangs of riotous young men from the surrounding districts going into Halifax, getting drunk and setting off in search of fun, which apparently involved knocking down local people and other acts of violence. This was in the context of the death of a fourteen year old local youth. Friedrich Engels reported of Manchester in the 1840s:

> On Saturday evenings, especially when wages are paid and work stops somewhat earlier than usual, when the whole working class pours from its own poor quarters into the main thoroughfares, intemperance may be seen in all its brutality. I have rarely come out of Manchester on such an evening without meeting numbers of people staggering and seeing others lying in the gutter.

For James Scurrah Saturday night was the 'Drink Carnival'. His estimate of the number of men in pubs on that night is equivalent to over two-thirds of those aged twenty to thirty-nine and around one in ten of the women in that age group in the town.[37] Sunday evening, in contrast to Engels who reported the same scene as Saturday only less noisy, was for Scurrah a much quieter affair. He also observed the effect of the afternoon break in the Bolton Road slum district: 'At every house I saw men standing outside waiting to go in and especially near opening time.' Some would be returning after a meal and sleeping off the lunchtime session. In working-class London this was exclusively a time for men. Even steady and respectable Battersea railway workers went to the pub before dinner, though they were careful to get back on time. In other households late arrival could lead to nasty confrontations.[38] In addition to Sunday at the local, fine days saw people heading out to the countryside and its pubs, not least because travellers were exempted from its restriction, like the thousands reported going from the East End to Epping Forest and Wanstead Flats in the 1890s.[39] Finally, one must note that as the pubs were open every other morning except Sunday, it was the habit of some to call in on their way either to or from work. Thus men at the huge Elswick works at Newcastle had their glass of spirits before work, and then the nightshift men replaced them.[40]

Alcoholic drink was central to pub life. This perhaps obvious but essential point is reinforced by the failure of temperance reformers to recreate the pub experience without it. Similarly, the working-men's club movement, which originated in efforts to create a place for drink-free sociability, fairly quickly found it necessary to allow it, for this as well as financial reasons. Our focus here is on drink and the pub, but well into the nineteenth century beer particularly was regarded as a necessity of life. As such it was consumed at home, work and in institutions like schools, hospitals and workhouses. Broadly speaking, however, and particularly from around mid-century, its consumption came to be increasingly focused on the pub as a more purely rec-reational activity. Home brewing, for example, declined to negligible amounts by the 1870s. Tea consumption in contrast soared.[41] Having said that, there continued to be a lot of home drinking. Commercial brewers also catered for the family trade, and from its creation in 1834 the off-licence provided beer for home consumption, in addition to the public house itself. With more restrictive licensing from 1869, which however limited the justices' discretion with regard to new beer off-licences, their number rose from 3,000 at the beginning of the 1870s to almost 12,500 by 1881. From 1882 that discretion was restored, but numbers remained over 12,000 into the new century. To them must be added grocers' licences to sell spirits, introduced in 1861 to allow respectable people to buy spirits without going to a public house, which numbered by then over 10,000. They were con-stantly criticised as providing a cover for female drinking, although the House of Lords Committee on Intemperance at least found the case not proven.[42]

Beer was the essential pub drink. It finally replaced old-fashioned unhopped ale by the end of the seventeenth century. It in turn was varied, produced as it was by hundreds of common brewers and thousands of individual publicans well into the nineteenth century, reflecting the use of local malts, water, yeast and brewing practices. These local brews were always most important, including cider in the West Country, although it and provincial beers were already being brought into London from the later seventeenth century. In the capital, from the 1720s porter became the dominant variety of beer.[43] Although it is difficult to reconstruct the precise development of changes in taste, Richard Wilson has provided a broad outline for the nineteenth century. Around 1830 the 'beer map' showed porter dominant in London and some other large cities and 'an infinite variety of mainly strong beers in most regions'. During the century this changed in two key ways. With London taking the lead there was an increasing demand for mild, sweet ales to replace porter. Second was the growth of demand for Burton ales, or versions of them, pale, sparkling bitter beer. These beers were still strong, but the revolution in the science of brewing from the 1870s aided the move to lighter beers, which was helped in turn by shifting the basis of taxation to the strength of the brew in 1880. According to type and strength, this generally cost between 2d and 4d a pint.[44]

The changing strength of beer is one of a number of difficulties we face in assessing trends in the overall amounts of beer that were drunk. The statistics themselves present problems, which are exacerbated by such variables as the changing age structure of the population and the effects of shifting patterns of drinking by sex or social class. We can at least be confident that in the past levels of consumption were high. At the beginning of the eighteenth century, depending upon different estimates for the amount of private brewing, consumption per head was of the order of twelve to sixteen pints a week, although a proportion of this was small beer by women, children and servants. Individual male consumption could be much higher. In the mid-eighteenth century ordinary labourers were said to drink about four pints of strong beer a day, London printers six pints a day and coal heavers, unloading from ships on the Thames, as much as eight pints.[45] To this one must add the huge amount of gin consumed. From those levels consumption fell, but remained high. By the beginning of the nineteenth century, excluding now private brewing, it was still over five pints a week per head. This declined during the sometimes economically troubled 1840s and 1850s, before rising again with the mid-Victorian boom to over six pints per head a week by the late 1870s. From this high level it again now declined and reduced by more than a quarter to 1914 at four-and-a-half pints, still high but clearly diminishing. Of course this is once again an aggregate figure; the drinkers are drinking more. Making allowances for children, abstainers and lower female consumption, one late nineteenth-century estimate of male consumption put it at between eleven and twelve pints a week. At these levels drink was always a major item of working-class expenditure, amounting among the poorest families to perhaps a quarter of their incomes, and of course underlay the tensions we have noted.[46]

Those levels of alcohol consumption were rooted in a number of practices and beliefs. It was an essential item of diet, and despite improvements to the water supply or the spread of alternatives remained so for many people, to which all those children with jugs and bottles testify. Similarly, its perceived contribution to strength and health, when so many men and women continued to work long and hard, endured through all attempts to discredit the connection. There were other psychological satisfactions, not least from intoxication. Whether one views it crudely as the quickest way out of Manchester or London, or as a variety of religious experience – 'the great exciter of the *yes* function in man', bringing the drinker 'from the chill periphery of things to the radiant core' – they were undoubtedly powerful. As Robert Roberts wrote of his father: he 'loved liquor as he loved life'.[47] Central to drinking too was what has been called symbolic exchange, the immense variety of rituals which bound the drinkers together. The temperance campaigner John Dunlop documented that variety in the 1830s, grouping about 300 different customs into no fewer than twelve types. These included the footings and loosings to begin and end a job or apprenticeship, the celebration of particular points in a job, like the rearing ale when the roof of a building was completed, as well as familiar occasions like marriages, births and funerals. He felt that many of them were of relatively recent origin, and was gratified that masters

and foremen were by then ending some of them. But drinking rituals, above all that basic one of treating – buying someone a drink
– remained an essential part of pub life.[48] It is impossible in the space
here to examine all that drinking meant to people. Something of the
pub's essential appeal to men is captured by D.H. Lawrence in *Sons
and Lovers*. Morel escapes to his local:

> The Palmerston windows were steamed over. The passage was paddled
> with wet feet. But the air was warm, if foul, and full of the sound of
> voices and the smell of beer and smoke.
>
> 'What shollt ha'e, Walter?' cried a voice, as soon as Morel appeared in
> the doorway.
>
> 'Oh, Jim, my lad, wheriver has thee sprung frae?'
>
> The men made a seat for him, and took him in warmly. He was glad.
> In a minute or two they had thawed all responsibility out of him, all
> shame, all trouble, and he was clear as a bell for a jolly night.[49]

The chief elements of a jolly night were described by Joseph Lawson,
looking back on his Pudsey alehouses, as talking, playing games and
music. The talk he characterised as village gossip, 'spinning long
yarns of various sorts and cracking jokes'. Sport and gambling were
other favoured topics. James Burnley was struck by this on visits to
Bradford pubs in the mid-1880s, and the 'sanguinariness' of the language. In one pub the talk was mostly of horses, and in another it was
'running on dogs and coursing in one corner; in another pigeon-
flying is the topic of discussion; while on a longsettle near the fire
sit three men who are offering to bet fabulous sums with each other
on some pedestrian match'. In rural East Anglian pubs work was the
chief topic of conversation, the men going over the day's tasks in
minute detail. No doubt too, current affairs sometimes came under
discussion, as it was common for newspapers to be available in pubs
to read or hear read. Although as Dickens characterised it at the
Three Jolly Bargemen in *Great Expectations*, a 'popular murder' was
of more interest to the group assembled round the fire. Later in the

century it might be the divorce cases from the *News of the World* on a Sunday night. But more elevated discussion was also to be heard. In mid-Victorian Birmingham, for example, regular impromptu political discussions took place in pubs as well as more formal groups like the Hope and Anchor Sunday Evening Debating Society, which chose a wide range of political, literary and social topics. At one pub scientific lectures were accompanied by practical experiments.[50]

There was an enormous variety of pub games. Lawson, for example, identified in the 1820s dominoes, 'shuvving the penny', 'marrowing each other's coins', 'odd-man-ing' and puff and dart, whilst played outside the alehouse were brasses, quoits and skittles. In rural areas games like these were still played in Edwardian times. In east Kent there was ringing the bull, matchboxes, tip it and smoking contests and in East Anglia skittles and quoits were still played outside nearly every pub, as well as darts or ring-the-bell. In urban pubs dominoes, darts (the throwing version eventually replacing the blowing one) and cards were the chief games. Some pubs provided bagatelle boards or billiard tables. In London in the early 1850s, 326 pubs were licensed for the latter and 1,269 for the former.[51]

Sport also maintained its 'symbiotic link' with drink and the pub. Boxing in particular was closely linked with it from the days of the prize fight through the greater respectability of the gloves, which some London landlords provided.[52] Other blood sports were still staged at pubs, although by then illegal. In November 1841, for example, Samuel Hird of the Rock Inn in George Street, Bradford was convicted of allowing the baiting of a fox and a badger in the brewhouse. And in that same district another beerhouse landlord received three months in 1861 for staging a dog fight in an upstairs room. In Liverpool pubs at this time they were said by one observer to be held several times a week, usually in the early morning, especially on Sunday, when the police were going off duty. In both towns dogs were also used to kill rats in contests. Henry Mayhew was informed of dog fights at London beerhouses and that rat pits were kept at around forty pubs, like the King's Head in Compton Street, Soho for which printed bills were produced: 'Killing To Commence At Half past 8 precisely.'[53] The killing then seems to have become unusual at pubs themselves, but continued to be organised from them, like shooting birds or coursing, which were important up to the First World War.[54] And the followers of legal blood sports, like fox hunting, continued of course long beyond this time to begin and end at public houses. Other traditional sports also continued. Bowling retained its popularity: in Edwardian Norwich publicans organised bowling clubs and a firm of brewers ran the Anchor League. Knur and spell was especially popular in the north of England: in 1920 it was still the most commonly advertised pub sport in the *Yorkshire Post*.[55] Landlords, though, were always willing to try new pastimes. Ping pong, for example, was reported at Huddersfield pubs in 1902.[56] In the case of football, although some teams were based at pubs, and the electric telegraph was used to provide customers with match updates, the real locus of the game was the ground. Thus a Blackburn publican complained in 1883 that, apart from a few pubs, football was bad for business.[57] In this sort of way, one can argue, the symbiotic link was beginning to weaken.

Bound up with the love of games and sport was the equally passionate devotion to gambling. Lawson's alehouse games were all played for beer. It was a source of constant contention with the authorities throughout the period, as gambling for money or money's worth was illegal. Whatever the law said, however, it was widespread, and indeed increased in the later years of the century. In horse racing, for example, the electric telegraph provided starting-price odds and speedy results, and pubs in some areas came to be used extensively for betting.[58] Other sports also provided suitable objects for a bet. In addition, numerous sweepstakes, raffles and lotteries were held, often for the social, sick and Christmas clubs which were run at the pub. From about 1900 slot machines appeared. By 1912 there were said to be hundreds in Yorkshire, for example, delivering to the winner a check to be exchanged for beer or cigarettes.[59] The latter, we might note here, had by then become essential features of the pub scene, eclipsing from the 1880s the clay pipes once often provided free by landlords.[60] And whilst spittoons remained a feature in the tap room in particular, ash trays would eventually replace them as essential pub fixtures for another century at least.

Music was the third of Lawson's essential pub activities. He meant informal pub songs, mostly on 'love, drink and war'. Francis Place remembered some of the songs in his father's parlour either glorifying criminals or dealing with sex, like 'A Hole to Put Poor Robin In', or 'Morgan Rattler':

> First he niggled her, then he tiggled her
> Then with his two balls he began for to batter her
> At every thrust, I thought she'd have burst
> With the terrible size of his Morgan Rattler

In Edwardian East Anglian pubs the songs were remembered as patriotic or romantic, but the tone of aggressive masculinity is there still in this ditty:

> Oh, she makes me do the washing;
> She makes me scrub the floor,
> She makes me run all errands
> Until my feet are sore.
> But I'll be level with her;
> Oh I'll be level with her.
> I'll cut her throat
> And away I'll slope
> I will! So help me never!

Landlords would give a pint to the first man to start the singing. Instruments like a squeeze box or a fiddle were used. Contests were held, with teams each side of the balk – the beam across the pub ceiling.[61] Informal singing like this was common throughout the period, and itinerant musicians provided accompaniment or entertainment in their own right. Mayhew for London documented these street entertainers, like Whistling Billy who performed in as many as forty pubs in an evening, doing the hornpipe and the brandy jig and playing his instrument up his nose.[62] The 'free and easy', or the 'harmonic meeting', were rather more formal, with a chairman and a mixture of amateur and professional talent. It was but a step then for some publicans to establish purely professional concert rooms. These flourished from the 1830s. Charles Rice was a part-time professional comic singer in London who recorded in his diary thirty-three pubs with concert rooms where he performed. They were established in towns of any size.[63] Some in turn began to style them 'music halls', one step away in turn from the hall to be separated from the pub itself. Thus in Bolton, for example, Thomas Sharples opened the Star Concert Room at the Millstone Inn in 1832. When he moved to another inn in 1840, which he renamed the Star, the concert room was in a building to the rear, which also housed a museum. The concert room could hold up to 1,500 people. It was arranged like a theatre and entry was by a 2d token redeemable at the bar. By the 1860s the site had become a veritable entertainment complex, with two pubs, a theatre, a music hall, a museum and a games room.[64] The Star, and pub music generally, attracted considerable criticism from those who worried about the morals of the lower orders. This prompted efforts to regulate it, either through the existing licensing system or the imposition of a requirement for a separate music licence. Legislation for music, dancing and other entertainment had in fact been passed for London in 1752, and now other local authorities took similar powers. In practice the licences were usually routinely granted, in a manner more bureaucratic than reformist, as in Leeds, for example, from 1867. In 1890 the Public Health Acts Amendment Act provided model regulations for local councils to adopt.[65] In yet another small way the pub world became subject to official interference.

In addition to providing a venue for this recreational trio, pubs continued to perform a range of other functions. In the provision of accommodation the new purpose-built hotels may have been replacing inns, but pubs still catered for travellers. Two men enjoying a long walk across Yorkshire from Clapham to Scarborough in 1875 stayed at pubs on the way, just as John Byng and others had done before them, and with similar mixed fortunes.[66] Some pubs acted as lodging houses. In Manchester around 1850 a quarter of the beerhouses let off apartments to lodgers. In Bradford at that time just over half took in lodgers, usually a single individual, but others clearly functioned as lodging houses. By 1891 this had fallen to one in ten. Elsewhere, however, the practice continued. Plymouth pubs were letting rooms in the 1890s to help make the business pay, and in rural east Kent pubs too had permanent lodgers.[67] The provision of food presents a similar story. Although restaurants and other types of eating house proliferated, pubs continued to serve food. Late Victorian and Edwardian pubs offered coffee and food in the morning, hot dinners like hot-pot, or the traditional set meal or 'ordinary'. They allowed customers to eat their own food, or cooked it for them, providing mustard, salt and even pickles. Itinerant food sellers visited pubs, as Mayhew saw, with fried fish, shrimps, pickled whelks and periwinkles, baked potatoes or sheeps' trotters. Others displayed the goods outside, like early takeaways. For all of them the fish and chip shop was to be a great competitor. Robert Roberts noted how Salford pubs were avid for trade, and put on free snacks, or supplied potato pie, cheese and pickles, a pint of beer and a piece of thick twist tobacco – all for 4½d.[68]

Many of these diners of course were workmen, like the Salford carters enjoying their cheap 'carters' pint' with the free snack. But the pub was bound up with the world of work in more ways than simply as a place for meal breaks or to relax at the end of the working day. Carriers did not just enjoy their pints there: carrying services continued to be based at pubs until motorised transport superseded them, as commercial directories show.[69] Where casual labour predominated, as in the docks for example, pubs acted as clearing houses and employment exchanges and also as pay places. In Liverpool, for example, the lumpers – the middlemen who contracted to unload the vessels – and the foremen who selected the daily gangs, used pubs and were themselves sometimes publicans. In London the same was true of the business of unloading coal from ships on the river. It was the object of a long campaign from the eighteenth century to break its link with the pub, but it was only later nineteenth-century mechanisation which effectively ended it.[70] The campaign covered the payment of their wages in public houses, and this practice generally was the object of repeated efforts to stop it from at least the mid-eighteenth century. Nineteenth-century legislation eventually dealt with it. It was banned in the mining industry in 1842, but a general prohibition was not finally enacted until 1883. Probably more important in the decline of the practice was the development by employers of proper payment methods on the premises. But it still continued, particularly where the payment required changing.[71] More broadly, pubs still functioned as informal clearing houses for work. This was as true for the unemployed in urban Salford as in rural East Anglia, where a man requiring a draining or a ditching gang, or harvesters or beaters, would put a notice in a pub window and ask the men to meet there.[72]

As a meeting place, finally, the pub was absolutely essential right through our period until the First World War, even after the removal, as we saw, of such as administrative or political gatherings. Space here permits only a limited summary of the extent and variety of groups and organisations which made use of pubs. Workers' organisations like friendly societies or burial clubs were there from the early eighteenth century. The 'lodge' or 'club' room became a feature of many pubs, and the names Oddfellows, Druids or Foresters were used for them. For the authorities, more overtly trade or political groups were problematic until later in the nineteenth century, as we saw. During the years of fear generated by the revolution in France this was especially the case – the London Corresponding Society was formed at the Bell, in Exeter Street in October 1791. Parliament in 1799 legislated to prohibit such groups on licensed premises, in addition to local initiatives by licensing benches.[73] But following relaxation of the law, trade unions, for example, were based at pubs. Branches associated themselves with particular houses, as in early Victorian Nottingham, where the shoemakers met at the Butchers' Arms, the lacemakers and printers at the Durham Ox and the framework knitters at (most prominently) the Dove and Rainbow, Seven Stars and King George on Horseback. The organisation of industrial disputes was thus pub based, like the miners who operated from the White Cow during the strike of 1844.[74] By the close of the period there was some removal of these organisations to alternative premises, but the pub was still the favoured one. Around 1900 over two-thirds of the branches of the Manchester Unity of Oddfellows and the Ancient Order of Foresters, and over 80 per cemt of those of the Amalgamated Society of Engineers, met on licensed premises. In York the use of pubs for such meetings was said to be 'less general' than it was, but that the demand for such rooms still exceeded supply.[75] A variety of other social or hobbies clubs also met at pubs. In Edwardian Norwich, for example, at least 100 fishing clubs were connected to pubs and the club meetings of canary breeders too were invariably held there, with the landlord usually a prominent official.[76]

In Edwardian England then the pub was without doubt a central institution in working-class life. It was far more than the mere drinking den portrayed by its opponents. It has been argued, however, that its role had changed, with the loss of many of its former economic functions, to become more narrowly a place for leisure and relaxation.[77] But whilst this is to some extent true, it would be wrong, as the preceding discussion has suggested, to overstate that narrowing process before 1914. Nevertheless, trends are clearly discernible, particularly from the 1870s, which would ultimately work to contract that role much further. Levels of drinking, for example, remained high, as we saw, but per capita consumption had begun to decline from the end of the 1870s. In an analysis which has been widely accepted, it has been argued that the essential cause of this was a shift of working-class expenditure towards foodstuffs, mass produced clothing and household goods as the price of those commodities fell.

The price of drink, in contrast, remained stable and thus became relatively more expensive.[78] From this time too, home life began to improve. Although terrible slums survived into the twentieth century, the process of removing the worst housing had begun, and new housing built from the 1870s not only was better, but with stricter licensing the resulting neighbourhoods were no longer filled with pubs as they once had been.

More particularly, increased disposable income could be spent on the growing number of alternative leisure opportunities. The development of the music hall and, from 1900, the rapid growth of the cinema, the popularity of day trips and holidays, and the coming of sport as a mass spectator pursuit all provided alternative opportunities for leisure. It was not that drink or the pub ceased to be part of the leisure world. Pubs quickly began to organise trips, for example. But taken together those developments were inexorably reducing its central role. As one Bradford landlord put it of his falling trade in the face of the cinema: whereas before people stayed there all evening, now they just called in for a drink on their way to and from the picture house.[79] Further, as the home itself became more comfortable so it too became a place for relaxation, to read the Sunday paper there, to take just one example, rather than be in the crowd at the Three Jolly Bargemen. But the most direct alternative to the pub was the working men's club. It actually originated as an attempt to provide alcohol free 'places of resort' for working men, but a combination of the preferences of the working men themselves and the economics of running a club led to the majority of them providing drink. As Booth commented of London clubs, in a generally positive assessment of their role: 'The bar is the centre and support of a working man's club – the pole of the tent.' From 1902, they were required to register with the licensing authorities if they supplied drink to members. In 1904 there were 6,371 clubs of all kinds, including political, trade, sport and social clubs, rising to 8,738 by 1914, of which 1,613 were affiliated to the Club and Institute Union with 489,000 members. This meant one club for every ten on-licensed premises. And even though clubs by that date only accounted for 1.5 per cent of the gross expenditure on alcohol, or 2.4 per cent on beer, they were clearly important alternatives. As Booth again noted of the London clubs: beer, music, games and discussion were what were wanted – just as at the pub. But they clearly also provided something which the pub did not, and better-off working men in particular, with a desire for independence, participated in the club movement with enthusiasm.[80]

8

Policing the Pub

It will be clear by now that the State was concerned with drink and drinking places in a large number of ways. It required retailers to obtain an annual licence from the magistracy, which placed upon them various obligations in running the business. It specified at what times of the day they must close. These, and the other restrictions we have noted, were rooted in concerns about public order and morality. The State had a third area of interest – its revenue. This was considerable. In the eighteenth and nineteenth centuries a major proportion of government funds came from drink taxation. At its highest level, during the wars with France, it counted for over half of its revenue, and through the succeeding century it continued to average around one-third. There was thus more than the possibility of a conflict of interest with its concerns over order and morals, although it was feasible to justify taxation as itself a measure of moral reform.[1] The other essential point of tension, which must be emphasised before we examine how the pub was policed, was that the State increasingly problematised activities – drink and drinking in pubs – which the majority of the population regarded as unproblematic parts of everyday life. It will thus be an important part of my aim here to chart not only the express desires of the State in the laws which it passed and the policing arrangements which it created, but how those desires fared in the actual world of pubs and their customers.

Public order and morality were not new concerns. During the medieval period a wide range of measures were implemented concerning drunkenness and drinking places, although they tended to be local and temporary. The principal national legislation was the thirteenth-century assize of ale, which sought to regulate prices and ensure uniformity of quality and measures.[2] During the Elizabethan and Stuart periods there was a 'storm of criticism' of alehouses, founded on concerns over public order, fears of the apparently rising numbers of the poor and vagrant and religious hostility to drink itself.[3] This led to the development of a regulatory framework for drinking places and to the passage in the early part of the seventeenth century of several statutes dealing with the conduct of premises and individual drinking behaviour. By the middle of the eighteenth century this system of regulation, as we have seen, was largely in place. Its basic outline was as follows. To sell drink required an annual licence, which was granted by magistrates at special licensing (brewster) sessions. A further licence was then required from the Excise to retail spirits, extended to beer in 1808. Until 1828 recognizances had to be entered into and sureties provided. The terms of both licence and recognizance were that the licensee should keep the assize of bread and ale, not open during the hours of divine service, permit no unlawful games, drunkenness or any other disorder, but in general maintain in the house good order. In addition, there were other statutory offences covering the use of proper measures, Sunday trading, gaming and permitting tippling (drinking bouts in effect). Tippling was an offence for publican and customers. So too was drunkenness.[4]

Under this quite elaborate system regulation of drinking places could be achieved in two ways: through the licensing process itself, as we have seen, and in the courts. It is with the latter that I am here concerned. Formerly, manorial and ecclesiastical courts had dealt with offences, but with some local exceptions this practice had ceased by this time.[5] Quarter sessions heard the more serious offence of keeping a disorderly alehouse. Most cases were dealt with by local justices sitting in petty sessions. Disorderly cases were by this time rare, if the quarter sessions of the West Riding or Northumberland are typical.[6] But nor were petty sessions much more likely to deal with offences. A study of summary court records in Essex, for example, for selected years between 1770 and 1813, found just eight hearings for licensing offences out of a total of 1,200. Similarly, of 1,375 convictions reported for Middlesex between October 1773 and December 1786 just thirty-four were drinking or licensing offences. In the largely rural North Riding there were a mere eight convictions in the whole period between May 1781 and February 1800 and none at all from August 1814 to November the following year.[7]

Selling without a licence was the most common offence. It is surely significant that it was one which involved a loss of revenue to the State, whatever its moral or public order aspects. As such it had been reflected in the efforts of the Excise against unlicensed spirit sellers during the gin period in London.[8] It accounted for more than half the Middlesex cases and all but one of those in the North Riding. Similarly, petty sessions held in June 1744 at the Bell Inn, Great Cheverell, in rural Wiltshire, heard twenty cases involving spirits, but also cider and traditional cowherds' and clerks' ales. It was the largest category of offence recorded by Edmund Tew, the rector of Boldon in county Durham, but who dealt with cases over a wide area of Tyne and Wear. Through the years 1750 to 1764 Tew recorded just two cases of permitting tippling, and one of the individuals involved was an illicit trader. William Hunt, the Wiltshire justice whose notebook revealed the preceding cases, also in five years recorded just two instances, involving five men in each, of frequenting alehouses on Sunday and tippling. Finally, a petty sessions book covering Hackney in the 1730s and again briefly in the 1750s, when it was a mix of farms, market and nursery gardens, elegant suburbia and some industry, recorded forty-three cases of Sunday trading or serving during divine service, roughly five or six a year.[9]

One might have expected to see the growing concern over drinking and drinking places from the 1760s and 1770s reflected in increased court appearances. Magistrates throughout the country had after all asserted their determination to carry out the intent of the royal proclamation of 1787 and had indeed implemented a variety of measures tightening up the licensing system. In this the North Riding justices were typical, resolving to enforce 'with the utmost severity' the laws for preventing excessive drinking and tippling. A single conviction of a labourer for drunkenness in just under nineteen years, however, was scarcely severe.[10] Fundamentally, the absence of proceedings in this period was due to the system of policing and the context within which it operated. In contrast to the centralised efficiency of the Excise, this relied upon a small number of part-time, unpaid (except for expenses) local parish constables. They lacked both the time and resources to enforce the law with any rigour. More especially, they were subject to community pressures and the dictates of their own inclinations.[11] Head constable John Carrington, for example, a farmer by then in his seventies, was responsible for seven parishes in Hertfordshire. He was fond of a drink himself and kept on good terms with the local publicans, who included his son and two of his tenants. Little wonder that his diary from 1798 to 1810 makes no reference at all to dealing either with drunks or licensing offences. Or a man like Obediah Martin, a butcher and constable at South Cave in the 1830s, who also liked a drink and was also on good terms with the local victuallers, who were no doubt his customers. Moreover, despite the law's attempts to prevent it, many publicans also acted as constable, as we saw.[12] Community pressures were therefore internalised through the desire not to antagonise customers or fellow parishioners, or simply by sharing the feeling that no real wrong was being done. At times those pressures could be more explicit. This point was made by several witnesses to the 1833 Select Committee on the Sale of Beer, which focused in particular on the rural south of England and the disturbances known as the Swing riots. As many constables were farmers, they feared reprisals ranging from arson to 'odium' and thus were inclined to ignore evasions of the law. And even had they wished to brave them, they were hindered further by the reluctance of people to give evidence. As one witness succinctly put it: 'There are not many people who like to turn informers in country places.'[13]

Clearly the relative infrequency of proceedings is an uncertain guide to the actual incidence of the offences. To take the one that did appear most frequently – illegal selling – it was probably quite common. It cannot have been easy to detect, not least given the continued prevalence of home brewing. It would seem to have increased as the number of legitimate public houses contracted, both absolutely and in relation to population. In Devon, for example, the restrictive licensing policy was blamed, admittedly by an opponent of it, for the opening of unlicensed cider shops.[14] In populous Lancashire and the West Riding they were common enough to acquire their nickname of 'hush' or 'whisht' (from the dialect word for 'be silent') shops. Samuel Bamford described one of the former in the country near Bury in the mid-1810s. It was a thatched building with two rooms. In one a table was formed from an inner door lifted off its hinges and placed on bricks and logs, on which were placed two candles in clay sockets. Seating also consisted of bricks or logs, empty firkins, upturned mugs, stools or 'any other article affording a seat'. The company comprised farm servants, factory workers and weavers as well as 'sots, bullies and occasionally thieves'. They may of course have preferred the more rough-and-ready ambience to the more respectable licensed premises.[15] In the West Riding whisht shops were widely reported in the 1820s. In November 1826 twenty-nine people, including one woman, were fined for keeping them in several villages around Bradford. In January the following year the incumbent of Haworth, Patrick Brontë, chaired a public meeting in the vestry calling for the 'Suppression of Whisht Shops', which were said to 'abound' in the district. A correspondent to the *Leeds Mercury* offered this reason for their spread: 'Bad ale being sold by many publicans at high prices, forces their customers into these illegal houses.' Another felt they were so common as virtually to represent the free trade in beer then demanded.[16] Free trade might have been expected to reduce the incidence of illegal houses, but they continued to be reported in the succeeding decades, from Lancashire hush houses to the 'wabble shops' of the Midlands.[17] Illegal distilling was also a problem. In the

early 1850s detections for this reached over 500 a year. It was especially common in places with significant Irish populations.[18]

Illegal drinking shops were believed to act as receiving houses for
stolen goods, by the Haworth meeting for example, as well as havens
for thieves generally, as Bamford saw. Formerly, licensed public houses
were used for criminal activities. In mid-eighteenth-century Sussex,
inns acted as bases for the smugglers. In Staffordshire at that time
travelling thieves depended on a network of provincial 'flash' public
houses, like the Rose Tavern in the parish of Kinver, where the stolen goods could be disposed of.[19] By the early nineteenth century
it is likely that such activities were more confined to illegal houses.
In London these flash houses, used that is by thieves and prostitutes,
were much discussed before the parliamentary committees looking at the capital's policing. Although some witnesses denied their
existence, the report of that of 1828 unequivocally drew attention to
them, but noted that they were often unlicensed houses.[20]

Concern specifically about crime, together with the wider anxieties about the lower orders which fed into the movement for the
reformation of manners, led to attempts to improve the existing system of policing. As Clive Emsley put it, 'men of property in England
appear to have developed a new threshold for order maintenance ...
and sought improved policing to achieve this.' Improvement came
through attempts to make the parochial system more efficient, in local
ad hoc arrangements and from centrally driven institutional reform.
Overall, however, it was a protracted process, displaying continuity
as much as change.[21] But whatever the particular improvements to
policing, one thing that united them was their interest in drink and
drinking places. London exemplifies the process. Before the creation
of the metropolitan police in 1829 there were already, it has been estimated, well over 800 watchmen on patrol at night. Although it is not
possible to link them definitely with action against drinking places,
given that private individuals acted as informers, in a little under two
years, from 1815 to 1817, 267 informations were laid against publicans
at the eight London police offices, which represents one for every

thirteen establishments. Gaming, Sunday opening and permitting tip-pling formed all but four of the offences. The new police stepped up this effort. Between 1830 and 1838 an annual average of 905 licensed victuallers and beerhouse keepers were charged before police mag-istrates with breaches of the law, roughly one for every six to seven establishments.[22] In London, as elsewhere, the beerhouse keepers were, and continued to be, more likely to fall foul of the law. This in part reflected the well attested fact that they *were* as a group more badly run, as we saw, but also that the law on opening times was stricter for them.[23] To take another example, in Leeds an improved borough force of day constables and night watchmen secured an annual average over four years of forty-three convictions against publicans and beerhouse keepers. After the Municipal Corporations Act of 1835 obliged such boroughs to establish professional forces under a watch committee, this rose to sixty-one in the three succeeding years.[24] In Horncastle, a Lincolnshire market town, the provisions of the 1833 Lighting and Watching Act were used to create a local force whose prime aim was to police public houses and to keep the streets free of noisy drunks.[25] In the final example, in Keighley, a smaller West Riding industrial town, the parish constables were augmented from 1842 by salaried watchmen under the provisions of local legislation. The diary of one of them, James 'Pie' Leach, shows clearly their concerns. Of the inci-dents he dealt with, by far the largest category was drunkenness, but public houses and beershops also came in for particular attention as he noted where company was served after hours or gaming permitted.[26]

This Keighley force was superseded by the new West Riding police created under the County and Borough Police Act, which in 1856 finally brought professional policing (with officers paid, full-time and in uniform) to the whole country. It was in part through an exam-ination of this new force, which instantly imposed a more efficient supervision of pubs and beerhouses, that Robert Storch argued the case for the police's particular role as a 'bureaucracy of official moral-ity', intent on imposing discipline on working-class communities. At the same time he was careful to point out the 'serious problems' facing the new police in carrying out this 'moral reform mission'. Many of those problems in fact were to prove 'utterly intractable', but notwith-standing this the nineteenth century did see 'the forging of a modern and generally effective technique of order keeping'.[27] There was, in the first place, the question of manpower. In London in 1840, for exam-ple, there would have been about 900 men divided between morning and afternoon patrols at a time when there were over 6,000 licensed premises. In Hampshire a force of fewer than 200 men policed in 1850 a huge, largely rural, county with over 1,400 public and beerhouses.[28] There was also a fairly large question mark over the quality of many of the new policemen, or indeed existing policemen in new uniforms. The experience of the Lancashire county constabulary was typical. Of its first 200 recruits 50 were discharged within six months, including 30 for drunkenness.[29] Officers of course shared the culture of drinking and the pub they were policing; hence the efforts of their superiors to separate them from it. Force instructions typically forbade drinking or entering pubs on duty and publicans too faced a penalty for serving them.[30] As often as not the police adopted a pragmatic approach to their task. The London force, for example, in the 1840s warned publicans in the first instance over drinking after hours and observed a tacit period of drinking-up time, although the law made no provision for it.[31]

The police also faced the wiles of publicans and their customers. Lookouts were commonly employed to watch for them and evidence was hard to come by.[32] Where a case did get to court, a further com-plaint from the police was the difficulty of securing a conviction. The customers might now happily give evidence, but to support the publi-can. Magistrates too were often chided with their reluctance to convict, as for example in 1850 by John May, the superintendent of police in Chelmsford, that they were very 'tenacious' in accepting evidence in cases involving harbouring disorderly characters. These complaints are to some extent supported by statistical evidence. In London between 1830 and 1838, 5,592 licensed victuallers and 2,551 beerhouse keepers were charged before police magistrates. Of the former, 64.8 per cent were convicted and just 49.9 per cent of the latter. There was, however, much local variation. The Hampshire force in 1848 secured convictions in over 80 per cent of cases involving both types of house, although the chief constable still complained of the difficulties this involved.[33] As to specific offences, although we lack detailed evidence, opening in prohibited hours was probably the most common. In Bradford, for example, in the four years 1855 to 1858 this formed almost two-thirds of offences prosecuted. Fewer than one in five were gaming offences, with the same proportion for those of permitting drunkenness or disorderly conduct, prostitution and harbouring notoriously bad characters.[34]

To reiterate, the statistics of prosecutions in any case bear an uncertain relationship to the actuality of the offence. During those four Bradford years there were just thirty-one cases of permitting drunkenness or drunk and disorderly conduct. It seems unlikely that the pubs of Bradford, or the pubs of anywhere else, witnessed just eight drunken incidents a year. But what was the reality of behaviour? Clearly the complaints and fears of contemporaries, those fears of course which led to the improvements in policing, suggest substantial levels of drunken behaviour in pubs. But to set against this, there was a persistent belief that behaviour was actually improving. A number of witnesses to those London police committees of the 1810s and 1820s thought so. So too did the radicals Francis Place and Samuel Bamford.[35] Historians have concurred in this view, whilst acknowledging the many complexities of the question, as Brian Harrison did in examining the relationship between industrialisation and drinking. In some ways it worked to reduce drunkenness: employers in the new factories wanted sober workpeople, for example. In others it made it more attractive: the escape route from the harsh life in the new industrial towns.[36] The anxieties produced by the troubled early decades of the nineteenth century, which collectively have been called the Condition of England Question, may have obscured the extent of improvement. But with the receding of these fears from mid-century, improvement was now increasingly perceived, even during the surge of drink consumption in the 1860s and 1870s. Thus at the height of consumption the House of Lords Committee on Intemperance was able to conclude that there was no evidence that things had got worse over the longer term. Drunkenness had declined among the 'more respectable portion' of the working classes and the apprehensions for drunkenness were 'becoming more and more confined to the lowest grades of the community'.[37]

The noble lords also noted the improved character of licensed houses. This they attributed partly to the effect of public opinion on police energies in dealing with them. But they also stressed the effects of recent legislation.[38] That of 1869 had, as we saw, the effect of allowing licensing magistrates to get rid of the most disorderly beerhouses. The return of all drinking places to their control also heralded a much stricter licensing climate. Further, the Licensing Act of 1872 codified the variety of offences which a licence holder might commit and increased the penalties. The offences were now to be recorded on the licence. Repeated convictions might lead to its forfeiture. Breaches of the law thus placed the licence at greater risk. The context of the greater profitability of the trade, coupled with the fact that pubs were increasingly part of much larger brewery businesses, together with the restrictive licensing climate, all combined to put pressure on publicans to avoid falling foul of the law. The effect on proceedings was marked. In London, for example, in the five years to 1870 there was an annual average of 1,156 summonses against drink houses. In the succeeding five years this dropped to 421. In Manchester the proportion of reports to licensed premises fell from 23.5 per cent in the five years to 1869 to 7.5 per cent in the succeeding five. Other towns and cities showed falls of a similar degree.[39] This was in the context of increased police efficiency and vigilance. Despite accusations to the contrary, it seems that forces had got to grips with drunkenness amongst officers. There was also greater routine surveillance of licensed premises. In Manchester over 31,000 visits were made annually to the more than 3,000 pubs by the mid-1890s; in Bradford around 10,500 visits were made to some 600.[40] Falls in the number of prosecutions in the context of increased police vigilance point strongly to the conclusion that *actual* behaviour in pubs was becoming more orderly.

1 The late seventeenth-century galleried courtyard of the Bull and Mouth Inn, St Martin's le Grand, by Valentine Davis, *c.* 1806. To the left is the coffee room. This great coaching inn was rebuilt in 1830 as the Queen's Hotel

2 The Plough, Kensal Green, engraving by Mary Banks of *c.* 1820. A basic, unadorned public house in what was then a rural setting north of London. A popular local in the eighteenth century of the artist George Morland

3 William Hogarth, An Election II: Canvassing for Votes. The painting shows the centrality of drink and the public house to the electoral process. Note the landlady to the left counting the takings, the central figure taking two bribes at once and the gifts offered to the female relatives of voters. Note also the elaborate inn signs

4 The Nine Elms Tavern, Grigg Street, Portsmouth, *c.* 1875. This basic, urban beerhouse, but with 'palatial' surrounds to the doorways, shows the landlord's other occupation

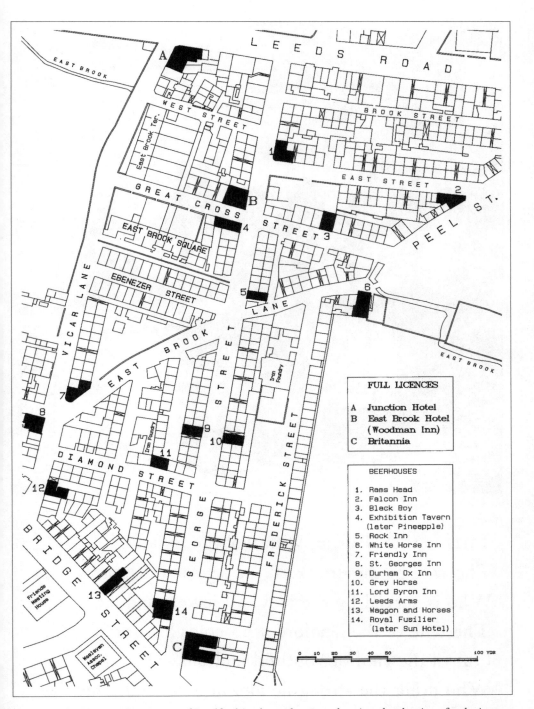

5 The George Street area of Bradford in the early 1850s showing the density of pubs in a poor working-class district. Contrast the three larger fully-licensed premises at prominent corner positions with the general dominance of small, back-street beerhouses. Not one of the pubs remains today

THIS is the *Woman*, with wobegone face,
The wife of the drunkard, in rags and disgrace,
Who is served by the lady, all jewels and lace,
The wife of the landlord who coins his bright gold,
Out of the ruin of youthful and old,
Who drink the strong liquors he sells night and day,
At the bar of the Gin-shop, so glittering and gay.

6 George Cruikshank, Interior of the Gin Shop Showing the Drunkard and his Wife, c. 1850.
Note the bar counter, the bar-back and the barrels of spirits in this temperance view of the
evils of drink

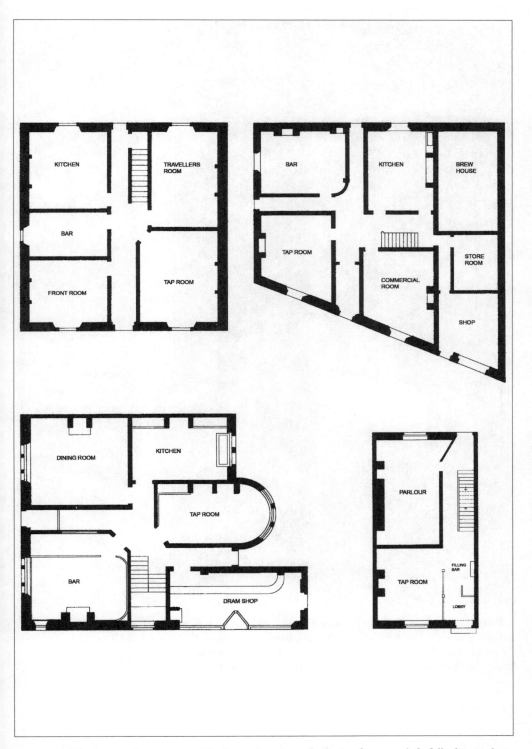

7 Mid-nineteenth-century public-house interiors: clockwise from top left, fully-licensed pub on a main road; same with brew house and attached shop; two-roomed basic beerhouse; and former inn with dram shop

8 Running a pub: landlord and landlady Arthur and Sarah Gray with staff – barmaid, barman and waiter (plus neighbouring shopkeeper to right) at the Black Swan Tavern, Thornton Road, Bradford, *c.* 1915. Arthur had previously worked for a wine merchant and been a head barman. Sarah was noted for her ability to deal with rough customers

9 The Old King's Head, Euston Road, 1906, showing the full splendour of the late Victorian and Edwardian gin palace. Note the prominent advertising and the ornate lamps

10 Crown and Anchor, North Street, Leeds, 1901, showing provincial splendour in a working-class district of the city. Note again the prominence of the brewery name. To the left is the Victoria Inn, a beerhouse

11 Public bar at the White Horse, Congreve Street, Birmingham, photographed in 1908 by Bedford Lemere. Note particularly the bar-back with its mirror glass and woodwork and the ceiling covered with tiles, a particular feature of Birmingham pubs

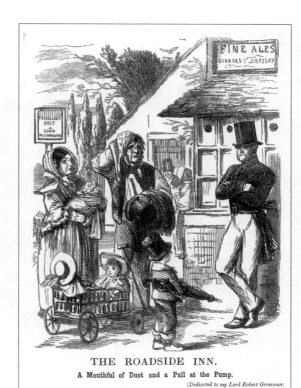

THE ROADSIDE INN.

A Mouthful of Dust and a Pull at the Pump.

[Dedicated to my Lord Robert Grosvenor.

12 Popular opposition to Sunday restrictions on pub opening is expressed in this *Punch* cartoon from 7 July 1855. Lord Robert Grosvenor was the author of a bill to restrict Sunday trading which provoked rioting in Hyde Park

13 The Doings of Drink, or The Publican Versus the People, from the painting by Robert Summers, a railwayman from Darlington, whose depiction of the evils of drink graced many a temperance home from the 1890s. Summers is rumoured to be depicted as the man in the check suit between Misses Whilde and Loose. The prosperity of the publican and his family are contrasted with the horrors produced by drink

Above and below: 14 *and* 15 Popular opposition to the 1908 Licensing Bill is expressed in these cartoons which were produced by the Trade as part of its campaign against the measure. From the *Brewing Trade Review*, 1 June 1908

Above and below: 16 and 17 The effects of improvement on the pub are displayed in these two photographs of the Golden Lion at Carlisle, contrasting the garish gin palace with what some hoped was to be the pub of the future

18 Brewers' Tudor displayed at the Barrack Tavern, Bradford, an older pub rebuilt in
1927–28 for Bentley's Yorkshire Breweries. Photographed here in 1995, it was later closed
and converted into a restaurant

Opposite above: 19 Pub interiors: clockwise from top left, late nineteenth-century island bar
arrangement; 1930s pub; 1950s pub with traditional layout; 1960s open plan with lounges

Opposite below: 20 The pub trip: ready for the off at the Delvers Arms, Bolton Road,
Bradford in the early 1920s. Such outings were an essential part of pub life

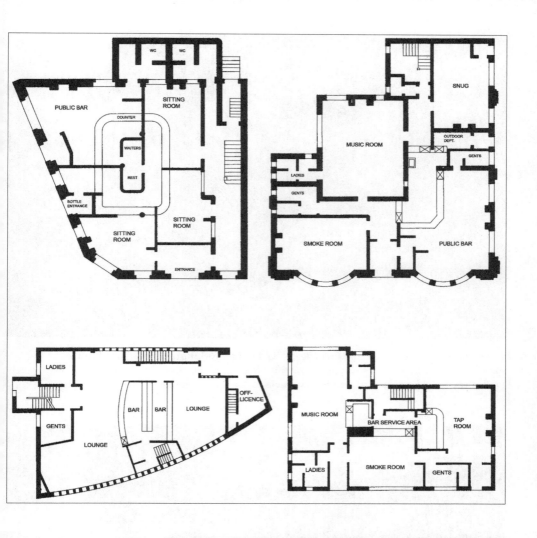

21 Snug at the (High) Ship Inn, Frenchgate, Richmond, Yorkshire, photographed in the summer of 1945 by J. Allan Cash of the British Council, to illustrate the life of an English market town. Older male and female customers in basic surroundings

22 The Red Ginn, Bowling Old Lane, Bradford, an estate pub of the late 1960s, which replaced an early eighteenth-century original but retained the old name referring to a device for drawing coal to the surface when mines were a feature of the area. Built by brewers Tetley of Leeds, it retained a public bar that featured Swedish-style seating

The early 1870s thus represent something of a watershed in the policing of the pub. The overall incidence of proceedings now remained low. In London the total had fallen by over half again by the mid-1890s. In Bradford convictions were annually in single figures by this time. What was the pattern of offences? In Leeds, in the twenty-four years from 1872 to 1895, just over half of all convictions were for permitting drunkenness or selling to a drunken person. The incidence of the latter fell away after 1882 and indeed there were no convictions at all in either 1886 or 1887.[41] As temperance campaigners and others tirelessly pointed out, however, this was in marked contrast to the number of proceedings against drunks. Nationally in 1899 these reached their highest ever figure at over 214,000, although in relation to population this was actually down from the peak years of the 1870s. As an academic study of the question put it: 'A drunken person is a common object; the conviction of a publican for serving a drunken person is a rare event'.[42] It is true that the police faced difficulties in securing convictions, as indeed they always had. It was not easy to prove that a person was drunk. There was no legal definition. Thus in 1864 the landlady of the Blue Bell at Beverley defined it as the inability to stand up, referring to a customer who had been drinking on Christmas Eve from ten in the morning to seven in the evening, and was 'merry, and quite jolly, but not lushy'. Hence the well-known lines:

> Not drunk is he, who from the floor
> Can rise again and ask for more:
> But drunk is he who prostrate lies,
> Without the power to speak or rise.[43]

It was also difficult to prove that a particular licensee caused the drunkenness or that the person was actually drunk when served. It could have resulted from drinking at various pubs or clubs or in a private house. It was not always easy to discern a state of drunkenness in a busy bar, unlike in the fresh air of the street outside, where they could be arrested for being drunk and disorderly. Licensees also made increasing use of legal assistance in court. Magistrates too tended not to accept the sole evidence of a constable and neither the drunk nor his fellow drinkers were normally willing to testify against the publican. Case-law on the offences did put the police in a stronger position and the Licensing Act of 1902 placed the burden of proof on the licensee that 'all reasonable steps' had been taken to prevent it. It also targeted customers by introducing a penalty for procuring a drink on licensed premises for a drunken person. But another reason finally for the low number of prosecutions was that put forward by a senior London magistrate: pubs were better managed by a better class of men.[44]

Elsewhere, serving in prohibited hours continued to be the most common offence. In Bradford, in the period 1875 to the outbreak of war in 1914, this accounted for just under half of all the proceedings.[45] The most vexatious for the authorities was Sunday trading. Its essential conflict with the main day of leisure raised the whole issue to that of music hall joke (Figure 12). An exemption had always existed for travellers, and as Sunday opening became more restricted this was retained. But then the Act of 1854 introduced the concept of a bona fide traveller to curb abuse of the existing exemption by those simply wanting a drink. The parliamentary committee which examined the workings of that Act felt that the new proviso was 'useless for the purpose of definition'. As its chairman had put it, having listened to the evidence of two 'eminent magistrates': 'one holds that nobody is a traveller, and the other holds that everybody is a traveller.'[46] But whilst its recommendation to rescind the 1854 restrictions on Sunday opening was accepted, the bona fide provision was retained, and in the Licensing Act of 1874 was given further definition as someone who was at least three miles from his previous night's lodging. 'Travelling' three miles for a drink seems then to have become something of a national institution. It was particularly so in Wales, where complete Sunday closing was enacted in 1881. Between Porth and Pontypridd, for example, a distance of four miles, sixty-three 'breaks' – small trams for seven passengers – operated a two-way traffic to the latter's fifty pubs. The joke would certainly thus not be lost on the readers of *The Diary of a Nobody*. An indignant Pooter is refused admission to the Cow and Hedge, having given his correct address to the porter in charge of the gate, whilst his companions claim to have travelled the necessary miles and are let in to enjoy their brandy and soda.[47] A judgement of 1893 removed the status of bona fide traveller if the main object of the travel was to obtain liquor. But another decision confirmed that in effect the three-mile rule did not apply to railway travellers, who could thus buy a ticket and enjoy a drink in the station refreshment room. The Royal Commission on the Liquor Licensing Laws of 1896 to 1899 heard yet more tales of the traveller. These again confirmed the extent of the practice and the absurdities involved, although it did not question the principle of limited Sunday opening.[48]

The clash between the law and popular preference was also illustrated in the third group of offences, for gambling. This had been and remained a hugely popular pub pastime, which seems to have increased in the later nineteenth century. Certainly concern grew, as seen in the founding of the National Anti-Gambling League in 1890.[49] This did feed into prosecutions. In Bradford, for example, they formed almost a fifth of offences in the period 1875 to the First World War, and the proportion grew to become the single largest group after 1900, although still only averaging four proceedings a year. The same was true of Edwardian Southampton. Convictions for gambling offences were the third highest category after permitting drunkenness and opening-hours offences, but totalled just five in eleven years.[50] But the law, as a study of the 'national evil' put it, was 'enigmatic and conflicting'. This is illustrated by a Batley case of 1912 involving one of the new slot machines on the bar at the Commercial Hotel, which offered a prize of a check to be exchanged for beer or cigarettes. The defence argued that some districts allowed them and that in any case competition for prizes was lawful. In darts, it was contended, whereas playing for a pint of beer was gambling, if the landlord were to offer a quart of beer for three bull's eyes with six darts it was not. For the prosecution precedent was cited that the issue of skill was irrelevant – any game for money or money's worth was gambling. The landlord was duly convicted of suffering gaming.[51]

If the number of proceedings for these three groups of offences was low, for the most serious ones, relating to prostitution and allowing thieves and other disorderly characters, it was lower still. Even in a port city like Southampton there were just two convictions between 1903 and 1914 for harbouring prostitutes, at the Vine Inn in High Street in 1912 and the Greyhound in Bridge Street the following year. In Bradford there were only ten proceedings in the whole period from 1875 to the war. The same was true of a range of other miscellaneous offences, including some of the newer ones. The laws regarding children and licensed premises, for example, were rarely used. In Southampton in those years there was just one conviction for serving a child under fourteen. In Bradford during the entire period from 1872 to 1914 only two cases of selling spirits to children were prosecuted, the Child Messenger Act was never invoked against a landlord and the 1908 provision as to children under fourteen in the bar was prosecuted a mere five times. As we have observed before, this may tell us little about the actual incidence of the practices. Even if the use of pubs by children did decline, as I have argued, it seems unlikely that it did to the extent suggested by proceedings. Similarly, prostitution may have become less common in the late nineteenth century, but it certainly did not disappear.

By the Edwardian period the publican was undoubtedly subject to a wide range of complex laws. *The Licensed Victuallers' Official Annual* for 1908 listed the offences under no fewer than sixty-three categories, far more than I can detail here, let alone assess their individual use.[52] The police paid attention to the conduct of licensed premises as they had done since their inception as professional forces. They, and reformers on their behalf, constantly argued for greater powers. They, and licensing justices, also wanted pubs to be more amenable to effective supervision. They thus took exception to multiple and side entrances to pubs and to compartments and snugs within them.[53] Not until the Licensing Act of 1902, however, was a clear power over structural alterations given to magistrates to address those concerns. But in the end, the extent to which the police brought licensees to court was tempered by a range of pragmatic considerations. And overall, I have argued, pubs were simply better run and less the scene of drunken and disorderly behaviour, or worse, than they had been. This in turn was the result of external pressures, which included policing, but also the enhanced value of the licence to their owners, increasingly brewery companies. It was also more fundamentally the result of slowly improving behaviour generally, a 'civilising process', or a greater diffusion of 'respectability' throughout the population, however one chooses to describe it.

This is not to suggest that pubs were now complete strangers to drunkenness or disorder. That would be absurd. One could fill a volume with examples. Like the beershop which James Burnley visited in the White Abbey slum district of Bradford, where 'drunk and disorderly' seemed to be the motto of the establishment. At closing time two women started to fight and were ejected by the 'bullet-headed' waiter. Outside, as scores of White Abbey residents came out to see the excitement, two men took up their quarrel until two policemen turned up to separate them. As Burnley passed on, to his ears came 'sounds of weeping women and cursing men, shrieking children and howling dogs', prompting his concluding thoughts: 'let us improve our slums away as much as we may, slummy people will still continue to exist, and men and women will congregate in wickedness and wretchedness.'[54] I leave the last words, however, to Charles Booth, certainly not one to minimise the misery caused by drink. For him, 'the ordinary public house at the corner of any ordinary East End street' presented this scene:

There, standing at the counter, or seated on the benches against wall or partition, will be perhaps half-a-dozen people, men and women, chatting together over their beer – more often beer than spirits – or you may see a few men come in with no time to lose, briskly drink their glass and go. Behind the bar will be a decent middle-aged woman, something above her customers in class, very neatly dressed, respecting herself and respected by them. The whole scene comfortable, quiet, and orderly.[55]

9

Politics and the Pub

We have seen how the State was concerned with the threats which drink and public houses might pose to public order and morality and how it sought to regulate and police it. We have noted too its significant dependence on the drink trade for revenue. These were thus important political concerns. They had been so indeed since the medieval period and at times, such as with the fear of alehouse culture in the Tudor and Stuart periods or the early eighteenth-century gin epidemic, had been intensely so. But that political salience increased from the later eighteenth century, not only as a result of familiar concerns about order and morals, but in, for example, the arguments for free licensing. In the nineteenth century it went on to become a key issue in political life, a centrality conveyed by the idea of a Drink Question or a Liquor Problem, however contested the actual questions and possible solutions might be.[1] It is not here my aim to attempt to examine the issue in all its complexity. That, as George Wilson's seminal temperance oriented study noted, would be a 'stupendous task'.[2] Rather, what I wish to do is explore in what ways this intense level of political debate had actual consequences for the pub and its customers.

My concern is with the effect of temperance sentiment broadly conceived as the belief that excessive drinking was a social problem which had to be addressed (Figure 13). At one extreme of this conviction was the teetotal advocacy of complete abstinence from alcoholic drink. In its early phase it sought to achieve its ends through a policy of 'moral suasion', of drinkers to give up drinking voluntarily. Whilst some did respond to the call, clearly most did not, as consumption figures and patterns of pub use amply testify. As Bradford publican Jeremiah Rudd, also a member of the town council, put it to a public meeting at the Temperance Hall on the proposed repeal of the 1854 Sunday Closing Act: 'Gentlemen who were in the habit of addressing societies composed chiefly of teetotallers, too generally supposed that they were addressing the people of England.'[3] The alternative to persuasion was prohibition, and in 1853 was formed the United Kingdom Alliance for the Suppression of the Liquor Traffic. It sought to achieve its aim by giving people the opportunity to 'veto' the sale of drink in their locality. This too was not successful, either in a series of so called Permissive Bills or in local veto legislation introduced by the Liberal Government in 1893 and 1895.[4] But whilst the practical impact of teetotalism or prohibition was limited, their contribution to a broader temperance sentiment did produce some results. The progressive reduction of Sunday drinking hours was one, although here too there were definite limits to what could be achieved. The 1854 Act, alongside another measure to curb Sunday trading in the capital, provoked rioting there and immediate legislative repentance the following year.[5] The return of beerhouses to magistrates' control in 1869 was another. This was followed in 1871 by an attempt by the Home Secretary Henry Bruce to advance the cause of temperance reform in a further measure of licensing reform, including more limited opening hours and a reduction in the number of licences. The measure produced a storm of protest and this, coupled with the failure of its likely temperance allies to support it and Bruce's inept handling, doomed it to failure.[6]

In the event a Licensing Act was passed in 1872, which whilst shorn of any attempt at licence reduction, may be bracketed with the measure of 1869 as an important turning point in the history of licensing. The 1869 measure was now made permanent.

The policing and opening hours sections of the Act have already been noted. There were a number of changes to the administration of licensing. The grant of a new licence had now to be confirmed by a further body of magistrates. Properties granted new licences were to have a higher annual value. In order to renew their licence publicans no longer had to attend in person unless required to do so. Objections to the grant or renewal of a licence had to be made in writing and evidence given on oath. Licences could now be removed to another district and provision was made for a six-day licence to exclude Sunday, which attracted a proportionate reduction in duty. Taken together, the measures of 1869 to 1872 had two important consequences. First the furore surrounding the 1871 Bill in particular made governments wary of the whole thorny and complex issue of licensing reform. Second they ushered in a new climate of strict licensing. The number of on-licences in England and Wales peaked in 1869 at 118,499, comprising 69,369 full- and 49,130 beer only licences, about one licence for every 192 people. The number of beerhouses, as we saw, was immediately reduced, and fell to 42,590 by 1871. It continued to contract until by 1901 there were 29,064. By that date the number of full-licences had actually risen to 73,784, but the reduction of beerhouses by more than 20,000, over 40 per cent of the 1869 total, meant that there were then 102,846 on-licences, one for every 316 people.[7]

The operation of the licensing system was the principal means of bringing about this overall reduction. Justices were still willing to grant new licences, but this willingness decreased over time. In the eight years from 1873 to 1881, 3,699 new full-licences were granted; in the ten years from 1887 to 1896 the figure was 1,930. Many of these were not, however, strictly speaking new licences. Of the 3,699, 15 per cent were upgrades of existing beerhouses. Further, many represented removals from one location to another, or were granted in return for the surrender of one or more (usually beer) licences. In the latter period some 61 boroughs and 107 petty sessional divisions were said to pursue this policy; others, however, found it objectionable.

Everywhere the licences were often granted to hotels or restaurants. The number of actual new pubs was thus comparatively small. An examination of particular localities sheds further light on what was happening. In a small number of places, like Crewe, Derby or Southampton, the number of licences actually increased, although nowhere did it keep pace with population growth. In many places the number of on-licences was practically stationary, but in others there was a decrease.[8] Thus in Portsmouth the licensing justices granted twenty-eight new full-licences between 1870 and 1900. All were substantial properties. Costs exclusive of the purchase of land were normally in excess of £1,500, and on occasion substantially above this figure. A further seventeen licences were granted to existing beerhouses, whose owners made the transition by capitalising on good locations and rebuilding them. But to establish pubs in newly developed parts of the town the justices began to ask that beerhouses in particular in the older parts of the borough be given up. In time their demands increased. Thus the Festing Hotel in Festing Road secured its licence in 1894 through the surrender by its brewer applicant of two of its beerhouses and the transfer of the licence from the Buckingham Arms in Cromwell Street. In that same year the licence of the Stamshaw Hotel required that four beer licences be given up. Overall in Portsmouth the number of full-licences fell slightly from 332 to 318 between 1875 and 1900, but the number of beerhouses contracted from 526 to 459.[9] In Bradford the licensing bench operated in a slightly different way. The total number of licences fell from 535 in 1870 to 447 by 1900. Whilst the number of full-licences actually rose from 137 to 174, that of beerhouses fell from 398 to 273. New licences were granted to a small number of commercial hotels, like the Northgate in the centre of the town, to remedy a perceived deficiency of accommodation. But more numerous was the grant of full-licences to existing beerhouses with the express purpose of improving such properties. This, however, was a short-lived experiment, largely confined to just the two years 1873 and 1874. Only to a limited extent did the Bradford bench pursue a policy of granting licences if another beerhouse were given up. Such was the Park Side Hotel, built in a newly developing district and granted a licence in 1879 in exchange for that of the Old Dusty Miller beerhouse in the centre of the town.[10] The most important example of brewers giving up licences in this way was Birmingham, where the chairman of the licensing bench, Arthur Chamberlain, proposed in 1897 what came to be called the 'Birmingham Surrender Scheme'. Under it brewers and bench cooperated in the closure of selected city centre pubs, with the brewers setting up a company to compensate owners for the loss. In the six years to 1904, 222 houses were closed, or 10 per cent of the existing stock of pubs. This, however, did not fulfil Chamberlain's aspirations, and the brewers too were disappointed in their hope of getting new licences in suburban areas.[11]

More negatively, the operation of the licensing system effected a reduction by the non-replacement of demolished pubs. The redevelopment of the central areas of Victorian towns and cities for new streets, public and commercial buildings and railway infrastructure accounted for many in this way. In Leeds, for example, twenty-eight pubs disappeared as part of such schemes in the years 1873 to 1896.[12] Finally, and the least significant statistically after the cull of 1869, was the refusal of licences for misconduct. In Bradford, for example, down to the First World War just twenty-two pubs disappeared in this way, the last one in 1888, comprising two full- and twenty beer licences.[13] But there were other influences on the number of licences. In some places landowners deliberately closed pubs, as they had in the eighteenth century. The local treasurer of the Church of England Temperance Society in the diocese of Ely noted two parishes in the late 1870s where the owners had limited their number to two, in one case having closed no fewer than six pubs. A corollary of this was for landowners not to permit the establishment of pubs in new developments. The most celebrated example of this was Titus Salt's model industrial community of Saltaire in the Aire valley near Bradford, lauded by the Reverend Dawson Burns of the United Kingdom Alliance as one of eighty places in Yorkshire with such a prohibitive arrangement. It was, however, common in new housing developments generally through the use of restrictive covenants.[14]

During these years the view that the number of pubs was excessive and ought to be reduced continued to gain ground. Bruce, in his abortive Bill of 1871, had already advanced the proposition that there were far more licences than were required for 'the public convenience'.[15] Although they varied in particulars, the great majority of licensing benches were clearly pursuing policies which helped to attain the result of fewer pubs. In general this was done without too much contention, as when misconduct was gross enough to merit closure, when demolished pubs were simply not replaced, or when brewers worked with them to secure new licences in more financially promising localities. But if the pace of reduction of licences were to be increased, or in any way made compulsory, this was bound to take the issue qualitatively much further and inevitably raised the question of compensation for their loss. This was to prove enormously controversial. For brewers and publicans, and indeed much mainstream opinion, compensation was only right and proper, but for temperance advocates it meant paying money to a trade that was inherently evil. Moves in the direction of compensation thus foundered on the strength of feeling aroused. On taking office in 1880 Gladstone favoured the principle, but in the face of vehement temperance opposition nothing came of it. In 1888 the Conservative Government included proposals for a compensation scheme in its local government legislation, but these too were sacrificed to secure the passage of the main measures. A further attempt to set up a compensation scheme in 1890 also failed.[16]

A central issue in the controversy was the status of the licence. In law it was granted for one year at the discretion of the licensing magistrates, as set down in the consolidating Act of 1828, which nothing had since altered. In practice renewal had come to be seen as a formality, except in cases of misconduct. The existing beer licences had in fact been explicitly protected to that effect in the legislation of 1869. Further, it was contended that the law did differentiate in fact in that the procedures for the grant of a new licence and the renewal of an old one differed. The licence was also treated as a form of property in several ways: in bankruptcy cases, for insurance purposes and in assessing compensation in cases of compulsory purchase for such as street improvements. The Inland Revenue certainly thought it was.[17]

The issue came to a head over the licence of a little public house in the remote and beautiful Kentmere valley in Westmorland, the Low Bridge Inn. In addition to catering to local farmers and occasional tourists the pub also played weekend host to the workers in the slate quarries at the head of the valley. The objections of local respectability to the resulting scenes precipitated the refusal of the licence in 1887 by the justices in Kendal, chaired by one Wakefield, although no reasons were forthcoming at the time. The owners of the pub, sisters Jane and Susannah Sharpe, who had in fact rebuilt it but lived in the original premises, appealed the decision to the quarter sessions. At the appeal reasons now given for its refusal were that it had been badly run, was too remote at five miles from the nearest police station for effective supervision and that as Kentmere had a population of just 176 it was not necessary. Appeals were now made all the way up to the House of Lords, which in 1891, in Sharpe v. Wakefield, finally affirmed the absolute discretion of magistrates over both the grant and renewal of licences as laid down in the statute of 1828. That discretion had to be exercised in a 'legal and regular fashion', but, in so doing, magistrates need not be limited in their inquiry to the character of the applicant and the suitability of the premises.[18]

The immediate impact of the decision, which affected only full-licences, and in any case merely confirmed what the courts had repeatedly upheld, was limited. A number of licences were refused renewal, but the scale of this was not great. Most magistrates deferred using their newly affirmed power until the royal commission, which the government appointed in 1896 to examine, as the Prime Minister Lord Salisbury put it, this 'thorny and difficult' subject, produced its report. In the event the commission worked for three years and produced two separate reports, signed by the majority and minority of its members respectively, with its chairman, Lord Peel, in the latter camp. The majority report recommended a large reduction in the number of licensed houses with compensation.[19] As no legislation was forthcoming, however, the movement for non-renewal now resumed. In 1901 the bench at Farnham, Surrey, convinced of the superfluity of pubs, submitted a voluntary scheme of licence reduction to local brewers and retailers. When the latter proved reluctant to negotiate, the justices the following year refused to renew all forty-five licences in the town. Eventually nine pubs were deprived of their licence, with just two reinstated on appeal. This success inspired benches throughout the country. More licences were denied renewal in 1903 than in the previous six years combined. Brewers and publicans now implored the government for legislation to restrain these attacks on their property, but opposed the suggestion that they should provide the finance for compensation. Temperance opinion, and most Liberals, still found the idea of compensation anathema. The Prime Minister, now Arthur Balfour, in a meeting with a trade deputation, did condemn the moves to reduce licences, however well intentioned, as little short of 'unjust confiscation of property', to which neither government nor Parliament could remain indifferent.[20]

Balfour accordingly grasped the nettle in the Licensing Bill of 1904.[21] This established the principle of compensation for licences extinguished on grounds other than misconduct, but the source of the compensation was to be the trade itself. Opponents dubbed it the Brewers' Endowment Bill and attacked it ferociously. To Lloyd George, it was raising up 'a barrier almost insuperable, a wall, an impregnable rampart, around the worst and most dangerous enemy that ever menaced this Empire'. All the major trade organisations, whilst dissatisfied with the source of compensation, gave the Bill grudging assent. Some local trade bodies came out more strongly in favour, whilst some individual brewers were more hostile, like the chairman of Heys brewery in Bradford, who found it more or less problematical, calling it a Brewers' Disendowment Act.[22] The compensation was to come from a levy on licensed premises, payable on a graduated scale. The amount to be paid out of the fund thus created was the difference between the value of the premises with and without a licence. Where a licensing bench refused renewal on the ground that it was not required by the public, they had to refer the case to a further committee, of all the justices in county boroughs or of quarter sessions elsewhere, which determined whether the decision should stand and if so granted compensation. Appeal as to the amount of compensation was in the first instance to the Commissioners of Inland Revenue, then to the High Court. The actual division of the payment between the interested parties – owner, or owner and lessee, and licensee – was to be decided by the compensation authority; the latter's share to be based on any legal interest in fixtures and fittings, length of time in the pub and its general conduct. A corollary of compensation for the loss of a licence was a payment for the so called monopoly value of a new one.

The Act certainly led to a reduction in the number of licences. In the ten years of its operation to 1914, 9,801 licences were extinguished, of which almost two-thirds were beerhouses. The total represented a little under 10 per cent of those in existence at the beginning of the century and in both absolute and relative terms compared favourably with the pace of licence reduction over the previous thirty-two years after 1869.[23] It was, however, fewer than had been anticipated, either by the government, brewers and certainly temperance reformers. Not only that, but licensing benches and compensation authorities were, in the words of a 1911 pamphlet surveying the first years of the Act's operation, increasingly disposed to let its machinery 'slow down': fewer licences were referred to the compensation authorities for refusal and fewer authorities levied the maximum charge. The pamphlet's author, Arthur Sherwell, attributed this partly to sympathy on the part of magistrates for the licensed trade, recently burdened with higher licence duties. But the principal reason was the scheme's cost. As licences were eliminated so the cost of removing those remaining increased. Less valuable licences were initially targeted for referral, so that as they were removed those that were left were the ones worth more and whose value in turn was enhanced by the removal of competitors. Fewer pubs also meant that the levy brought in less money. Further, the amount of compensation was inflated by the Kennedy judgement of 1906, which held that the value of the premises was to be the amount it would fetch on the open market. This included the rent and the brewer's profit from the sale of beer, both of which had to be capitalised over a number of years' purchase according to the circumstances of the house, its location and the state of the market. As the Bradford authority found in trying to get rid of just ten of the 'worst and lowest class' pubs in the city, the compensation payable was more than the amount raised by the levy.[24]

It was poorer, run down pubs which in general were removed. Urban and rural authorities alike targeted them. Quite typical was the Southampton bench, which referred, for example, the Atlantic Arms in Mount Street in 1913, a beerhouse in a 'filthy condition' in a 'very poor neighbourhood'. Or in rural north Lancashire in 1909 the Queen's Arms at High Newton similarly was referred, a beerhouse in a bad state of repair with an earth closet in the garden and the urinal flowing into a field. Structural considerations like these were taken into account, alongside evidence of the number of licensed premises in relation to population, the state of trade, previous convictions, effectiveness of police supervision, the number of times the licence had been transferred and the character of the clientele. A 'class of people particularly interested in dogs', for example, who used the Lord Byron Inn in Diamond Street, were a consideration for the Bradford bench. In some areas population decline had removed the pub's customers. In Newcastle the magistrates looked in particular for closures at areas of the city where dwellings had been demolished for warehousing and business premises. In Cornwall, where the decline of mining had led to de-population, at Gwennap and Chacewater, for example, the Miners' Arms and the Miners' Inn respectively were closed in 1912. At the latter place the Crown, with an average custom on police visits of just seven, also was closed.[25]

It was because it commonly removed run down, unprofitable houses that the Act in the end worked to the advantage of brewers. Suffolk brewers Greene King & Company were well pleased to offload some of their least economic houses. Fellow East Anglian brewers Steward & Patteson similarly found that compensation payments and the proceeds of the sale of the closed premises more than covered their contributions to the levy. Most of the closed pubs were averaging under a hundred barrels a year, and thus the barrelage of the rest actually rose.[26] Licensees were probably less pleased. The measure's detractors had predicted that 'the brewer will get the corn and the publican the sack'. Certainly the licensees' overall share of the compensation was just 11 per cent in the first ten years of the measure's operation. Evidence from Portsmouth shows that this at least usually amounted to more than the licensee paid to go into the pub, although it was not possible in that case to comment on the overall amount of profit or loss. They were of course out of a job unless the brewer found them another pub, which as former tenants of run down unprofitable premises was perhaps optimistic.[27]

The movement to reduce the number of licences thus had results not always gratifying to its proponents. The sentiments that drove it also produced a whole series of proposals for further restrictive modification of the licensing system. These received an exhaustive hearing from the royal commission of 1896 to 1899. As Arthur Shadwell tartly commented on the overall effect of its deliberations: 'It merely took up one point after another, without any plan or order, found them all in an unsatisfactory state, and proposed a long and promiscuous list of amendments, based on no principles and sometimes inconsistent.'[28] Some of them did, however, find their way into the Licensing Act of 1902, usually those endorsed by both of its reports. Some have already been noted, but two important changes should be added here. One which had long been desired, and sometimes sought, was a power over the structure of licensed premises. The creation of dram shops, with drinkers standing at long bars, the proliferation of snugs and compartments, the opening of multiple entrances to pubs, or straightforward extensions to the drinking area all excited opposition. All were variously seen as encouraging excessive or secretive drinking, particularly by women.[29] In practice it had proved difficult for licensing benches to prevent such developments, however much they might assert it as a policy. This was certainly the experience of the Bradford bench, for example, with dram shops, beerhouses in old and run down premises and attempts to create additional drinking rooms. Elsewhere, as at Newcastle, where the 'long bar system' was a concern, justices had used powers under local legislation to look at structural alterations.[30] Now, to the existing power in the 1874 Licensing Act to look at the plans of proposed new premises the new Act gave magistrates additional control over their structure on renewal of the licence. Consent was now required if alterations created additional facilities for drinking, or concealed any part of the premises from effective observation, or affected communication between the drinking areas and other parts of the premises or the street. On renewal the justices could also ask to see plans of the premises and could now request that such alterations be made as were reasonably necessary to secure the proper conduct of the business. A second change covered clubs. In response to a growing concern over their proliferation, and in particular over 'bogus' clubs whose aim was actually simply to sell drink, all such institutions had now to be registered. Magistrates were given power to strike off clubs on a variety of grounds relating to their conduct and authenticity.[31] There was, finally, to be one further attempt in 1908 by the Liberal Government to effect a more rapid reduction in the number of licences, but this foundered in the House of Lords. Instead, a new consolidating Licensing Act was passed in 1910 to replace that of 1828. It made little material change and remained the basis of licensing law for almost half a century.

A massive effort was thus expended trying to prohibit pubs altogether, reduce their numbers, or place upon them ever more restrictions, with the results overall that we have seen. But there was a further reform movement which sought to address the alleged evils of the pub through engaging more directly with its vital role as a social institution, one which people actually liked. One earlier manifestation of this had been the creation of alternatives to the pub. Such was the British Workman movement, which followed efforts by philanthropists to provide 'public houses without the drink', selling coffee and snacks to working men. It was launched in Leeds in 1867 and spread to other towns like Bradford, Liverpool, Manchester and Newcastle. Sometimes the premises were former pubs, like two opened in Bradford in 1871, and as well as cheap tea and coffee provided rooms for reading, smoking, discussion and meetings. There were also classes, social gatherings for men and their wives and a free and easy on Saturday nights. They were not a financial success. Of three opened, one closed and two became clubs. But in Liverpool thirty-one were operating by 1878 near the docks and other busy parts of the town and the company's capital was said to have doubled.[32] A similar venture was the coffee tavern, again using pub names and sometimes pub premises. London, for example, had the Edinburgh Castle Coffee Palace in Limehouse opened in 1873, or the Dublin Castle in the Mile End Road in 1876. In the latter years of that decade 156 coffee tavern companies were incorporated in England and Wales. But the phenomenon in the end was short-lived, often undone by its earnestness and of limited appeal to the pub devotee.[33]

Of greater significance were attempts to reform the pub itself. Inspiration came from the Swedish town of Gothenburg and its 'system' of liquor control. The essence of this was that the provision of drink should be organised so that the managers of outlets had no pecuniary interest in its sale, and that surplus profits should accrue to the wider benefit of the community. One variant of this, municipal control, came to nothing, but disinterested management, as it came to be known, was tried in a number of experiments. One of the earliest was at the Boar's Head in the village of Hampton Lucy in Warwickshire. The pub was held in the trust of the rector, the Reverend Osbert Mordaunt, for the good of the parish. One of his servants managed it, receiving a salary and the profits on non-alcoholic drinks and food. Only beer was sold and most of the profits went to charity. Of greater significance, however, than such isolated experiments were companies established to run pubs on disinterested lines. The first was the People's Refreshment House Association, formed in 1896, which within five years had eighteen houses under its management. Here too managers – agents 'in the cause of temperance and good behaviour' as the Association dubbed them – were paid a fixed salary plus the profit from food and non-alcoholic drinks. Shareholders were to receive no more than a 5 per cent dividend and surplus profits to go to 'objects of public utility'. The second were trust companies, running pubs in trust that is for the benefit of the community along the same disinterested lines. A Central Public House Trust Association was established in 1901, and within two years over £300,000 was subscribed in forty-two companies. As its founder, Earl Grey, put it, their managers similarly were to be 'missionaries behind the bar' in the cause of moderation. Grey was involved in the Northumberland Public House Trust Company, which built two new pubs, the Grey Arms at Broomhill and the Delaval Arms in Scottswood Road, Newcastle, close to the great Elswick works. Both pubs had large dining rooms, that at the latter accommodating 150 workmen, and made non-alcoholic drinks readily available.

The overall impact of these experiments was limited. In the Northumberland case the trust struggled from the outset to make money, let alone generate surplus profits for community uses. Its estate was expanded to seven houses, but only by taking on pubs which no brewer wanted. By 1910 the arrears on dividends amounted to 23 per cent. In the whole of England and Wales by 1914 there were approximately 250 trust houses, a negligible number to set against a total of around 90,000 on-licences. Two-fifths of these belonged to the Refreshment House Association, a quarter to the Home Counties Trust (the product of the merger of several trust companies) and one-third to other companies affiliated to the Central Trust. In 1914 the Home Counties Trust ceased its affiliation with the Central Trust to pursue a more profit-driven approach and more middle-class customers, becoming after the war Trust Houses Ltd. Although about a quarter of the houses managed by the Refreshment House Association or the Central Trust were in industrial areas, the majority were rural or small-town pubs. The first acquisition of the People's Refreshment House Association, for example, had been the Sparkford Inn, in the Somerset village of that name. As a 'picturesque, old-fashioned country inn' with a small local trade and thus dependent on passing tourists and cyclists, it was scarcely the type of vile urban drinking den which reformers sought to eradicate. The chief legacy of the movement was its essential principle of improving the pub, as in the greater provision of food and non-alcoholic drinks for example, and this was to have a much greater influence during the war and in the years that followed.[34]

How did customers, publicans and brewers respond to this massive outpouring of concern with the object of their affections and livelihoods? Customers did, on occasions, react violently. They had rioted in London over Sunday closing in 1854. The new hours introduced in 1872 similarly lead to hostile direct action, often directed at the perceived class bias of restriction, which did not apply to gentlemen and their clubs. At Cheltenham, for example, a crowd turned out of the public houses at the new closing hour and forced two clubs to follow suit. A club was attacked at Coventry by a mob singing 'Britons never shall be slaves', as had the rioters of 1854. At Liverpool publicans distributed broadsides and talked of 'one law for the rich and another for the poor'. In the most serious incident, at Ashton in Lancashire, soldiers were called out to disperse the 'Rule Britannia' singing crowd of between 10,000 and 15,000 people.[35] More orthodox political means were also used. Customers and publicans turned up at temperance meetings to vote against motions on local option. At times of great passion, as over the Licensing Bill of 1908, thousands signed petitions and attended mass meetings and demonstrations (Figures 14 and 15). With the franchise extensions of 1867 and 1884 working-class voters were targeted by drink trade organisations at local and national elections. Publicans gave out voting cards to customers to persuade others to vote for favoured candidates.[36] Having said that, the most common response by customers would seem to have been to live with the restrictions. In truth they were neither overly restrictive, except on Sunday, nor especially rigorously enforced. Pubs were still open most of the day and men (and women) could enjoy them pretty much in 1900 as they had in 1800. If you got drunk, or had a bit too much, in the pub itself you would be likely enough left alone unless you created a disturbance. Outside in the street you would be equally unlikely to attract police attention unless you were sufficiently aggressive or comatose to force it. One powerful reason for these facts was that in the end most policemen, as we saw, and indeed probably most politicians, doubted the wisdom of trying seriously to restrict the chief pleasure of the working man.

The drink trades, a heterogeneous mix of retailers and producers, did organise. In the eighteenth century there were many ad hoc protests, notably for example over the billeting of soldiers. A London-based Friendly Society of Licensed Victuallers was established in 1794, with its own newspaper – the *Morning Advertiser*. Publicans too had organised to oppose the campaign for free licensing. For the brewers, to the medieval Brewers' Company of London was added the Country Brewers' Society in 1822, composed chiefly of Home Counties and East Anglian firms.[37] From around 1830 local organisations of licensed victuallers and beersellers were established, which acted as pressure groups and enjoyed social activities like their annual dinners.[38] Prompted by the legislative activity of 1869 to 1872, national organisations were established, like the Licensed Victuallers', and the Beer and Wine Trade, National Defence Leagues. For brewers the National Trade Defence Fund was set up in 1888. The Trade, as it thus came to be called, campaigned strongly against perceived threats to its livelihood, like the local veto proposals of 1893 and 1895. In the general election of the latter year the unpopularity of those proposals and the vigour of the Trade's campaigning were widely seen as bringing about the defeat of the Liberal Government, when eighty-seven English and Welsh seats were lost, including those of several staunch prohibitionists. Again in 1908 vigorous opposition was offered to the government's proposals, with monster meetings and demonstrations throughout the country.[39]

It was this kind of activity, together with what were regarded as the unlimited financial resources of the drinks industry, which raised the Trade to the position of national menace in some eyes. Gladstone's attribution of his 1874 election defeat to a 'torrent of gin and beer' and Rowntree and Sherwell's 1899 analysis of the 'social and political menace' of the Trade, in their respective ways exemplified this belief.[40] But the reality belied this image. The Trade was not a unified entity, but was divided both geographically and by the frequently conflicting interests of its constituent parts: brewers and retailers, publicans and beersellers, on- and off-licence holders. The potential for disunity increased during the Edwardian period with the divergent effects of the compensation scheme, adverse trading conditions as beer consumption fell and the tax increases in the People's Budget of 1909.[41] As to political weight, although the industry was bound to be a force simply because of its economic scale, it is easy to mistake that for influence. Politically, once the Liberals had become identified, however reluctantly by some of them, with the cause of temperance, the industry had nowhere else to go but the Conservatives. But that party had by no means always been supportive of its interests, and it proved unwilling to denounce the budget increases at the 1910 elections. By 1914 trade organisation was deteriorating and brewers and retailers were 'frustrated and apathetic'.[42] In this shape the industry was soon to face the challenges of world war.

10

The First World War and the Pub

In a survey of the public house covering some three centuries, to devote a single chapter to something over four years warrants justification. This lies in the extent and nature of the changes which those years witnessed in the use of the pub and the wider context in which it functioned. For the ways in which the pub was used were indeed radically transformed. Opening hours were dramatically reduced, eliminating early morning, afternoon and late-night drinking. Essential pub practices, like treating, giving credit and the long pull (serving more than the correct measure to attract custom) were made illegal. With the sole exception of treating, all of them were retained after the war. Writing in the mid-1980s, one historian of the war's social consequences could regard those regulations as 'still today ... perhaps the most tangible long-term legacy of the First World War'.[1] Other changes also outlasted the war. The price of the drink consumed soared, whilst its strength fell. Women resorted to the pub in greater numbers. More broadly, the war accelerated the trends already evident, if hitherto still limited, to reduced consumption of alcohol and less drunkenness. And in the political salience of drink and the pub, which I explored in the previous chapter, the war marked a real turning point. From being given maximum prominence by its perceived threat to the war effort, drink as an issue was ultimately to be largely neutralised by its effects.

The outbreak of war had immediate effects on the pub. Anti-German feeling found expression in the renaming, for example, of the King of Prussia pub in Halifax as the King of Belgium. Or in the harassment of the German-born, like Bradford publican William Sonnenberg, who was fined for failing to provide particulars to the authorities as an enemy alien, although he had lived in the country for the previous twenty-two years.[2] More significantly, the armed services quickly obtained new powers under the first Defence of the Realm Act (DORA), and subsequent extensions to it, over the supply of drink in military and naval areas. Such restrictive orders multiplied rapidly, with nearly 500 made in the first ten months of the war. They covered opening hours of pubs (including for civilians), the treating of servicemen and the serving of women at certain times. Licensing magistrates were also given the power, if the chief constable so recommended, to suspend the sale of alcohol in the interests of order and the suppression of drunkenness. Subject to Home Office approval they might also close pubs before nine o'clock in the evening. These measures also covered registered clubs, putting them in this way for the first time on the same footing as pubs. By the close of 1914 justices had made restrictive orders in at least 427 of the 1,000 licensing districts. In London, for example, the powers were immediately used. To combat the problem of provincial recruits enjoying the capital's later opening hours and lavish treating by civilians, closing time was brought forward from 12.30 to 11 p.m. The result, claimed the *Brewers' Gazette*, was a 'transformation', from 'immense crowds' lounging about the great traffic centres like the Elephant and Castle to scenes of peace and respectability. Closing was subsequently brought forward to ten o'clock and to nine in the capital's dock and arsenal districts.[3]

Alongside the concern over the effects of drink on the armed services went a wider call for greater sobriety in the nation as whole. George V found himself setting an example by declaring abstinence for the duration of the war, although in the event he availed himself of the exception for medical purposes. Many indeed followed the King's pledge, although the House of Commons for one felt unable to close its bars. It was the new Minister of Munitions, Lloyd George, who had manoeuvred the monarch and at the same time dramatically raised the temperature of the national concern over drink by linking it to the wider war effort. In one speech he had claimed: 'Drink is doing us more damage in the War than all the German submarines put together.' And to a deputation from the Shipbuilding Employers' Federation he now declared: 'We are fighting Germany, Austria and Drink; and, as far as I can see, the greatest of these three deadly foes is Drink.'[4]

Solutions in the form of nationalisation of the drink trade or of higher taxes in the end came to nothing. What happened was the creation in May 1915 of the Central Control Board (Liquor Traffic). This body, chaired by prominent banker and former Liberal MP Lord D'Abernon, comprised politicians, employer and labour representatives, civil servants and later brewery and temperance men. It was given powers in specifically defined areas where servicemen assembled, or in which war work was in progress, to increase the efficiency of labour and to prevent it being impaired by 'drunkenness, alcoholism or excess'. The selection of areas to be scheduled was undertaken by the local military authorities or a government department. This was followed by an investigation by the Board of local conditions involving a wide range of interested parties from the armed services, police, local councils, licensing justices, employers and unions, church, temperance and liquor interests. From initial scheduling of quite small areas the process was quickly applied to coincide with larger administrative units and to create a 'protective fringe' around the restricted districts to stop hopeful drinkers going beyond them. Within six months most of the ports, the industrial Midlands and the West Riding and about two-thirds of Scotland had been scheduled. In the end, however, most of the country except for agricultural and sparsely populated areas, and the vast majority of its population came to be covered by the Board.[5]

The Board worked both restrictively and constructively. There was a dramatic reduction in the hours of sale. In London, for example, weekday opening fell from the pre-war total of nineteen-and-a-half hours to just five-and-a-half. Early morning, afternoon and late evening drinking were prohibited. By restricting sale to meal times it was hoped that alcohol's effects would be diluted by food, and by creating gaps in the drinking day that 'soaking' would be prevented. Whilst concessions were made, for example for early opening for pubs near the London docks and markets, in other ways the restrictions were made tighter. Sunday closing was extended to some areas felt to be too close to dry Wales and Scotland. The exemption for the bona fide traveller ceased. Further, a number of pub customs were now prohibited: treating (except with a meal), giving credit and the long pull.[6]

Constructively, the Board worked to achieve a number of objectives conducive to sobriety. It particularly sought to encourage the provision of food in pubs and the sale of lighter beers. The success of its efforts was, however, respectively 'modest' and 'limited'. Its most dramatic action was to take direct control of the drink trade in three areas: Enfield Lock (where the Royal Small Arms Factory was situated), Cromarty Firth (in response to an appeal from the Admiralty) and the Carlisle and Gretna district (also the site of munitions works). The latter was the most significant. The Board acquired there over 200 licences, about half of which were in Carlisle itself. To these were later added another 136 licences when the area was extended to Maryport. In addition to the usual restrictions noted, powers were taken to suppress redundant or 'undesirable' licences, to forbid the sale of drink to those under eighteen and to control the use of advertising on pubs (Figures 16 and 17). Constructively, the sale of food was promoted. As part of this strategy the Board converted the old post office in Carlisle to the Gretna Tavern. It sold only wine and beer and included a restaurant seating about 180 people. Six other 'food taverns' were established and all were run on the 'disinterested management' lines of the pre-war experiments. Both these taverns and other pubs under the Board's control were also consciously created, or reconstructed, to do away with features deemed to be obnoxious, such as partitions, snugs and concealed entrances, part of a general aim to secure 'air, light and publicity'.[7]

Direct control in this way was in the end geographically limited compared to the much wider remit of the Board in the scheduled areas. There, the most drastic of its powers – to close a pub – was used relatively infrequently. In the whole of England and Wales to the end of March 1918 just eighty-five had been closed for the remainder of the year.[8] Looking at the other restrictions, these could certainly be irksome, affecting as they did deeply ingrained pub habits, and were resented. This was especially true of the no-treating order. When a man went into the Boltmakers' Arms in Keighley with three women and in traditional style asked: 'Now, lasses, what are you going to have?', no doubt he, the women, the barman and the publican were none too pleased to be heavily fined as a result of observation by plainclothes policemen. Similarly in Bradford, the local trade paper complained of excessive police supervision and trivial prosecutions. In March 1916, for example, it fulminated over the conviction of the landlord of the Old Crown for allowing two men to buy each other drinks and muttered about the 'positive scandal' of the plainclothes officers 'of military age' who had reported them. In another case, the landlady of the Crescent Hotel was fined after giving the brewery draymen their customary beer. In this instance the presiding magistrate explicitly acknowledged how the regulations cut across long established practices. Hearing appeals into such cases the recorder also noted that point and how 'every man's hand seems to be against the Control Board'.[9] In fact, the actual number of such prosecutions was limited. In Bradford, for example, the combined total for treating, the long pull and giving credit was actually matched by those for contravening wartime lighting restrictions. On the other hand, perhaps not unsurprisingly, proceedings for opening in prohibited hours were four times higher than for the equivalent pre-war period.[10]

The war created further difficulties for the publican. The inadequate allowances under the ancient billeting obligation were once again a source of grievance.[11] But the greatest changes, for publicans, customers and brewers, were in the price, strength and availability of drink. As a result of tax increases and the rising cost of raw materials the price of beer soared. It doubled in the first two years of the war, reaching 4*d* for an ordinary pint of draught bitter in a public bar. Added to this, production was restricted and limits placed on the strength of beer brewed. This was in turn accompanied by price fixing according to original gravity. At its lowest in 1918 the average gravity of beer was not to exceed 1030 degrees. The name 'Government Ale' being attached to such brews, the government retaliated by prohibiting brewers from advertising it as such. In April 1917 the *Brewers' Journal* was noting that even in large urban areas many pubs were receiving only a barrel of beer a week, while in rural districts the situation was even worse. A month later the closure of beerhouses on certain days of the week was reported from many urban areas. As one Portsmouth pub informed its customers one Tuesday in August:

SOLD OUT

No Beer
No Spirits
No Nothing

OPEN AGAIN FRIDAY[12]

These changes strained relations between brewers and publicans. The latter claimed constantly that they were having to bear the brunt of price increases and shortages. The local trade and general press in Bradford, for example, documented their complaints. By the spring of 1917 a meeting of the licensed trade in the city claimed it was facing 'overwhelming difficulties' and urged brewers to 'make a little more sacrifice' than they were. And at another meeting in April the president of the local Licensed Victuallers' Society accused brewers of viewing them as 'mere lackeys to sell beer for their aggrandisement'.

One landlord told the meeting that his house cost him £200 a year in rent and rates, but at that dinnertime he had taken just 6s 8d, to which a voice responded: 'You're lucky; we've only taken 6d.' Tenants also alleged that managed houses were given preference in the allocation of the available beer.[13] Underlying these tensions was the contrast between the publicans' difficulties and the brewers' profits. From being little affected in the early part of the war, from 1917 they offered companies everywhere a 'welcome bonanza' as the move to weaker beer lowered unit costs and consumer demand held up with full employment and the absence of peacetime leisure pursuits.[14]

The actions of government had then a range of important effects on pubs, publicans, brewers and customers during the war. But what of the long-term consequences and overall significance of wartime changes? Controls on the production of beer and spirits, and on prices and strength were removed progressively to the summer of 1921.[15] But there was of course no return to pre-war prices. Nor did beer regain its pre-war strength: the average gravity of English beer had been 1052.58 degrees in 1900, in 1920 it was 1038.57.[16] Many of the restrictions also became permanent. Although the Central Control Board itself was wound up, despite the hopes of its leaders for 'a new authority, suitable to peacetime conditions' to continue its work, a Licensing Act passed in 1921 preserved much of its legacy. The unpopular no-treating order had already been revoked in 1919, but the new legislation confirmed the prohibition of credit and the long pull. Restricted opening was maintained, closing pubs for most of the morning and in the middle of the afternoon. Stated permitted hours within overall parameters gave a degree of local flexibility, which produced some anomalies between licensing districts, notably the extra evening hour on one side of Oxford Street compared to the other. The bona fide traveller made no more journeys. Two years later, in 1923, a further Act prohibited the sale of alcohol to anyone under eighteen.[17] All these changes appreciably altered the world of the pub and helped to shape its character for much of the rest of the century.

The war years also witnessed an important change to the pub's customers as women began to use them more. They were now drawn into the workforce in large numbers and the State provided allowances to soldiers' wives. Income and independence, plus of course a desire for company, led more women into the convivial world of the pub. This inevitably aroused hostility. In Keighley, for example, early in the war the licensing bench was urging publicans to discourage women's drinking, especially of servicemen's wives. Clergymen, with very few exceptions, deplored the trend. E.A. Burroughs, later Bishop of Ripon, blamed the 'heedlessly liberal scale' of the separation allowances for creating for women a 'heaven' of 'eighteen shillings a week, and no husband', whose chief delight was the public house. In some areas, like the North East, restrictions were placed on women using pubs.[18] But this did not detract from the general trends. First existing pub goers now went more often. This was the conclusion of a committee of women set up in 1915 to advise the Control Board on the allegations of excessive drinking: there was no evidence of it among any considerable number of women and girls who had not drunk before. Another committee looking at the experience of Birmingham the following year also found the allegation of increased intemperance to be unfounded, but that women munitions workers with money to spend 'caused a visible concentration of numbers at particular times'.[19] Second the pub habit began to move up the social scale, drawing in some women for the first time. In Bristol, for example, the majority of the new female customers were employed lower middle- and working-class women, chiefly shop assistants and factory workers. Against these customers the city's chief constable asserted, 'no possible imputation could be made as regards loose character'. Robert Roberts recollected the shocked surprise of Salford's respectables as unaccompanied women began to enjoy their glass of stout in the Best Room of the local pub. As the Control Board set an example in its Carlisle pubs of catering to respectable women, so this facet of the movement to improve the pub was to be developed after the war.[20]

It was in its contribution to this movement for pub improvement that the state control scheme exerted an influence wider than its rather limited geographical application. The example which it had set of a 'coherent philosophy' of improvement towards drink and the pub was a potent one to some brewers. It comprised fewer licences, the provision of food and weaker, or non-alcoholic, drinks, new pub designs emphasising light and space and a socially broader clientele, including women. This philosophy was to find greater expression in the approach to their public houses of some brewery companies in peacetime.[21] For them the war also taught other lessons. Although they had chafed at the controls, their profits had in fact increased. Reduced beer consumption was thus not necessarily a calamity, any more than fewer licences had been. Further, the overall position of the trade, despite Lloyd George's earlier fulminations, had been strengthened. In the end the government had sought to ensure a rea-sonable supply of beer, as one brewer representative on the Control Board put it, for 'industrial content'. In the pursuit of its aims in this and other ways the government too had necessarily forged much closer links with the industry.[22]

Part of the reason for the enhanced position of the industry also lay in the ways in which the war represented a watershed in the social and political history of drink. The trends already evident before the war towards reduced consumption and declining levels of drunken-ness were accelerated. Consumption fell markedly, especially with the restrictions on output: UK per capita beer consumption was 27.8 gallons in 1913; by 1918 it had fallen to just 10; per capita spirit consumption fell from 0.7 gallons to 0.33. Similarly, convictions for drunkenness plummeted from 183,800, or 49.7 per 10,000, in 1914 to 29,100, or 7.9 per 10,000, in 1918.[23] On the political front, drastic measures towards the trade, like prohibition or total state purchase, had not materialised. Having begun the war as the supreme threat to the nation's survival, drink ended it as a support to morale whose supplies government was keen to maintain. As John Greenaway has expressed it: 'The "heroic" days of the temperance versus Trade struggle were over.' Once again this shift reflected existing developments which were accelerated by the war, such as the decline in militant nonconformity and the acceptance of excessive drinking as a social rather than a moral problem, with roots in housing, education and working conditions. A 'distinctly new phase in the history of the Drink question' had begun.[24]

II

Improved Pubs and Locals
1920–1960

Although another world war within a generation was to have marked effects on the pub, their significance was much less than in the earlier conflict. In the history of the pub it makes sense to extend our analysis to include the immediate post-war years. No period in the history of the pub has been without change, and the inter-war years are certainly no exception. But there was much continuity from those decades into the 1950s, in the social world of pubs, for example, or in the stability of the licensing regime established at the end of the First World War. Moreover, those continuities are highlighted when viewed alongside the enormous changes from the late 1950s to the present day.

One area of continuity was in the consumption of alcohol. The pre-existing fall, which the First World War had greatly accelerated, proved to be permanent. Looking at beer consumption, although there were short-term fluctuations – falls in 1920–2 and 1929–32, recoveries in 1922–4, 1932–7 and notably during the Second World War – the overall trend was downward. In the 1930s the average UK per capita consumption per year was 13.1 gallons; in 1913 it had been 27.5 gallons. In 1955 it fell to just twelve gallons, as raw material shortages, high taxation and severe restrictions on output persisted through the period of austerity following the war.[1] Excess consumption followed the same trend, at least when measured by police action against drunkenness. Having risen briefly at the end of the war, the number of convictions in England and Wales fell steadily to a low point of 30,100, or 7.5 per 10,000 population, in 1932. Although convictions then rose, it was a long way from the 183,800, or 49.7 per 10,000, of 1914. During the Second World War charges (rather than convictions) fell steadily to reach a low of 5 per 10,000 in 1946, although this to a degree probably reflected greater police tolerance.[2] There was of course still drunkenness. Oral evidence from Manchester and Salford shows that drink (and gambling) were most likely to feature in accounts of disrupted family relationships. Similarly, Richard Hoggart, recollecting his childhood in south Leeds, saw that drink 'was still regarded as the main pitfall for a working-class husband'. Viewed another way, however, of Lancashire women interviewed in another oral study only two had trouble with a drunken husband. Rowntree's second survey of York in the mid-1930s found that whilst the number of heavy drinkers was still 'by no means insignificant', the habit had definitely declined: as one publican put it: 'Conditions today are infinitely better in our business than they were.' The Royal Commission on Licensing was emphatic, concluding in 1931: 'by almost universal consent, excessive drinking in this country has been greatly, even spectacularly, diminished.'[3]

This change had many causes. The depressed state of the economy for much of the inter-war period, particularly in the staple industries of coal, iron and steel, shipbuilding and textiles, was an important influence in the areas affected. The Manchester and Salford oral evidence testifies to the way in which drinking and visits to the pub were regulated by economic fortunes. Similarly, a survey of Sheffield attributed its below average level of convictions for drunkenness in part to the depression in the city's staple industry. Or as a Bolton barmaid put it to Mass Observation's investigator, in what remains the most intensive and valuable study of pub life: 'They just wait for the last hour; never mind what time you open or what time you close. It's all they've got the money for.'[4] Compounding this, drink continued its pre-war trend in becoming more and more expensive. In real terms the price of beer may have been 40 per cent higher in 1931–33 than in 1920–23 and was still 25 per cent higher in 1934–38. The war added to this: the average price of a pint of draught beer more than doubled and there were further tax rises in the austere peace.[5] It therefore cost more to drink less. But the proportion of working-class expenditure on drink now declined, as money (for those with some to spend) went on goods and services whose prices fell or were more stable, in the way we saw from the late Victorian period. In particular, more spending went on other leisure pursuits.[6] This was true of established pleasures, like the seaside, or those more recently developing before the war, like the cinema. By 1934 there were on average 18.5 million admissions to the cinema every week, rising to between 20 and 22 million by 1939. This did not mean that the pub was forsaken, but it did represent a diminution of its central importance. As the Lancashire oral study reported: on Saturday night whole families might go to the cinema, but afterwards father might adjourn to the pub while wife and kids went for fish and chips.[7] In addition to cinemas and seaside resorts there was also huge investment during the inter-war years in such as dance halls or sports stadia, including for new forms like greyhound racing. The leisure pound also went on gambling, notably the football pools with ten million coupons a week filled in by the late 1930s, and in the home: nine out of ten having a wireless set, for example, on the eve of the war.[8]

It is to housing that we must look for the most significant development affecting the pub. The inter-war years saw a massive programme of slum clearance and new house building. Altogether more than four million new homes, including over a million by local authorities, were constructed in England and Wales, constituting a third of all houses by 1939.[9] But whilst slum clearance removed many pubs, the operation of the licensing system continued severely to limit their replacement. Bradford exemplified the process. The slums that ringed the city centre were largely cleared. In one of the poorest areas, White Abbey, five beerhouses were closed and demolished in the process, whilst just one fully-licensed pub was permitted to be rebuilt on the same site. In the city as a whole the cumulative effect was that the number of beerhouses fell by a third. At the same time the licensing justices set their faces against new licences in areas of population growth. In the only instance when a licence was removed from a central location to premises adjoining a new corporation housing estate, the justices in fact resisted until the brewery won on appeal.[10] This restrictive outlook was common. The licensing justices of cities like Liverpool, Sheffield and Manchester were equally reluctant to provide the residents of new estates with pubs. In the latter case, its huge Wythenshawe estate, housing some 35,000 people by 1939, had to make do with just one pub.[11] Elsewhere justices were more forthcoming, but this was frequently to only a limited extent. Between 1915 and 1939 the Portsmouth bench granted nine new full-licences, raised the status of three beerhouses, permitted two others to be transferred to new sites because of road improvements and granted one beer licence to a refreshment house; but over the same period 43 full-licences and 137 beerhouses closed.[12] Taking the country as a whole, during the inter-war years the number of full on-licences fell from 59,377 in 1921 to 55,961 twenty years later. But the number of beerhouses fell much more steeply by almost a quarter, from 22,677 to 17,249. In total the number of on-licences fell by more than a tenth to 73,210.[13]

The restrictive outlook of Victorian justices, who sought both to prevent or limit the increase of drink outlets and to restrain the 'facilities for drinking' of existing houses, thus persisted well into the twentieth century. It was to pose a problem for those who advocated a policy of improvement of the public house. The movement to achieve this end had begun, as we saw, in the late nineteenth century in a number of experiments of so called disinterested management. It received a boost from the experience of State control during the war. Its essence was succinctly stated by George Sims in a pamphlet published late in the war by the True Temperance Association. In contrast to the 'vindictive' assaults of 'teetotal fanatics', True Temperance said to a man:

You shall have your glass of beer, or your glass of spirits, but in order to get it you shall not have to fight your way through a crowd of noisy topers. You shall have it in a place of sweetness and light where you may sit with your friends or your wife and family and be surrounded not by a mob of drinkers for drinking's sake, but by quiet people who are passing a leisure hour in a reputable place of general refreshment. You shall have public-houses provided for you where you may have either your beer or your spirits, or, if you prefer it, tea or coffee; and where, while you take your refreshment, you may if you wish it, play certain games and listen to good music.

It was through the influence of its environment that the new public house would produce improvement.[14] The movement represented, in the words of its historian, a 'coherent philosophy', which drew on the pre-war Progressive faith in rational solutions to society's ills and its goals of 'efficiency, order, discipline, social control, and bourgeois uplift'. Practically, it comprised fewer licences, the provision of food and weaker beer, new pub designs, a wider clientele and the creation of a 'venue for respectable family leisure'.[15] It was now carried forward by a number of committed brewers, driven by the ideology of improvement but sustained also by their belief in its commercial sense. For them the war had demonstrated that reduced beer consumption did not mean less profit. Widening the social base of the pub's patrons would boost the sale of more expensive and thus more profitable beers. Moreover, the necessary expenditure on improvement would tend to disadvantage smaller brewers, and licence reduction would further eliminate competition.[16]

The movement depended, however, upon licensing justices still largely imbued with an outlook of restriction. This obstacle in the way of improvement was noted by a parliamentary committee which reported on the disinterested management question in 1927. Sidney Nevile, who had served on the Control Board and became 'the de facto leader of the improved-pub movement', found such difficulties facing Whitbread's early efforts, for example in seeking to open a new pub on Tooting Bec Road, Wandsworth, which was finally achieved in the High Court.[17] It was thus where brewers and bench were of like mind that the policy found its most significant expression. This was particularly the case in Birmingham, where William Waters Butler of brewers Mitchells & Butlers (who had also served on the Control Board) and chairman of the licensing bench George Bryson, together with the city's planners, carried the policy forward. Altogether the company spent £1.7 million on 142 pubs. Exemplifying the approach was its British Oak at Stirchley, with parking for cars, no garish advertising, gardens, bowling greens and a playground; inside it featured an assembly room for food, concerts, meetings and functions.[18] Brewers in the London area were eventually able to achieve similar results. Barclay Perkins was granted permission to build a pub on the London County Council's new Bellingham estate in 1923, the first brewery to be so favoured, and built the Fellowship in the following year. It set up its Anchor Taverns, under the management of Alexander Part formerly of the Home Counties Trust, which ran 30 pubs from its tied estate of some 400. On some of them it spent lavishly, notably the Downham Tavern, opened in 1930 on another London County Council estate at a reputed cost of £70,000. It comprised two big lounges, a concert/recreation hall for 1,000 people, tea room and children's room, no fewer than 36 lavatories, roof garden, bowling greens and tennis courts. At Whitbread Nevile had set up the Improved Public House Company in 1920 with the intention of recreating the 'continental cafe system where facilities are offered for the comfort of both sexes'. It ran sixteen of the brewery's new pubs, huge quasi-restaurants that ringed the capital and were aimed at the middle-class motoring public. But the emphasis on food pervaded Whitbread generally: by 1948 nine out of ten of its pubs were serving meals and snacks.[19]

It was large brewers like these which dominated pub improvement: twenty-seven companies with £1 million of shareholdings or more were responsible for one out of two pubs built or rebuilt in the inter-war years. It was also localised. Birmingham and London together accounted for one-sixth of the total. Of that total two-thirds were in suburban or rural locations. In a number of other towns, like Oxford, Coventry, Southampton, Sheffield, Leicester, Brighton, Leeds, Norwich, Portsmouth, Newcastle, Hull, Reading, Manchester and Sunderland, new pubs on improved lines were built, but in none did they represent more than a fraction of the existing stock. Towns of comparable size, typically with declining staple industries, more obstructive licensing benches and probably less innovative brewers, like Bradford, Blackburn, Bolton, Oldham, Salford or Gateshead, witnessed little such development.[20]

Architecturally these pubs largely looked backwards to recreate a version of the traditional inn, either in neo-Tudor or neo-Georgian style. Of the former, examples included the Black Horse Hotel, Bristol Road South, Birmingham of 1929, which used Cotswold stone, grey-brown Cotswold slates and silver-grey half-timbering to recreate the Midlands manor house. Or the 1932 Old Goat Inn at Enfield, of which the *Brick Builder* was moved to remark: 'Possibly the acme of design has been reached in a very beautiful house in brick with Tudor chimneys.' It was much derided as 'Brewers' Tudor' for the exterior or 'Tea-Shop Tudor' for the inside. The Royal Fine Art Commission, for example, later sniffed at the 'mockery of some historic style such as the Elizabethan – which only succeeds in looking as artificial as a film setting but is unfortunately more permanent …' (Figure 18). The Georgian tradition was emphasised in two architectural competitions. The first in 1920, sponsored by Samuel Allsopp and Sons, conceived its public house as 'a modern building, but one more on the lines of an Eighteenth Century Inn than of a Nineteenth Century Public House'. The second, the following year, held by the Worshipful Company of Brewers, looked for a pub 'quiet and simple in character', in a district where the architectural style was a 'quiet rendering of eighteenth century English classic.' Examples included the Southborough Arms on the Kingston Bypass or the Greyhound at Wembley. More modernistic designs were comparatively rare. Perhaps the most striking was the Comet Hotel at Hatfield, named for the aircraft of the nearby de Haviland aero-drome, with its exterior rounded like the eponymous plane and its interior mirrors featuring it streaking across them.[21]

In total some 5,900 pubs were built or rebuilt between the wars, concentrated in the second half of the 1930s, which represented about 7 per cent of the existing stock of on-licences in 1921. This was a huge financial investment. But much greater was investment in general improvement to pubs. Two surveys for the Brewers' Society of 1927 and 1930 showed that well over 400 brewers between 1922 and June 1930 spent £21 million (probably an underestimate) on improvements to over 20,000 pre-war premises, with more in the succeeding decade. Looking at a city where improvement in the reformers' sense was limited, Bradford, the licensing justices nevertheless approved 435 alterations to licensed premises, particu-larly from the late 1930s. This meant in effect that virtually all the pubs in the city were 'improved' in some way.[22] Much of this was simply modernisation as living standards rose. This included toilet facilities. For most of the pub's history these had been in the yard. Some urban pubs had added urinals to the premises, which might consist simply of a space between a stone flag and the outside wall, although these came to be seen as a nuisance. But sanitation remained basic to the turn of the nineteenth and twentieth centuries. In Blackburn in 1893 fewer than 10 per cent of pubs had modern toilet facilities. In Shrewsbury around 1901 about a fifth of the public houses and nearly half the beerhouses lacked separate WCs. Even into the inter-war period this was still the case. The Scott Hotel, a beerhouse in Bradford's White Abbey district, still in the 1920s had a privy midden, like a quarter of the houses in the locality, in a 'very disgusting state' according to the public inquiry into its redevelopment.[23] In addition to improved sanitation pubs fitted out their parlours, or 'best rooms', with more comfortable furnishings – carpets and upholstered seats – and the designations 'smoke room' or 'lounge' began to be common. But the accommodation in the public bar or tap room frequently remained basic. In London in the 1930s the poorest type of public bar had its 'brown walls, beer-stained bar, spittoons, a sawdust floor, a dart-board and a little knife-board ledge big enough for three or four customers to try and sit on'. In York at this time the majority of the city's pubs had a smoking room or lounge with horse-hair upholstered seating and a sawdust and spittoon public bar, or else the former rooms were larger and rather better furnished and the public bar lacked the spittoons and sawdust.[24] The war, and the restrictions on materials that followed, meant that improvement to pubs effectively ended for the remainder of this period. Although the efforts of reformers, and the more general modernisation of pubs, brought change and added diversity to the pub scene, there was much into the 1950s that was essentially as the Victorians had known it (Figure 19).

The diversity of pubs makes it difficult to generalise about how well publicans fared in this period. There is certainly evidence of difficult times. We have already seen how unemployment affected the pub's trade. Publicans in the North East, for example, were reported as facing difficulties in these years: in 1924 half of Newcastle's houses were failing to pay their way and this was true also of the region in the succeeding decade. Bradford's chief constable clearly had this widespread state of affairs in mind when he told the Royal Commission on Licensing that he was not aware of local publicans having difficulty carrying on.[25] One particular difficulty facing publicans was the continued growth of clubs. During the inter-war years their numbers in England and Wales almost doubled to 15,657. They enjoyed the advantages of lower prices and less onerous restrictions. But whilst clearly a threat to the publican's trade, its effect was muted by the relatively restricted share of the beer market which clubs enjoyed, varying between localities at between 5 and 7 per cent.[26] But the continuing attraction of the pub life cannot solely be assessed in cash terms. It was no doubt partly responsible for the flow of 'retired boxers, wrestlers, vaudeville artistes, billiards champions, footballers' and others into the trade reported from London, with the aside that they were 'not necessarily good business people', but who enjoyed an 'automatic working-class following'.[27] But the majority of publicans in an oral history of York pubs found it a rich and reward-ing life in the deeper sense of those terms. As one landlady expressed it, looking back over a life in the trade:

> Many times we didn't even have a night off, we just stopped in the pub
> and played darts with the lads. It was more a friendly, homely atmosphere.
> All your customers were friends. All my life I've had pleasant memories,
> I've had fun, I've really enjoyed it. If I went tomorrow, I've no regrets. My
> husband was the same, he loved the licensed trade. He didn't have hob-
> bies – his work was his hobby.[28]

Most publicans continued to be tenants, but there was a further shift to management. From forming 7.5 per cent of brewers' on-licences in 1925, the proportion of managed houses rose to 18 per cent by the mid-1930s, at which level it remained for the next 25 years. It contin-ued to be concentrated in particular areas: in both Birmingham and Newcastle, for example, 48 per cent of pubs were managed. For ten-ants the tie was generally extended, from being confined to draught beer to include bottled (now increasingly popular) and foreign beers, wines and spirits and in many cases soft drinks too. The number of brewing companies with which these publicans worked more than halved between the wars, but throughout this period the picture is one of retailing still dominated by local brewers.[29]

Probably the greatest change for the publican, as for the custom-ers, was the much more restricted drinking scene brought about by the war. Although more limited opening was probably to a degree welcome, the law and its complexity was in general perceived as a burden. As Alexander Part's guide to innkeeping put it, 'so long as you do not try to associate English licensing law with moral sen-sibilities, or common sense, there is hope for you.' Regarding the police, his advice was never to trust them, but at the same time to keep friends. He also noted that the police in general would only take action against a licensee where a specific complaint or com-munication had been made.[30] The police continued their now long-established practice of regular supervision of licensed premises. In Bradford, for example, 32,000 visits were made annually using a four-point classification system rising from not less than once a week to only when necessary. The York oral history study found that earlier friction between police and licensees gave way in the 1920s to an acceptance, and even welcoming, of the regular visits by a sergeant and constable. For the officers too, enjoying a pint in the kitchen, the visits were probably not unwelcome. Although the higher ranks were sometimes less friendly, like the Inspector who insisted that closing time meant precisely that – not a glass of beer anywhere.[31] Actual prosecutions remained at the low level attained in the late nineteenth century. Details of proceedings in Bradford for the years 1921 to 1931, for example, showed the main offences as serving outside time and allowing gambling, together averaging about seventeen a year. There were just ten cases of permitting drunkenness. The Bolton study quantified this as for every 5,000 hours a pub was open, one of its customers was drunk and disorderly. Of course trouble did sometimes occur, but as the York study shows, such incidents were individual and isolated. In Portsmouth during the inter-war period just one pub was deprived of its licence for misconduct. This was the William the Conqueror, a beerhouse in Silver Street, Southsea. Having been heavily fined in 1922 for selling alcohol outside hours, harbouring prostitutes and permitting drunkenness, a watch was kept by the police on the pub, and as prostitutes continued to use it the licence was refused in 1924.[32]

The prevailing social tone was thus much as Charles Booth had found in the ordinary East End pub. An observer in the mid-1920s, Ernest Selley, personally visiting hundreds of pubs throughout the country, found that the atmosphere was usually 'genial': 'There is companionship, refreshment, enjoyment, change, some recreation, warmth and light.'[33] During the period this traditional essence of pub life was articulated in the idea of the 'local'. As with the use of pub, which became general only late in the nineteenth century, it seems odd that it was not used earlier, given that pubs had always functioned in this way, and it is difficult to date precisely its origins. The OED cites examples from the mid-1930s, but its general usage and meaning is indicated by Maurice Gorham's 1939 study of simply *The Local*, with its sympathetic evocation of the traditional world of the pub and its 'regulars'. Mass Observation in Bolton found that the only nickname or slang term for the pub was boozer (although jerry shop was apparently still in local use), but the study throughout clearly documents the characteristics of the local, and in fact uses the term 'local pub'. Outside the town centre all pubs relied for the great majority of their custom upon people living in the immediate vicinity. In its characteristic way the study measured this. These regular customers either lived within a few minutes' stroll of their local, or if they didn't, either worked nearby or retained a habit formed on earlier association. But whilst there existed a maximum distance – two or three minutes' walk – beyond which the normal pub-goer in normal circumstances would not go, within that distance the actual choice of local was the product of a complex set of variables. Most important were previous relationships with existing regulars, such as through work, but others were the beer, the landlord or even the pub pianist.[34] A study of a working-class district of central Oxford in the early 1950s, St Ebbe's, shows the local in its fullest sense. Customers remained loyal to one or other of the sixteen pubs in the area. It was a 'friendly world', where regulars helped one another out at times of financial difficulty and the daily social world of talk and games was supplemented by pub trips and street parties for special events like the coronation[35] (Figure 20). Studies of the new estates built during these years highlighted the pull of the local. As a Mr Kemp put it, out in Dagenham in the late 1950s, speaking of the pubs serving an estate of 27,000 homes:'They did it all wrong when they built those places. Instead of little pubs that could be like little clubs for the people round about, like they are in Poplar, they built them whacking big places.'[36]

This point is conveyed by Mass Observation's conclusion on the life of the pub at the close of the 1930s that it was 'still essentially very much a pre-industrial institution. Format, ritual, traditions, nomenclature, games, have not changed very much in the past hundred years.'[37] Having examined the elements of the traditional world in an earlier chapter, I shall focus here more on areas of change. One thing to note at the outset, as indeed we have seen throughout this study, is the importance of local diversity. This applies to the use of pubs by women. During the war they had begun to visit them in greater numbers. Speaking generally this continued, but the evidence is sometimes contradictory. The *New Survey of London Life and Labour* reported that women were in fact a smaller proportion of pub frequenters than before the war. Its sample count of eight pubs on Friday and Saturday nights (when they were most likely to be out) showed that a quarter of the customers were women. Other evidence from the capital showed greater pub use. On a typical Saturday night in Fulham at that time over one-third of the patrons were women. In Bethnal Green in the mid-1920s it was a common sight on Saturday lunchtime to see women of all ages in the pub or standing outside. In Vauxhall many women used pubs regularly and Monday remained the traditional day for them to visit the pub and afterwards return home for a sing-song.[38] In Bolton's town-centre pubs at the weekend women were about a quarter of the customers, falling to about 15 per cent in main road pubs away from the centre, and lower still on weekdays. There, as the tap rooms and vaults were closed to them, the parlours or lounges might be half-full of women. In York women were making greater use of pubs, forming about a quarter of customers. But in the hotel type of pub on the main roads over 40 per cent of customers were women, suggesting that among middle-class women it was now possible to enter with relative ease an establishment not tainted with the vulgarity of the pub. For Selley, similarly, the increase in women drinking was chiefly in the better-class public houses. In other districts, such as mining communities, a woman definitely lost 'caste' going into a pub. Yet again, however, studies of Lancashire towns showed that for respectable women to go into a pub with their husband was now acceptable. Clearly it is a complex picture revealing, it has been argued, a range of distinct yet widely held attitudes from never entering a pub, to only when accompanied by husband, to independently, if modestly. As one Ordsall women remembered her mother as a regular at the 'King Billy', which also held a women's pub outing, in the 1920s:

> She'd put tenpence away … it was tuppence ha'penny a glass of mild … And Monday, Wednesday, Friday and Saturday, she had a glass of mild on each of those nights … she'd go in at 8 o'clock, and she'd stay till 10. She'd had that one drink.[39]

The Second World War, like the First, saw a rise in the use of pubs by women. This was especially the case in urban and industrial areas, and above all by young women. A Mass Observation report of one south-west London borough in 1943 found that 45 per cent of women under thirty claimed they were visiting pubs more often since the war began. This was based on increased spending power and freedom from neighbourhood and familial constraints where women were relocated to a new area. It reflected too the enhanced role for the pub as a centre for contact and socialising in the disruption of war, and the women's belief in their right to leisure as equal contributors to the general war effort. This produced among some observers the anxieties that characterised the First World War. But it is significant of changing government perceptions of the situation that when they were brought to the attention of the Home Secretary in 1944, and he was asked if he would do something to remedy the situation, he replied he would not. As to the extent to which this renewed growth of women in pubs was sustained in the post-war years, the evidence is mixed, once again varying between differing localities. Mass Observation, looking at Bolton, London and York in 1947 and 1948 found increases in the first two, but a return to pre-war levels in the third. The St Ebbe's, Oxford, study showed that women still formed a minor part of the pub world, typically coming with their husbands, or if alone preferring the snug. On the whole the real movement of women, and young women in particular, into the world of the pub was still to come.[40]

In general the evidence suggests an ageing of the pub's population in this period. In Bolton the thirty to fifty group provided the 'big body of regular drinkers'. Young people were not common there, preferring dance halls, the cinema or simply walking the streets. Only the town-centre pubs adjoining dance halls were patronised by them. In London similarly they formed only a minority of customers: those aged 25 or under making up just 8 per cent in the pubs surveyed, where three-quarters were over 35. In Derby in the early 1950s young people under 25 were also the least likely to go to pubs. In St Ebbe's too the age level was high (reflecting that of the district); young people who did drink tended to go to larger pubs than the basic locals there[41] (Figure 21).

As to the social class of customers, there is evidence that the pub habit was rising again up the social scale. This was particularly true of the newer suburban or rural pubs, where the arrival of the motorist introduced a better-off trade. Conversely, as Selley found, many village pubs suffered as the new buses took people into the nearest small town for the shops, the cinema and a more enticing pub than the 'poor, ill-lighted, cramped' village 'alehouse'.[42] But in general the pub remained a working-class institution. In the public bars of 20 London pubs the *New Survey* found only 4 customers out of 150 who were clearly above that class, with a further 19 borderline lower middle-class; the great majority were the skilled or unskilled working-class. Selley too found that other classes used the pub, but not so much in relation to their numbers; customers were largely working-class.[43]

Looking at what these customers were doing, there was much continuity with earlier years. In Bolton pubs people talked, played games like cards, dominoes, darts or quoits, and enjoyed music (most pubs had a piano). A variety of clubs, sports and hobbies were connected with them, from the Oddfellows to pigeon flying. This persisted. Male customers in the pubs of St Ebbe's exchanged banter and talked of horse racing or football or holidays, whilst the women

covered local news, health and children. A study of a Yorkshire mining community at this time found similar talk on work and sport,
games of dominoes, cards, billiards or snooker and meetings of the
union, British Legion or the Buffaloes. In York pubs there was usually a piano but customers would bring in other instruments like
accordions, ukeleles, violins or even a penny whistle.[44] But there was
change too. In music, for example, mechanised forms had appeared
late in the nineteenth century, like the Polyphon, which played over
1,000 tunes, the Symphonium and the musical clock. These were
succeeded by the wireless, the gramophone or radiogram, and after
the war by television and the juke-box. The landlord of the Bay
Horse in Marygate, York, for example, got a TV in coronation year
and later both a juke-box and a record player.[45]

In analysing the pub's customers by sex, age, social class or activities, however, one should not lose sight of the immense variety of
individual pub worlds. As Maurice Gorham enthused in *The Local*:

> There are pubs around Portland Place where you will feel lost if you do
> not know the jargon of the rag trade, the used-car market or the B.B.C. . . .
> At the Victoria Stores, opposite the stage door of the Victoria Palace, you
> can see the chorus boys, all made up for the second house, struggling to
> the bar through the press of broad-backed draymen from Watney's brew-
> ery round the corner, on a Friday night. The pubs of Covent Garden of
> course, are full of market porters in the Public Bar and fruit salesmen in the
> Saloon, but the Nag's Head has the Opera house custom as well. There is a
> pub near Cambridge Circus where you will always find Negroes.[46]

The capital had a number of pubs popular with homosexuals, like
the Running Horse in Shepherd's Market, where 'respectable men
in evening dress and camp queans solicited sailors and workmen'
until it was closed in 1937 at the instigation of the Admiralty and the
Canadian military. Pubs in working-class districts, like the Prospect
of Whitby at Wapping Stairs or Charlie Brown's on the West India
Dock Road formed a 'protean milieu' where 'dock labourers, sailors

from across the world, and families mingled freely with flamboy-
ant local queans and slumming gentlemen'.[47] But pubs in general
displayed a complex individuality formed of design and decor, the
particular brewer's beer on offer, the publicans and their staff and
the varied mixes of customers and their favoured pursuits. So whilst
they displayed many common features, and one can categorise them
in a variety of ways, as in the title of this chapter, or as Selley did, distinguishing between Food Taverns, Social Houses or Drink Shops,
it was always still the Red Lion or the Black Horse or thousands of
other specific names.

I end this chapter with the Second World War. In sharp contrast
to the First, beer and the pub were from the outset seen as essential elements of the war effort. They were the ally, not the enemy,
and temperance voices were now ignored. For Lord Woolton, the
Minister of Food, in May 1940, the nation was now temperate and
it was: 'the business of the Government not only to maintain the
life but the morale of the country.' Maintaining the supply of beer
was vital to this, and with it the pub itself. For A.P. Herbert, a noted
friend to the pub in Parliament, it had 'been the one human corner,
a centre not of beer but bonhomie; the one place where after dark
the collective heart of the nation could be seen and felt, beating
resolute and strong'. The *Brewers' Journal* noted in April 1942 how
the term local was coming into increasing use, 'a neighbourly, part-
of-us phrase'.[48] The vital role of the pub in maintaining morale was
evidenced in contemporary research. In Fulham once the Blitz had
begun a decline in pub-going was reversed. In Plymouth it was
found that talk of air raids decreased in proportion to the consumption of alcohol.[49] The raids of course had tragic consequences for
some publicans and their pubs. Altogether eighteen tenants and
their wives of brewers Watneys lost their lives. Eighty-four of the
company's pubs were reduced to rubble. Charringtons, with many
East End pubs, was hardest hit with 149 completely destroyed. A
report on the damage to licensed premises found that by the end of
August 1943, 1,348 on-licences had closed through enemy action

and a further 876 through other circumstances caused by the war, forming together 3 per cent of existing licences. The losses were concentrated in particular cities and districts within them. 15 per cent of pubs were affected in Portsmouth, including the George where Nelson had stayed in 1805; 16 per cent in Hull. In the county of London 7.6 per cent of licensed premises closed, but in the City the figure was 29 per cent; in central Liverpool about 30 per cent were affected and in Swansea almost half.[50]

The war saw further huge increases to the price of beer. Although output did rise, it was achieved partly through a reduction in gravity of about 15 per cent (in contrast, the output of spirits was limited to one-third of the 1939 level). Moreover, because demand soared there were shortages, and pubs were obliged throughout the war to reduce their opening hours or ration what they had over the course of the week, naturally tending to favour their regulars.[51] The demand was swelled not only by domestic consumers, but by the influx of overseas service personnel. United States troops were advised that they would be welcome in British 'taverns' as long as they remembered one thing: 'the inn or tavern is the poor man's club or gathering place where men have come to meet their friends not strangers.' York pubs, close to a number of air bases, played host to many, like the Canadian aircrew who left their 'lucky charm' behind the bar at the Three Tuns. One publican's daughter recalled there a lot of 'argy-bargy after the pubs turned out, a lot of slanging'. A 'not ungrateful' Maurice Gorham coyly remembered 'that our overseas allies often brought with them drinking habits rather more violent than ours'. But perhaps the last word should be with the Agent-General of Ontario, after the war asking God to 'bless the British licensed house. It saved our lives from loneliness – it is a glorious institution, and may it live and prosper for ever.'[52]

12
Conclusion: Modern Times

Mass Observation had reached essentially two conclusions about the pub at the close of the 1930s. The first was its central importance: 'More people spend more time in public houses than they do in any other buildings except private houses and work-places.' As a social institution the pub was more important than church, cinema, dance hall and political organisation put together. But the second was its decline: 'The pub today plays a smaller part in the life of the town than it ever did.'[1] In that sense the war years may be seen as something of a swan-song for the pub in the central role which it had performed. Certainly in the post-war period the theme of decline has been a dominant one. An ethnographic study of pubs in the South West in the mid-1980s found that 'pubs have declined a great deal since the late 1960s', although the rate later flattened out. Another general survey similarly dated the decline from around 1970, a time when the pub had been 'at the peak of its prestige and popularity'.[2] Decline has been a note particularly struck by those critical of the way they have seen the traditional world of the pub and beer disappearing, usually linked to a variety of social changes which the writers have found more or less objectionable. Notable here was Christopher Hutt's 1973 book on *The Death of the English Pub*. A history of the pub published in 1994 reached a similar, although not altogether hopeless, conclusion in its final chapter: 'The End of the Road: Recent Years'.

The chairman of the Campaign for Real Ale's Industry Group put this emphatically, also in that year, at 'The Pub in 2000' conference: 'We have to stop the downward spiral gripping the pub.'[3]

To some extent, of course, judgement will depend on one's perception of what a pub should be, as I discussed at the beginning of this study. The departmental committee under Lord Erroll, which looked at liquor licensing at the beginning of the 1970s, made the point:

> It is impossible, in our view, to generalise about the public house. Everyone has his own ideal image. For some, the term conjures up a vision of an old country town coaching inn; for others, it may mean a small village pub, a city discotheque or a dockland bar. It makes little sense to commit oneself to a particular view of what should constitute a public house.[4]

A public house was thus all of these and this study continues to encompass that variety as it charts developments towards the present day. The period from the late 1950s has been one of an unprecedented rate of change for the pub and its world, whose long-term significance cannot yet be determined. For these reasons, and given my space here, the discussion will be suggestive rather than exhaustive.

Between 1951 and 1971 the number of on-licences in England and Wales fell by 13 per cent from 73,421 to 64,087. This represented then one on-licence for every 761 persons; in 1921 the figure had been one for every 458 and in 1871 one for every 201. There had clearly been a massive reduction in the availability of drink outlets for the English people. As not all on-licences were held for pubs, their number within that total in 1971 was estimated at 61,000, roughly 1 for every 800 people. By 1971 the beerhouse, that cause of so much complaint in the nineteenth century, had virtually disappeared. Numbers fell from 13,664 in 1951 to just 447.[5] Some were removed through the redundancy process established in 1904, which continued disproportionately to affect them, although the financing of the scheme still kept the overall number low.[6] The scheme itself was finally wound up by the Licensing (Alcohol Education and Research) Act of 1981, which allocated the remaining assets where its title suggests. Beerhouse licences were also surrendered in return for the grant of full-licences, a process which was now further stimulated by a provision of the 1947 Finance Act empowering justices to accept this in the same area at a reduced monopoly value. Finally, beerhouses were themselves granted full-licences. In Bradford, for example, between 1950 and 1965, 47 were upgraded in this way; in Portsmouth between 1948 and 1963 no fewer than 131.[7]

Portsmouth was one of a number of towns and cities whose pubs had suffered badly in air raids. In 1942 it had been provided that licences affected in this way might be suspended so as to avoid the payment of duty and the necessity for annual renewal. In 1945 the Home Secretary was given powers to create Licensing Planning Areas with special committees composed of representatives of licensing justices and local planning authorities. In Portsmouth local brewers quickly set up an advisory delegation to the committee established there to press for the transfer of a dozen of the 106 suspended licences to the proposed new housing development at Paulsgrove. In the end the transfer of just six was agreed to in 1949.[8] It was, however, an indicator of a more forthcoming attitude among licensing justices than had commonly been the case before the war. Even one of the stricter benches, as Bradford's had been, now began to take a more accommodating line. From 1960 new premises in developing areas, including corporation housing estates, were granted licences in return for the surrender of one or more existing ones. In this way a number of new pubs were built, but the overall trend, as nationally, was downward. The 425 on-licences of 1940 had contracted to 343 by 1970.[9]

From the mid-1970s this decline was reversed, for the first time in a century. The number of on-licences now rose by some 27 per cent to reach 81,455 by 2004. Licensing justices became increasingly willing to grant new licences to a rising number of applications. In 1976, 1,297 new licences were applied for, of which 90 per cent were granted; in 1986 the proportion granted fell, but the actual number was now over 2,000; applications continued to rise, however, and in 2004 98 per cent of 3,550 were granted.[10] But we need to look more closely at those on-licences. First, many existing licences were in fact disappearing. Taking the five years to 1980, for example, 5,998 new on-licences were granted, but as the total of licences rose by 2,064, then 3,934 had been lost. These disappearing licences were existing pubs in both urban and rural areas. In East Anglia, for example, between 1966 and 1977 Watneys closed twenty-seven pubs in sixteen villages within the Downham Market licensing division. They were mainly sold as private houses. Nationally by the mid-1990s more than a quarter of rural parishes were without a pub.[11] In urban areas redevelopment for housing, commercial or road purposes progressively reduced the stock of pubs built in the nineteenth century. In Bradford, typically, slum clearance and the development of two major roads decimated the pubs within a huge area to the south of the city centre.[12] But a number of social, economic and demographic developments also produced the decline. Chief among them was the demise of heavy and manufacturing industry. Just as the troubles of the steel, shipbuilding, textile and other trades caused problems for pubs in the inter-war years, their collapse from the late 1970s effectively removed an essential support of the urban, male-dominated pub. Demand for beer, although not for alcoholic drinks generally, fell sharply in the 1979 to 1981 recession and did not recover thereafter, partly as a result of the increase in real terms of its price. The average pub price of beer was 25 per cent higher in real terms in 1986 than 1980.[13] Demographic change worked to produce the same result. The working class who had always formed the great bulk of the pub's customers continued the trend established in the inter-war years to move to private housing or council estates in the suburbs. The inner-city housing that escaped demolition was now often occupied by immigrants from the New Commonwealth, for many of whom the pub was not a part of their cultural landscape.

The stock of what one might term traditional pubs, built that is before the twentieth century, thus contracted. But what of the new on-licences? They were granted in many instances to what were clearly not pubs by any definition, as they had been to railway refreshment rooms or concert halls, for example, from the mid-nineteenth century. A selected year from Bradford illustrates this point. In 1981, of ten new licences granted two were to casinos, one to a bingo and social club, two to church halls but restricted to functions, one to a wine bar, one to a student-oriented bar/concert hall, two to places principally restaurants and one to a hotel. Although of course then open to the public for the sale of alcohol on the premises, could they fairly be described as pubs? Using the definition of the trade body, the British Beer and Pub Association, the number of pubs in England and Wales by 2006 was 51,479, representing a fall over the previous 35 years of some 10,000 establishments.[14]

Alongside this contraction was the expansion of places to drink other than pubs. This was facilitated by the introduction in 1961 of separate restaurant, residential and combined restaurant and residential licences, whilst at the same time the discretion of licensing justices to refuse them was limited. By 1971 there were 11,228 of these new licences, rising to 20,622 in 1980 and peaking at over 31,000 in 1997. The number of registered clubs also rose, reaching a high in 1983 of over 27,000, although their number then contracted to under 20,000 in 2004. But equally significant was the expansion of places to buy drink to consume at home, notably at the supermarket. From 28,166 in 1971 the number of off-licences rose to almost 48,000 twenty years later.[15] Quite clearly there was a dramatic decline in the number of pubs relative to other licensed premises, both on and off. Further, as part of that trend the pub's share of the drink trade contracted. Its share of the beer market fell from an estimated over 80 per cent in 1955 to 63 per cent by 1980.[16]

As to the pubs themselves, they too were changing. New pubs were built, for example on new estates, or existing pubs rebuilt (Figure 22). But to the overall stock of pubs the most significant change was to their interiors. These continued to be refurbished in line with the general rise in the standard of living, and consequent desire for comfort, as well as to comply with health and safety standards.

This was commonly done in some version of the 'traditional', incorporating stained oak furniture, horse brasses and the like. But a number of pubs were decorated along particular 'themes', a development castigated by the traditionalists, like Hutt, decrying examples like the George IV at Hounslow, rebuilt as the Honeycomb and decorated accordingly with even the cash register hidden in an imitation wooden hive. The creation of self-consciously 'Irish' pubs, as with the O'Neill's or Scruffy Murphy's concepts, was another development along these lines.[17] Overall, however, the biggest single change was the opening out of the interiors as the traditional variety of rooms was consolidated into just one, two, or at most three (Figure 19). This permitted greater supervision of the premises by the staff and dispensed with the use of waiters. It also reflected the decline of heavy and manufacturing industry: fewer men in working clothes meant a diminished need for a separate public bar or tap room. It was the result too of changes in the social world of pubs, as women and the young increasingly began to use them. They became more a place for a night out rather than an extension of work or home. Customers still formed their social spaces, but they did so within a physically much more open setting. A sociological study of a 'traditional' working-class pub with its interior opened out in this way identified a range of such spaces. There was the 'public space' of the middle-aged regulars at the bar, the 'negotiable space' of the non-sitting areas by various groups using the pub, including some all female, and the 'closed social space' where couples sat alone. As the pub filled up and more alcohol was consumed, so the social spaces imploded or dissolved, although never totally.[18]

The cumulative effect of the varied refurbishments and opening out of premises was the virtual disappearance of pub interiors predating the 1950s. The CAMRA National Inventory of Historic Pub Interiors, compiled from 1991, sought to include all historic pubs from every period of its development. In the whole of the UK just 205 were identified with intact or largely intact interiors of outstanding historic importance, plus a further 43 with interiors with particular features of such importance. It included gin palaces like the Philharmonic in Liverpool or the Bartons Arms, Birmingham; rural pubs like the Luppitt Inn, Luppitt, Devon or the Sun Inn at Leintwardine in Herefordshire; and inter-war pubs like the Holly Bush at Hinckley in Leicestershire or the Test Match Hotel at West Bridgford, Nottinghamshire.[19] Of course realistically one would not expect many to have survived, any more than the interiors of shops, or indeed private houses, have survived. But if the pub is an English institution to stand alongside its churches, then clearly there is a case for documentation and preservation.

Returning to the modern pub, an important trend was the opening of entirely new outlets in the centres of towns and cities throughout the country. The resultant agglomeration of pubs and bars, and including night clubs, restaurants and takeaways, has been characterised as the 'night-time economy'. A number of developments produced it. First was the more liberal approach of licensing justices. As we have seen, this dated back to the late 1950s, but was carried significantly further in the late 1990s by the relaxation of the judgement of 'need' in the grant of new licences, so important for their Victorian predecessors. This came about following trade criticism of the continuing inconsistencies of policy between licensing benches and the 1998 report of the government's Better Regulation Task Force, which specifically recommended against the use of a judgement of need. Faced with this, and the report's other recommendation that jurisdiction over licensing be transferred to local authorities, the *Good Practice Guide* of the Justices' Clerks' Society conceded abolition of the criterion of need as 'out of date and unnecessary'. Instead, market forces and planning law would together effectively regulate the number of premises. Whilst not free licensing in the early nineteenth-century sense, since magistrates retained their licensing role, it did arguably embody the old idea that 'no man would sell liquor to his ruin'. Second was the declared belief of both central and local governments in the vital economic importance of the leisure industry, and of drink outlets as part of it.

Some local authorities in particular were attracted to this as a way to civic renewal in the vision of a twenty-four hour city, in imitation of what was believed to be the urbane, cosmopolitan culture of their European counterparts. To an extent some police forces embraced this, or else gave up on their traditional role of objector to new licences. A third reason, it has been argued, was the desire of the drinks industry to retarget young people it feared losing to the 'rave' culture, with its alternative venues and new substances to consume. A result was the controversial promotion of so called alco-pops. Fourth was the growth of a number of branded outlets, such as J.D. Wetherspoon, Edwards, Hogshead, Firkin, O'Neill's, Slug and Lettuce, Pitcher and Piano, All Bar One and Walkabout.[20]

Within this latter development was the opening of massive new pubs utilising a range of premises previously put to other uses. J.D. Wetherspoon, for example, with 130 pubs by early 1996, opened them in former banks, post offices, cinemas, shops, supermarkets, department stores and hotels. Examples included the former Natwest building in Irongate, Derby which opened as the Moon Under Water or, with the same name, a former cinema in Deansgate, Manchester, with three bars on two floors covering 8,000 square feet and costing over £2 million. The average cost of conversion and fitting out was £750,000. An established retailer, Yates's Wine Lodges, which had from the 1880s sought to educate the working man and his wife to good wine and food in plain and simple surroundings, now reviewed its operations. It too then converted former retail units in Coventry, Leeds and Luton, with a normal criterion of between 3,500 and 5,000 square feet.[21]

In all these new pubs food was an important part of what was now offered to customers. This new emphasis on food in pubs was a result of the competition of other places at which to enjoy a drink, including the home, and the relative decline of beer as the mainstay of the pub's economy. To put it another way, the pub needed to tap into the affluent society's love of eating out. Food had in fact always been a part of the provision of the public house, from the innkeepers of the coaching days through to their putative heirs in the improved pub. But equally it had often been limited. Ernest Selley's survey in the mid-1920s had found his category of 'Food Tavern', 'which definitely sets out to provide meals', the least common type and chiefly confined to towns and cities. The working population limited itself to bread and cheese, pickles, ham rolls or taking in their own food, still common as it had been in the nineteenth century. Similarly in Liverpool in the early 1930s, only a few pubs were reported as providing food. Or as the landlord of the Phoenix in York in the 1930s and 40s put it: 'You get food in a cafe, you get beer in a pub.' In many pubs crisps, a new delicacy from the 1920s, was as much as was on offer.[22] This situation changed from the 1960s. Restaurant-oriented pubs, like Berni, Beefeater, Harvester or Vintage Inns were developed. Between 1977 and 1984, for example, food sales in public houses grew by 375 per cent and went from 12 per cent of all food catering sales to 22.5 per cent. At the close of the 1990s pubs headed the list of number of meals taken in commercial establishments, not including snacks, at 345.5 million, comprising 248 million in pub restaurants and a further 97 million bar meals.[23]

From the foregoing discussion it will be clear that the 'pub' came to cover a highly diverse set of premises. To an extent that has always been the case, but this study has argued for a relatively greater degree of homogeneity from the mid-Victorian period coincident with the increasingly general use of the term pub. But in the later twentieth century the pub became once again a more heterogeneous institution. This is notwithstanding the view that some writers have taken of increasing 'sameness', in the development of the single drinking area and the use of a 'pattern book' of styles, which produced only variations on the basic theme of pub 'traditional'. For others, in contrast, the fragmentation of the pub 'into a number of separate identities' has been the dominant theme. And from a post-modern perspective, the contemporary pub world has been presented as offering a variety of venues to restless consumers seeking 'a range of different public house experiences'.[24]

This great variety makes it difficult to generalise as we turn once again to the publicans and their customers. There were important changes in the ownership and running of pubs. The pace of concentration in the brewing industry accelerated markedly from the late 1950s in the so called merger mania. By 1967, according to the Monopolies Commission Report on the Supply of Beer, the six largest brewers – Bass Charrington, Allied, Whitbread, Watney Mann, Courage and Scottish and Newcastle – between them accounted for nearly 70 per cent of total beer production and owned over half of all the on-licences in Great Britain.[25] One consequence of concentration was rationalisation and greater scale economies in production. Thus the Big Six closed 54 of their 122 breweries over the period 1958 to 1970. Smaller, independent brewers did survive, 'sometimes by luck, more often by shrewd judgement'.[26] Another consequence (and indeed cause) of this merger activity was the development of new products. First the production of 'keg' beer (brewery conditioned, filtered, pasteurised and carbonated) reversed the trend from draught to bottled beer. Pioneered on a small scale by Watneys in the 1930s, the company promoted its Red Barrel vigorously from the late 1950s. Ind Coope Tetley Ansell/ Allied followed suit with their Double Diamond from 1962. Second was the growing popularity of lager. Led by Ind Coope with its Skol brand of 1959, sales rose to 2 per cent of the British market by 1964. But the introduction of draught lager from the mid-1960s helped to give it the boost that by 1989 it formed over half of all beer sales. One response to these trends was the formation of the Campaign for Real Ale in 1971. Whilst it clearly did not succeed in returning traditional cask-conditioned beer to its dominant position (it accounted for just 15 per cent of the market in 1989), it did contribute to the preservation of real ale and the creation of a further market segment of pubs specialising in its service.[27] It also helped to prevent the disappearance from bars of the hand pump in favour of other forms of dispense.

It was the level of concentration in the industry which led to another inquiry by the Monopolies and Mergers Commission into the supply of beer. It concluded that a monopoly existed which operated against the public interest and that the degree of vertical integration should be reduced in order to encourage lower retail prices and improve consumer choice. The Department of Trade and Industry endorsed the report, but ultimately watered down its proposals. Nevertheless, the government in its Beer Orders of 1989 made important changes. Brewers owning more than 2,000 full on-licences were required either to dispose of the brewery business or to dispose of or free the tie on half of the number in excess of 2,000 by 31 October 1992. Tied premises were also to be allowed to sell a 'guest' cask-conditioned draught beer and to buy non-beer drinks and alcohol-free and low-alcohol beers from outside the tie. One consequence was a shift in the ownership of pubs and the development of pub companies, the so called pubcos. The largest of them, Punch Taverns, had over 9,200 pubs in its estate by 2006.[28]

For the publican one change was the continuation of the shift from tenancy towards management. At the close of the 1960s, 23.6 per cent of houses were managed but over 76.4 per cent continued to be tenanted, although there remained differences between brewery companies. Twenty years later the national brewers managed between 27 and 38 per cent of their properties.[29] The changes in the ownership of pubs produced continuing variation in their relative incidence. The remaining national brewers who both produced and retailed beer – Scottish and Newcastle, Bass and Whitbread – had shifted strongly towards management. Some regional brewers had also taken steps in this direction, notably Marstons with their Pitcher and Piano pub chain. But smaller local breweries largely remained with the more traditional tenancy. This picture, by the close of the 1990s, was reversed with the new pub companies. Here the national companies with their large inheritance of tenanted pubs from the major brewers stayed with the older form. Smaller chains, often with particular branding strategies, were more likely to use management as a form of retaining control. But tenancy remained the main way of running a pub: by 2006 some 29 per cent of brewer-owned pubs in the UK were managed, compared with a little under a quarter of those owned by pub companies.[30]

Looking at the individuals in the trade, there were continuities from earlier generations. The more personal rewards remained of prime importance. A survey of nearly 600 licensees published in 1970 showed that 86 per cent liked the job itself – meeting people and so on – whereas only 4 per cent put money first and foremost. It also showed that 37 per cent of them claimed to work between 90 and 109 hours a week. The liking for the sociability and the perceived independence similarly served to mitigate the long hours and poor financial rewards of the publicans in a study of the trade in Kent at this time. Many tenants in a study of two south-west towns in the mid-1980s were demoralised by the low return on their investment, the fact that managed houses were more profitable and the extra work produced by such as the trend towards food service.[31] Other continuities were revealed in a survey of managers in 1999. One was the tendency to move from within the trade to the position of publican. 17 per cent of one or both partners in couples and 41 per cent of single managers had previously worked behind the bar for the company surveyed, in line with that company's aim to reduce staff turnover and promote the idea of a career ladder. 5 per cent had a family background in the trade. But entry from an entirely distinct occupation was still the most common route, and skilled manual or non-manual working-class occupations dominated, although retail management was typical among single managers. Three changes stood out, however. One was a greater acceptance of women, either running the business themselves or as the main partner. Although, as we saw, where the man typically had another occupation the wife had in practice filled this role. The others were the entry of younger, and often single, people, reflecting partly the orientation of pubs towards the young. An exemplar of all those trends was the Scottish and Newcastle run Rat and Parrot in Leeds, a branded outlet covering 9,500 square feet, employing a hundred staff serving 5,000 drinks a day and managed by a twenty-seven year old woman.[32]

Turning finally to the customers and their world, one point must be made first. If we accept its fragmentation into a wide variety of forms, but which may be subsumed under the title of pub, the pub has remained central to the country's leisure habits. In 1970 nearly three-quarters of the adult population visited a public house at least occasionally. Regular users, visiting that is once a month or more, comprised 44 per cent of the adult population, with 67 per cent of men and 26 per cent of women. Local studies confirm this general picture. One of a north-east Derbyshire mining village in 1968 found that of its 157 interviewees only 18 said they never went to the pub. In the 1990s it remained the most common free-time activity outside the home among adults, with 65 per cent having done so within the previous three months.[33] But there were important shifts among the customers. The young returned to the pub after half a century. Whereas young people in three Lancashire towns in the 1940s and 1950s most frequently mentioned the dance hall as the place to meet a potential boy- or girl friend, with pubs referred to by very few, by 1970 the pub had become the only public meeting place regularly mentioned. Dance hall, church hall and cinema had all declined. This was linked to the increasingly younger age at which alcohol was being consumed, both generally and in pubs. In a survey of 1980, 70 per cent of underage respondents had had a drink in a pub or other venue.[34] The young now had more disposable income to spend on what increasingly came to be perceived as an essential part of a more affluent lifestyle. At the same time supervision of pubs was being relaxed. The Bradford police, for example, made fewer than half the number of routine visits, to many fewer pubs, than their late-Victorian counterparts. In the 1960s and into the 1970s the practice largely ceased. This was not necessarily welcomed by publicans. As one York landlady remembered the regular weekend visits of sergeant and constable and the consequent flight of the underaged: 'Now that was stopped, and it was the worst thing that ever happened in pubs.'[35]

By the mid-1990s among those aged 16 to 24, 78 per cent had visited a pub within the previous three months, the second highest category after those 25 to 34. The young from the first had a central role in the growth of the night-time economy. This was being noted from the mid-1980s. A study of Sunderland showed how thousands then converged at weekends on the town centre to do a round, or 'circuit', of nine or ten establishments. It contrasted the old pub, where customers stayed for most of the night, with the new pub as 'fashion item'. Twenty years later another study of the by now greatly expanded night-time economy similarly highlighted the shift from the pub as 'poor man's club' towards a themed environment of 'aspirational consumption'. Excessive consumption of alcohol to the point of 'off your face' drunkenness, it has been argued, is central to a 'hedonistic release' from a variety of work, educational, parental and environmental pressures. A police officer in a north-east city put the general picture this way:

> I think until recently people just didn't know what it was like in a city cen-
> tre like ours. There was kind of the perception that it was just a few drunks
> and nothing much to worry about, but if you go into the city centre, about
> two o'clock Sunday morning then you can't help but see the extent of the
> problem, because you've got literally thousands and thousands of mostly
> young kids, and they're mostly drunk out of their minds.[36]

The potential for violence was a major focus of concern, but this tended to be on the streets outside rather than on the premises themselves, with their own internal security arrangements. Pubs generally remained safe environments. This was shown, for example, in a two-year research study published in 1980, which suggested that a customer spending two hours a day in a statistically average pub would wait eight years to see a fight. It found that the key variable in pub violence was in fact the publican, with the young and inexperienced in handling sometimes difficult situations more likely to be on the receiving end. The amount that some publicans drank was also a factor, with fifteen pints or a bottle of spirits cited as 'not exceptional'.[37]

Young women, as television and press coverage of the phenomenon was fond of observing, made up a major proportion of the night-time revellers. The greatly increased use of pubs by women generally was another significant modern change. This, however, took some time to develop after the post-war reverses to the trend to greater use in the Second World War. The 1970 survey cited above had found that just over a quarter of women visited a pub at least once a month. This was close to another survey for the National Federation of Licensed Victualler Associations in 1969, with 15 per cent in public bars and 34 per cent in all others. The use of pubs by women was still circumscribed. 90 per cent of women in 1970 said they would not enter a pub alone (among regular pub users it was still 85 per cent) and fully 43 per cent would never from choice even go into one.[38] This was most marked in the traditional pub. In a rural Herefordshire parish the pub least used by women, just a few older marrieds, was the most strongly working class. Younger wives were occasionally taken by their husbands to more 'sophisticated' pubs on main roads away from the parish. Only young non-farming wives sometimes went to pubs with female friends. A study of an urban, 'rough working-class pub' found the women comprising older women with their husbands at the week-end, some young female 'acolytes' of the young male regulars and a small number of prostitutes. The same observer found in a 'respectable' working-class pub that just 20 per cent of regulars were women, again accompanying men especially on Friday or Saturday nights. In a 'posh' middle-class pub, however, some two-fifths of regulars were women. In an East Anglian village in the early 1980s, similarly, although the pub was an important social centre for working-class women (they also had a darts team), their use of it was only acceptable at certain times and only when accompanied by a man. And within the pub they were very much guests in a male world, constrained by social conventions, such as not buying rounds or drinking pints, which allowed them 'a prescribed place in the pub they were free to inhabit'.[39]

From about this time, however, this situation began to change, as the economic and social bases of the traditional male-dominated pub were eroded, together with other influences producing greater independence and equality for women. The study of the South West in the mid-1980s found that all-male pubs were then in a distinct minority.

Change in the labour market was leading to a more varied group of customers, including more women and particularly young, single women. By the mid-1990s nationally, 57 per cent of women now reported visiting a pub within the previous three months. But at the same time, finally, there was evidence too of an overall decline in pub use by the young. One survey showed that whereas in 1987 the 18 to 24 age group accounted for 18 per cent of pub regulars, going that is at least once a week, over 15 years it fell to 11 per cent.[40]

Children were another group of customers making a return to the pub. The pub improvers had envisaged pubs as more family-oriented places. In the post-war period the growing desire to share leisure pursuits as a family pointed in that direction. In 1970 two-thirds of those people surveyed preferred a place for the whole family to the pub, but at the same time there was a lot of support for family places selling alcohol.[41] The growing emphasis on food also pointed this way. But the law remained restrictive on the presence of children. One development was the provision of 'family rooms' separate from the bar area. By 1984 there were reported to be between 2,500 and 3,000 of such rooms. Ten years later so called Children's Certificates were introduced, which could be granted by licensing justices to allow children under fourteen in bars where meals were sold, provided the 'environment' was suitable for them. After a slow start, amid accusations that some justices were insisting on prohibitive conditions to the certificates, their grant became more likely: from 72 per cent of applications in 1995 to 92 per cent in 2004, by which time 7,200 were in force.[42] It seems likely, however, given the professed desire of people to enjoy leisure as a family and the ending of routine police supervision of pubs, that the presence generally of children increased. The 2003 Licensing Act then effectively ended restriction, with children now to be allowed unless conditions specific to the premises forbade it.

For all the pub's customers a significant change was the great increase in opening hours. These had remained substantially unchanged since the First World War. In 1961 they were revised to allow a slightly extended time for drinking and permit greater flexibility in setting the hours. Also introduced was the ten-minute 'drinking up' period. The Welsh were given the option to remove the ban on Sunday drinking introduced in 1881. The people of South Wales did so immediately, with most of the rest of the principality subsequently following them. Also in 1961 provisions made in 1949 for late-night drinking in restaurants and clubs providing music and dancing in London were extended to the whole country, and now also covered premises where meals as well as entertainment were provided. Late-night drinking became much more prevalent and a key component of the night-time economy. In 2004 there were 12,200 Special Hours Certificates in force.[43] The ending of the afternoon break was a rather more protracted process, amid the conflicting claims of brewers, publicans, the tourist industry, the alcohol control lobby and others. In the end the liberalising trend of the times prevailed. It was abolished first in 1987 for parts of licensed premises used as restaurants, and then for pubs generally the following year, when drinking-up time also was extended to twenty minutes. Sunday, and Good Friday, afternoon opening followed in 1995, leaving only Christmas Day with a four-hour break.[44] The whole idea of permitted hours finally was replaced by the Licensing Act of 2003 with a system of agreed hours for specific premises.

More liberal times also had an impact on activities within the pub. The centuries old concern for gambling in pubs was relaxed. In 1960 the Betting and Gaming Act that legalised bookmaking also allowed dominoes and similar games to be played for small stakes. Although indicative of the changing climate of opinion it probably made little practical difference. More significant was the growth of fruit machines (technically Amusement with Prizes or AWP machines) after the 1960 Act rather ambiguously permitted their use in 'commercial' premises provided a local authority licence was obtained and stakes and prizes were limited. The appeal of their contribution to income was irresistible, and within twenty years there were around 78,000 fruit machines in pubs.[45] Change like this as ever took place alongside continuities. A 1970 study of Bolton and an

East Anglian market town noted the most common games as still darts, dominoes and occasionally cribbage, but things like bowls or skittles had declined. Pinball, billiards, pool and table football were all now played. Also declining was the pub sing-song as the piano disappeared and the juke box spread from the 1950s. More organised pub activities like the annual trip and the range of sick, slate or thrift clubs were also in decline. A survey in the mid-1980s found the traditional games like darts and dominoes still widely available, but noted too, for example, that two-fifths of pubs had pool tables and over a quarter video games. For music, over half had a juke box, with 3 per cent featuring a video version, but 17 per cent offered live entertainment and 11 per cent a disco. The south-west study similarly at this time found that every pub had some form of music be it the juke box, tapes or live acts.[46]

This latter study concluded that people still had a local and that pubs remained 'very important focal points in the community'. Moreover, because of the widening of their clientele they had become 'a focus point for a greater range of social relations'. This continuing use of a local by 'regular' customers was documented in other studies. These covered, for example, the intense sense of locality of a 'hard pub in a hard area' of Merseyside studied in the early 1970s, where no strangers even stopped, but a respectable working-class pub in another study also had a mostly local custom. The 1982 study of *The Public House in Transition* found that the public house was a 'strictly *local* institution whether it finds itself in a village, a town, a suburb or in the business quarter of an industrial or commercial centre'.[47] At the beginning of the twenty-first century Punch Taverns described the majority of its more than 9,200 pubs as of a 'community nature'. It categorised these locals under four types. There was the basic local still with a generally working-class custom and a relatively low proportion of women, largely dependent upon the sale of drink and offering little food. Mid market locals – the 'traditional British pub' as depicted in the television soaps – in middle market residential areas, mostly offered food and themed evenings, quizzes, darts or pool. City locals away from the bars of the night-time circuit catered to local workers and shoppers by day and residents by night. And upmarket locals, which were still community pubs but also high class outlets in low density housing areas for white collar workers and professionals, and with a higher proportion of women than most other locals. Together they made up 78 per cent of the company's portfolio of pubs. A further 13 per cent of its pubs, however, reflected some of the changes which I have noted: those oriented towards food service, those changing function from cafe by day to bar by night and those in or near the 'young person's circuit'.[48] As we have seen, places of these latter descriptions formed an important and growing proportion of the overall total of pubs. At the same time that trend was reinforced by the continuing closure of older pubs in both urban and rural areas.

In my concluding remarks, looking particularly at modern developments but also reflecting on the history of the pub, I would emphasise six key points. The first is the increased heterogeneity of the world of the pub. I have argued that the pub evolved from a diverse range of drinking places to become in Victorian England a recognisable and relatively homogeneous institution. But in the late twentieth century this pub once again fragmented into a variety of differing entities, albeit that the local remained essential among them. The second is the contraction of pub numbers within an overall context of significant expansion in what the Victorians called facilities for drinking. The 2006 figure of 51,479 pubs in fact was little more than the number at the beginning of the nineteenth century. The third is the liberalisation of the licensing system and other forms of control on pub activities. Whilst in the past in some areas, such as opening hours or the presence of children, regulation was minimal or non-existent, in other areas like gambling or drunkenness it was ostensibly strict. The historical trend was towards greater restriction. From the late 1950s this was reversed in the ways I have shown. The transfer of responsibility for licensing matters from the Home Office to the Department for Culture, Media and Sport in 2001 was symbolic of the change that had taken place. The Licensing Act of 2003 ended the 450-year jurisdiction of the justices in a radical transformation of the system. Licensing power was transferred to local authorities, the justices' licence replaced by separate licences for persons and premises, and the latter given individual operating schedules. All applications were to be granted unless objections were received.[49] The Act also embodied a fourth point – that of continuing concern about the effects of alcohol consumption – in its provisions for crime and disorder and the protection of children. But throughout recent years, whilst the Drink Question in the nineteenth-century sense of an overarching problem has not been revived, there has been continuing concern over a range of issues regarding alcohol. In addition to those in the Act these have included drinking and driving and the health consequences of excessive drinking, including so called binge drinking.[50] The fifth point is the definite arrival of women into the pub world in greater numbers almost certainly than at any time since the eighteenth and early nineteenth centuries, if not exceeding those periods. The final point then is the centrality of alcohol in society. It is an essential part of the affluent society as it was of the much poorer world (for most people) of the eighteenth and nineteenth centuries. Having fallen from the late nineteenth century, levels of alcohol consumption in the later twentieth century rose markedly.[51] Public drinking places were still essential to that consumption. As part of them the pub remains, as Mass Observation found some seventy years earlier, of central importance in society. But at the same time, the other half of their conclusion is still valid – the pub today has a smaller role than it ever did.

Reference Notes

ABBREVIATIONS

BO	Bradford Observer
LI	Leeds Intelligencer
LM	Leeds Mercury
OBP	Old Bailey Proceedings
OED	Oxford English Dictionary (2nd edn 1989)
PP	Parliamentary Papers
RC	Royal Commission
SCHC	Select Committee of the House of Commons
SCHL	Select Committee of the House of Lords
WYAS	West Yorkshire Archive Service
YO	Yorkshire Observer
YDO	Yorkshire Daily Observer

CHAPTER I INTRODUCTION: WHAT IS A PUB?

1   S. Orwell and I. Angus (eds), *The Collected Essays, Journalism and Letters of George Orwell, vol. 3, As I Please 1943–1945* (Penguin: Harmondsworth, 1970), pp. 63–5.

2   M. Gorham, *The Local* (Cassell & Co: London, 1939); *Back to the Local* (Percival Marshall: London, 1949); M. Gorham and H. Mc G. Dunnett, *Inside the Pub* (Architectural Press: London, 1950).

3   M. Girouard, *Victorian Pubs* (Yale University Press: New Haven and London, 1984, first published 1975); C. Hutt, *The Death of the English Pub* (Arrow Books: London, 1973), p. 116.

4   T. Burke, *The English Inn* (Herbert Jenkins: London, 1947, first published 1930), p. 143; *Will Someone Lead Me to a Pub* (George Routledge & Sons: London, 1936); A.E. Richardson, *The Old Inns of England* (B.T. Batsford: London, 1934), p. 22; A.E. Richardson and H.D. Eberlein, *The English Inn Past and Present: A Review of its History and Social Life* (B.T. Batsford: London, 1925); C. Dickens, *The Pickwick Papers*, ch. LI.

5   B. Oliver, *The Renaissance of the English Public House* (Faber and Faber: London, 1947), pp. 54, 69 and 92.

6   W. Scruton, *Pen and Pencil Pictures of Old Bradford* (Amethyst Press: Otley, 1985, first published 1890), p. 175.

7   Gorham, *Back to the Pub*, p. 90.

8   A. Crawford, *Birmingham's Victorian Pubs* in M. Binney and E. Milne (eds), *Time Gentlemen Please!* (SAVE Britain's Heritage: London, 1983).

9   Burke, *English Inn*, p. 7; M. Jackson, *The English Pub* (Collins: London, 1976), p. 5.

10 M. McLaren, 'The London Public-House', *London Mercury*, May 1928, pp. 30–8.

11 *What's Brewing*, December 1994; Punch Taverns, the Punch estate, www.punchtaverns.com (November 2006).

12 Mass Observation, *The Pub and the People: A Worktown Study* (Cresset Library: London, 1987, first published 1943), p. 108.

13 M. Adler, 'From Symbolic Exchange to Commodity Consumption: Anthropological Notes on Drinking as a Symbolic Practice' in S. Barrows and R. Room (eds), *Drinking: Behavior and Belief in Modern History* (University of California Press: Berkeley, 1991).

14 V. Hey, *Patriarchy and Pub Culture* (Tavistock: London, 1986); G. Greer, *The Female Eunuch* (MacGibbon & Kee: London, 1970), p. 142.

15 For example, T. Brennan, *Public Drinking and Popular Culture in Eighteenth-Century Paris* (Princeton University Press: Princeton, 1988); R. Rosenzweig, 'The Rise of the Saloon' in M. Chandra and M. Scudson (eds), *Rethinking Popular Culture: Contemporary Perspectives in Cultural Studies* (University of California Press:

Berkeley, 1991); E. Malcolm, *'Ireland Sober Ireland Free': Drink and Temperance in Nineteenth-Century Ireland* (Gill and Macmillan: Dublin, 1986); 'The Rise of the Pub: A Study of the Disciplining of Popular Culture' in J.S. Donnelly, Jr and K.A. Miller (eds) *Irish Popular Culture 1650–1850* (Irish Academic Press: Dublin, 1998); I. Donnachie, 'Drink and Society 1750–1850: Some Aspects of the Scottish Experience', *Journal of the Scottish Labour History Society*, vol. 13, 1979, pp. 5–22.

16   P. Jennings, *The Public House in Bradford, 1770–1970* (Keele University Press: Keele, 1995).

CHAPTER 2   THE EVOLUTION OF THE PUBLIC HOUSE 1700–1830

1   The survey is analysed in A. Everitt, 'The English Urban Inn 1560–1760', in his *Landscape and Community in England* (Hambledon: London, 1985), pp. 157–8; J.A. Chartres, 'The English Inn and Road Transport Before 1700', in H.C. Peyer (ed.), *Gastfreundschaft, Taverne und Gasthaus im Mittelalter* (Oldenbourg: Munich, 1983), pp. 165–9; and P. Clark, *The English Alehouse: a Social History 1200–1830* (Longman: London, 1983), pp. 41–3.

2   Clark, *English Alehouse*, pp. 195 and 215, n. 1.

3   C. Morris (ed.), *The Journeys of Celia Fiennes* (Cresset: London, 1947), p. 89.

4   11 & 12 Will. III, c.15.

5   D. Defoe, *A Tour Through England and Wales* (Dent: London, 1928), vol. 1, p. 205 and vol. 2, p. 205.

6   I used in particular the *Leeds Mercury* from 1719 onwards; The Proceedings of the Old Bailey, London, 1674–1834, www.oldbaileyonline.org (April 2006), which can be searched with keywords.

7   C. Bruyn Andrews (ed.), *The Torrington Diaries* (Eyre and Spottiswoode: London, 1934–8), vol. 1, pp. 98–9, vol. 3, p. 214, vol. 2, p. 235 and vol. 3, p. 136.

8   M. Dalton, *The Countrey Justice* (Classical English Law Texts, Professional Books: London, 1973), p. 27; Dalton, *Countrey Justice* (London, 6th edn, 1635), p. 31; 5 & 6 Edw. VI, c. 25.

9   R. Burn, *The Justice of the Peace and Parish Officer* (London, 18th edn, 1797), p. 22.

10   W. Blackstone, *Commentaries on the Laws of England* (London, 12th edn, 1794), Book the Third, p. 164.

11 Chartres, *English Inn*, p.160; and his 'The Eighteenth-Century English Inn: A Transient "Golden Age"?', in B. Kümin and B. Ann Tlusty (eds), *The World of the Tavern: Public Houses in Early Modern Europe* (Ashgate: Aldershot, 2002), p. 207.

12 T.B. Macaulay, *The History of England from the Accession of James II* (Longman, Brown, Green, and Longmans: London, 10th edn, 1854), vol. 1, p. 383.

13 R.C. Latham and W. Matthews (eds), *The Diary of Samuel Pepys* (Bell and Sons: London, 1970-83), vol. IX, pp. 228–31.

14 Clark, *English Alehouse*, pp. 11–13.

15 7 Edw. VI, c. 5; Clark, *English Alehouse*, p. 12; J. Hunter, 'English Inns, Taverns, Alehouses and Brandy Shops: The Legislative Framework, 1495–1797', in Kümin and Tlusty, *World of the Tavern*, pp. 70–2; 12 Cha. II, c. 25; F.W. Hackwood, *Inns, Ales and Drinking Customs of Old England* (Bracken Books: London, 1985, first published 1909), pp. 71–9.

16 Latham and Matthews, *Pepys*, vol. IV, p. 100, vol. IX, p. 78 and vol. III, p. 16.

17 Hackwood, *Inns*, p. 75.

18 W. Maitland, *The History of London From Its Foundation By the Romans to the Present Time* (London, 1739), pp. 519–20.

19 Clark, *English Alehouse*, pp. 21 and 43; Chartres, *Eighteenth-Century English Inn*, p. 207.

20 H. Murray, *A Directory of York Pubs 1455-2003* (Voyager: York, 2003), p. vii; WYAS, Wakefield: Brewster Session Paper, QE 32/2/44; East Riding Archives, Beverley: Certificate of Good Character, Bainton Beacon, QDT 2/1; 1 Ja. I, c. 9; *OED*.

21 Clark, *English Alehouse*, pp. 43–5; P. Mathias, *The Brewing Industry in England 1700–1830* (Cambridge University Press: Cambridge, 1959), pp. 542–3; E.A. Wrigley, et al., *English Population History from Family Reconstitution 1580–1837* (Cambridge University Press: Cambridge, 1997), p. 614; Maitland, *History*, pp. 519–20; L. Schwarz, 'London 1700–1840', in P. Clark, *The Cambridge Urban History of Britain Volume 2 1540–1840* (Cambridge University Press: Cambridge, 2000), p. 650, taking a population of 600,000.

22 Clark, *English Alehouse*, pp. 222–7.

23 Latham and Matthews, *Pepys*, vol. IX, p. 100, vol. II, pp. 89 and 178 and vol. I, p. 287.

24 Defoe, *Tour*, vol. 2, pp. 181 and 86; P. Borsay, *The English Urban Renaissance: Culture and Society in the Provincial Town 1660–1770* (Clarendon Press: Oxford, 1989), pp. 210–11.

Reference Notes

25 Defoe, *Tour*, vol. 2, p. 213; M. Younge, *Ripon Market Place: The Evolution of the Centre of a Historic Yorkshire Market Town* (Ripon Historical Society: Ripon, 2001), pp. 15–18; J. Markham, *The Beverley Arms: The Story of a Hotel* (Highgate: Beverley, 2000).

26 P. Hembry, *The English Spa 1560–1815: A Social History* (Athlone Press: London, 1990), p. 125; R. Dymond, 'The Old Inns and Taverns of Exeter', *Devonshire Association Transactions*, vol. VII, 1880, pp. 3–32; Adams, *Torrington*, vol. 1, p. 48; Everitt, *English Urban Inn*, p. 156.

27 E. Baines, *History, Directory and Gazetteer of the County of York Volume 1 West Riding* (Baines: Leeds, 1822); Hembry, *English Spa*, p. 308.

28 Chartres, *Eighteenth-Century English Inn*, pp. 211–12.

29 Clark, *English Alehouse*, pp. 195–7.

30 W. Cudworth, *Historical Notes on the Bradford Corporation* (Brear: Bradford, 1881), pp. 27–33; Chartres, *Eighteenth-Century English Inn*, pp. 214–16.

31 W.A. Pantin, 'Medieval Inns' in E.M. Jope (ed.) *Studies in Building History* (Odhams: London, 1961); J.A. Chartres, 'The Capital's Provincial Eyes: London's Inns in the Early Eighteenth Century', *The London Journal*, vol. 3, 1977, pp. 24–39.

32 Everitt, *English Urban Inn*, p. 162.

33 J. Larwood and J. Camden Hotton, *The History of Signboards From the Earliest Times to the Present Day* (Hotten: London, 5th edn, 1866), p. 10; Burn, *Justice of the Peace* (25th edn, 1830), p. 37.

34 Latham and Matthews, *Pepys*, vol. II, p. 184; R.W. Blencowe, 'Extracts from the Journal of Walter Gale, Schoolmaster at Mayfield, 1750', *Sussex Archaeological Collections*, vol. IX, 1857, pp. 182–207; Larwood and Hotton, *Signboards*, p. 39; Hackwood, *Inns*, pp. 304–8; R. Nettel (ed.) *Journeys of a German in England: Carl Philip Moritz A Walking Tour of England in 1782* (Eland Books: London, 1983), pp. 25 and 124; P. Corballis, *Pub Signs* (Lennard: Luton, 1988), pp. 50–2; and Jennings, *Public House*, pp. 28–9.

35 Hackwood, *Inns*, pp. 282–318; L. Dunkling and G. Wright, *A Dictionary of Pub Names* (Routledge & Kegan Paul: London, 1987).

36 *LM*, 14 March 1769; Baines, *County of York Volume 2 East and North Ridings*; H. Ritvo, *The Animal Estate: the English and Other Creatures in the Victorian Age* (Cambridge University Press: Harvard, 1987), pp. 45–6, 58 and 80.

37 Baines, *County of York*; E. Baines, *History, Directory and Gazetteer of the County Palatine of Lancaster Volume 1* (Wales: Liverpool, 1824).

38 Dymond, 'Old Inns and Taverns of Exeter'; Everitt, *English Urban Inn*, p. 188; E. Kennerley, 'Lancaster Inns and Alehouses 1600–1730', *Lancashire Local History*, vol. 5, 1990, pp. 40–51; W. Branch Johnson, 'The Seventeenth Century Hertfordshire Inn', *Hertfordshire Past and Present*, vol. 4, 1964, pp. 16–20; J.D. Marshall, *Kendal 1661–1801: The Growth of the Modern Town* (Cumberland and Westmorland Antiquarian & Archaeological Society: Kendal, 1975), p. 4.

39 OBP: t17641212-57 and t17670218-20; Clark, *English Alehouse*, pp. 197–8.

40 OBP: t17551022-28, t17350522-1 and t17450911-6; W.H. Chaloner (ed.), *The Autobiography of Samuel Bamford Volume Two Passages in the Life of a Radical* (Frank Cass: London, 1967, first published 1839–41), p. 109; *OED*.

41 Pantin, 'Medieval Inns', p. 188; Latham and Matthews, *Pepys*, vol. I, p. 301; OBP: t17650918-24.

42 Mathias, *Brewing Industry*, pp. 107-9; *LM* 14 March 1801; W. Branch Johnson, *"Memorandoms for …" The Diary Between 1798 and 1810 of John Carrington* (Phillimore: London, 1973), p. 117; Jennings, *Public House*, pp. 36–7.

43 Everitt, *English Urban Inn*, p. 188.

44 Clark, *English Alehouse*, pp. 198 and 275–6; OBP: t17521026-24; M. Thale (ed.), *The Autobiography of Francis Place (1771–1854)* (Cambridge University Press: Cambridge, 1972), p. 37.

45 J.D. Marshall, 'Rural Society Before the Victorians', in O.M. Westall, *Windermere in the Nineteenth Century* (Centre for North West Regional Studies, University of Lancaster, Occasional Paper 20, rev. edn, 1991), p. 17; J.E. and P.A. Crowther (eds), *The Diary of Robert Sharp of South Cave: Life in a Yorkshire Village 1812–1837* (Oxford University Press: Oxford, 1997), p. 192.

46 *OED*; *LI*, 15 December 1772; T.E. Casson, 'The Diary of Edward Jackson, Vicar of Colton, for the year 1775', *Transactions of the Cumberland & Westmorland Antiquarian and Archaeological Society*, New Series, vol. XL, pp. 1–45; J. Beresford (ed.), *The Diary of a Country Parson: The Reverend James Woodforde* (Clarendon Press: Oxford, 1924–31), vol. 3. p. 189; *Chaloner, Bamford Volume 2*, pp. 118 and 132.

47 C. Dickens, *Barnaby Rudge*, ch. 37; T. Hardy, *The Mayor of Casterbridge*, ch. 27; *OED*.

48 F.A. Pottle (ed.), *Boswell's London Journal 1762–1763* (Heinemann: London, 1950), p. 318; J. Boswell, *Life of Johnson* (Dent: London, 1960), vol. 1, p. 620; A. Swift and K. Elliott, *The Lost Pubs of Bath* (Akeman Press: Bath, 2005), p. 31.

49   *The Norwich Directory* (Chase: Norwich, 1783, facsimile edition published by M. Winton: King's Lynn, 1991).

50   Defoe, *Tour*, vol.I, pp. 153 and 130; OBP: t174000903-6.

51   Latham and Matthews, *Pepys*, vol.VII, pp. 385-6 and vol. IX, p. 78; Boswell, *Johnson*, vol.I, p. 262; Pottle, *Boswell*, pp. 263-4.

52   Report from a Committee of the House of Commons, appointed to enquire into the several Burglaries and Robberies committed in London and Westminster, reprinted as Appendix 8 to the Report on the Nightly Watch and Police of the Metropolis; PP 1812 (127) II.95; 32 Geo. III, c. 59.

53   SCHC on the State of the Police of the Metropolis; PP 1816 (510) V.1, p. 24; Hackwood, *Inns*, pp. 78-9.

54   See those of Baines cited or, for example, Pigot and Company, *National Commercial Directory 1828-9* (London, 1828).

55   M. Ellis, *The Coffee-House: A Cultural History* (Orion Books: London, 2005), pp. 173-4 and passim; see also A. Ellis, *The Penny Universities: A History of the Coffee-Houses* (Secker & Warburg: London, 1956) and B. Lillywhite, *London Coffee Houses* (George Allen and Unwin: London, 1963).

56   Maitland, *History*, pp. 519-20.

57   Pottle, *Boswell*, p. 237; Beresford, *Woodforde*, vol.I, p. 149.

58   Ellis, *Coffee-House*, pp. 211-15; Clark, *English Alehouse*, p. 297.

59   PP 1816 (510), p. 80; SCHC on the State of the Police of the Metropolis, and execution of Laws for Licensing of Victuallers; PP 1817 (233) VII.1, pp. 167 and 484-90; B. Harrison, *Drink and the Victorians: The Temperance Question in England 1815-1872* (Keele University Press: Keele, 2nd edn 1994), pp. 39-40.

60   Latham and Matthews, *Pepys*, vol.I, p. 76 and vol.VIII, p. 412.

61   J.A. Chartres, 'No English Calvados? English Distillers and the Cider Industry in the Seventeenth and Eighteenth Centuries', in J. Chartres and D. Hey (eds) *English Rural Society 1500-1800* (Cambridge University Press: Cambridge, 1990), p. 317.

62   Ibid., pp. 318-19; T.S. Ashton, *An Economic History of England: The Eighteenth Century* (Methuen: London: 1955), p. 243; First Report of Commissioners of Inland Revenue; PP 1857 (1) IV.65, Appendix 19; for smuggling, Clark, *English Alehouse*, pp. 240-1.

63   M.D. George, *London Life in the Eighteenth Century* (LSE: London, 3rd edn, 1951, first published 1923), pp. 29–30; Chartres, 'Calvados', p. 328; Clark, *English Alehouse*, pp. 239–40; 2 Will. & Mar. session 2, c. 9; 12 & 13 Will. III, c. 11; 1 Ann. St. 2, c. 14.

64   P. Clark, 'The "Mother Gin" Controversy in the Early Eighteenth Century', *Transactions of the Royal Historical Society*, 5th Series, vol. 38, 1988, pp. 63–84.

65   *OED*; P. Hyland, *Ned Ward: The London Spy* (Colleagues Press: East Lansing, 1993), p.255; Pottle, *Boswell*, p. 272.

66   Maitland, *History*, pp. 519–20; J. Warner, *Craze: Gin and Debauchery in an Age of Reason* (Profile Books: London, 2003), pp. 45–6.

67   L. Davison, 'Experiments in the Social Regulation of Industry: Gin Legislation, 1729–1751', in L. Davison et al., *Stilling the Grumbling Hive: The Response to Social and Economic Problems in England, 1689–1750* (Alan Sutton: Stroud, 1992), p. 27; Clark, 'Mother Gin', pp. 68 and 84.

68   Ibid., p. 70, J. Warner and F. Ivis, 'Gin and Gender in Early Eighteenth-century London', *Eighteenth-Century Life*, vol.24, 2000, pp. 85–105; Warner, *Craze*, pp. 46–50.

69   2 Geo. II, c. 17 and c. 28; 6 Geo. II, c. 17; 9 Geo. II, c. 23; 16 Geo. II, c. 8; 17 Geo. II, c. 17; 20 Geo. II, c. 39; 24 Geo. II, c. 40; 26 Geo. II, c. 13.

70   PP 1857 (1), Appendix 32a.

71   P. Earle, *The Making of the English Middle Class: Business, Society and Family Life in London, 1660–1730* (Methuen: London, 1989), p. 33; Warner, *Craze*, p. 39; H.L. Douch, *Old Cornish Inns and Their Place in the Social History of the County* (Bradford Barton: Truro, 1966), pp. 25–33; Clark, *English Alehouse*, pp. 240–1; J.A. Chartres, 'Spirits in the North-East? Gin and Other Vices in the Long Eighteenth Century', in H. Berry and J. Gregory (eds), *Creating and Consuming Culture in North-East England, 1660–1830* (Ashgate: Aldershot, 2004).

72   George, *London Life*, p. 42; W.E.H. Lecky, *A History of England in the Eighteenth Century* (Longmans, Green: London, 3rd edn 1883), vol. 1, pp. 479–81.

73   Clark, 'Mother Gin', pp. 83–4.

74   Ashton, *Economic History*, pp. 57 and 243; PP 1857, Appendix 19.

75   G. Jackson, *Hull in the Eighteenth Century: A Study in Economic and Social History* (Oxford University Press: London, 1972), p. 286; *LI*, 26 June and 18 September 1787; *LM*, 5 January 1790; Clark, *English Alehouse*, p. 262; Thomas Trotter, *An Essay, Medical, Philosophical, and Chemical, On Drunkenness, and Its Effects on the Human Body* (Routledge, London, 1988, first published 1804), p. 48.

76 PP 1816 (510), p. 50.

77 Ibid., pp. 27, 59, 64, 77 and 101.

78 PP 1817 (233), pp. 316–19; see also J. Bowles, *The Existing Law Respecting the Right of Retailing Spirituous Liquors Stated and Vindicated with Some Brief Remarks on the Baneful Effects, Physical and Moral, Produced by Ardent Spirits* (London, 1817).

79 PP 1817 (233), p. 186.

80 G.B. Wilson, *Alcohol and the Nation: A Contribution to the Study of the Liquor Problem in the United Kingdom from 1800 to 1935* (Nicholson and Watson: London, 1940), p. 19; Harrison, *Drink*, pp. 64–5; PP 1857 (1), p. 2 and Appendix 32a.

81 SCHC on Laws and Regulations which restrict Sale of Beer by Retail; PP 1830 (253) X.1, pp. 38–9.

82 J.P. Kay, *The Moral and Physical Condition of the Working Classes Employed in the Cotton Manufacture in Manchester* (E.J. Morten: Didsbury, 1969, first published 1832), p. 57.

CHAPTER 3   THE PUBLIC HOUSE AND SOCIETY 1700–1830

1 Chartres, *Eighteenth-Century English Inn*, pp. 208–9.

2 Maitland, *History*, pp. 519–20; R. Unwin, *Wetherby: The History of a Yorkshire Market Town* (Leeds University Press: Leeds, 1987), p 67; Everitt, *English Urban Inn*, pp. 159–61.

3 Chartres, *Eighteenth-Century English Inn*, p. 218; *LM*, 29 July and 2 September 1809.

4 H. Darbishire (ed.), *Journals of Dorothy Wordsworth* (Oxford University Press: London, 1958), p. 191.

5 T.P. Cooper, *The Old Inns and Inn Signs of York* (Delittle & Sons: York, 1897), p. 14.

6 P.S. Bagwell, *The Transport Revolution From 1770* (Batsford: London, 1974), pp. 41–9; *LM*, 6 May 1815 and 21 July 1836.

7 H.W. Hart, 'Sherman and the Bull and Mouth', *Journal of Transport History*, vol. V, pp. 12–21.

8 *LM*, 21 November 1807.

9 Andrews, *Torrington*, vol. 1, p. 53 and passim; Morris, *Fiennes*, pp. 79, 83 and 95.

10 Chartres, *Eighteenth-Century English Inn*, p. 213.

11 H. Whitbread (ed.), *'I Know My Own Heart': The Diaries of Ann Lister 1791–1840* (Virago: London, 1988), p. 65.

12 E.M. Butler (ed.), *A Regency Visitor: The English Tour of Prince Pückler-Muskau Described in his Letters 1826–1828* (Collins: London, 1957), pp. 114–15 and 135.

13 B.M. Ratcliffe and W.H. Chaloner (eds), *A French Sociologist Looks at Britain: Gustave d'Eichtal and British Society in 1828* (Manchester University Press: Manchester, 1977), pp. 63–6.

14 Chaloner, *Bamford Volume 2*, pp. 130–1.

15 D. Hey, *Packmen, Carriers & Packhorse Roads: Trade and Communications in North Derbyshire and South Yorkshire* (Landmark: Ashbourne, 2001, first published 1980), p. 150.

16 A. Groom, *Old London Coaching Inns and Their Successors* (LMS Railway: London, 1928), pp. 11–12; Chartres, *Eighteenth-Century English Inn*, pp. 216–17.

17 Baines, *County of York*.

18 T.M. James, 'The Inns of Croydon, 1640–1840', *Surrey Archaeological Collections*, vol. 68, 1971, pp. 109–29; Chartres, *Eighteenth-Century English Inn*, p. 219; Everitt, *English Urban Inn*, p. 171; *LI*, 24 August and 12 October 1762; Baines, *County of York*; R. Lloyd-Jones and M.J. Lewis, *Manchester and the Age of the Factory: The Business Structure of Cottonopolis in the Industrial Revolution* (Croom Helm: London, 1988), p. 36.

19 Contemporary newspapers provide abundant evidence, used by Chartres, *Eighteenth-Century English Inn*, pp. 220–1; Everitt, *English Urban Inn*, pp. 171–3; Jennings, *Public House*, pp. 65–6; W. Wicks, *Inns and Taverns of Old Norwich* (Norwich, 1925), p. 31 and passim.

20 M. Gillen, *Assassination of the Prime Minister: The Shocking Death of Spencer Perceval* (Sidgwick and Jackson: London, 1972), p. 20.

21 *LI*, 22 July 1766 and e.g. *LM*, 21 March 1775 or 10 December 1782.

22 Jennings, *Public House*, pp. 60–2.

23 Burn, *Justice of the Peace* (1797), vol. 1, p. 41 and vol. 4, p. 285; J.D. Marshall, *The Autobiography of William Stout of Lancaster 1665–1752* (Manchester University Press: Manchester, 1967), pp. 204 and 231; D.L. Powell, 'Billeting in Surrey in the Seventeenth and Eighteenth Centuries', *Surrey Archaeological Collections*, vol. XXVII, pp. 128–35.

24 Andrews, *Torrington*, vol. 1, p. 21.

25   D.Vaisey (ed.), *The Diary of Thomas Turner 1754-1765* (Oxford University Press: Oxford, 1984), p. 144.

26   Thale, *Place*, pp. 34–7; N. Rogers, 'Impressment and the Law in Eighteenth-Century Britain', in N. Landau (ed), *Law, Crime and English Society, 1660–1830* (Cambridge University Press: Cambridge, 2002).

27   G.E. Aylmer (ed.), *The Diary of William Lawrence Covering Periods Between 1662 and 1681* (Toucan Press: Beaminster, 1961), pp. 11–12; R, Newton, *Eighteenth Century Exeter* (University of Exeter: Exeter, 1984), pp. 81–2.

28   Borsay, *Urban Renaissance*, p. 144.

29   C.J. Billson, *Medieval Leicester* (Edgar Backus: Leicester, 1920), p. 30.

30   P. Clark, *British Clubs and Societies 1580–1800: The Origins of an Associational World* (Clarendon Press: Oxford, 2000), pp. 2 and 164; Murray, *York Pubs*, p. 14.

31   Hembry, *English Spa*, p. 202 and passim.

32   M. Reed, 'The Transformation of Urban Space 1700–1840', in Clark, *Cambridge Urban History*; Scruton, *Pen and Pencil Pictures*, pp. 120–2.

33   Chartres, *Eighteenth- Century English Inn*, p. 224; *Jackson's New Illustrated Guide to Leeds and Environs* (Jackson: Leeds, 1889, facsimile edn published by Old Hall Press: Leeds, 1990), p. 89; Wicks, *Norwich*.

34   B. Cozens-Hardy, *Mary Hardy's Diary* (Norfolk Record Society, vol. XXXVII, 1968), p. 23; D. Ayres and J. Hunter, *The Inns and Public Houses of Wokingham* (Berkshire County Council: Reading, 1994), p. 28.

35   A. Chadwick, *The Court: Pubs and Licensing* (Ripon Museum Trust pamphlet: Ripon, 2000).

36   RC on Liquor Licensing Laws, First Report; PP 1897 [C.8356] XXXIV.253, p. 138; *Paterson's Licensing Acts*.

37   Clark, *English Alehouse*, pp. 24 and 28; C.M. Iles, 'Early Stages of English Public House Regulation', *Economic Journal*, vol. XIII, 1903, pp. 251–62.

38   Clark, *English Alehouse*, ch. 8, for this and what follows; J.A. Sharpe, 'Crime and Delinquency in an Essex Parish 1600-1640', in J.S. Cockburn, *Crime in England 1550–1800* (Methuen: London, 1977), p. 103; K. Wrightson, 'Alehouses, Order and Reformation in Rural England, 1590–1660', in E. and S. Yeo, *Popular Culture and Class Conflict 1590–1914: Explorations in the History of Labour and Leisure* (Harvester: Brighton, 1981), pp. 1–2.

39   11 Hen.VII, c. 2; 5 & 6 Edw.VI, c. 25.

40 Dalton, *Countrey Justice*, pp. 19 and 27.

41 Gentleman of the Middle Temple, *The Publican Protected; Containing All the Laws Relating to Publicans* ... (London, 1800), pp. 52–6.

42 S. and B. Webb, *The History of Liquor Licensing in England Principally from 1700 to 1830* (United Kingdom Alliance: London, 1903), p. 8, n. 1; R.J. Robson, *The Oxfordshire Election of 1754: A Study in the Interplay of City, County and University Politics* (Oxford University Press: London, 1949), pp. 53–4; J.D. Chambers, *Nottinghamshire in the Eighteenth Century: A Study of Life and Labour Under the Squirearchy* (Frank Cass: London, 1966, first published 1932), p. 33, note 4 and 48, n. 1.

43 Dalton, *Countrey Justice*, p. 27; 1 Ja. I, c. 9.

44 P. Clark, 'The Alehouse and the Alternative Society', in D. Pennington and K. Thomas (eds), *Puritans and Revolutionaries: Essays on Seventeenth-Century History Presented to Christopher Hill* (Clarendon Press: Oxford, 1978), p. 70; S. and B. Webb, *English Local Government From the Revolution to the Municipal Corporations Act: The Parish and the County* (Longmans: London, 1906), p. 540; 2 Geo. II, c. 28; 26 Geo. II, c. 31.

45 Crowther, *Sharp*, p. 162; SCHC on Victualling-House Licenses (Holborn Division); PP 1833 (585) XV.261, pp. 40 and 47.

46 Webb, *Liquor Licensing*, chs II and III.

47 48 Geo. III, c. 143; Account of Number of Ale, Wine and Spirit Licenses issued in England and Wales; PP 1828 (164) XVIII.511; see above, ch. 2, n. 21.

48 Clark, *English Alehouse*, pp. 45–59; Murray, *York Pubs*, pp. xii–xiii.

49 North Yorkshire Record Office, Northallerton: Richmond Borough, Alehouse Keepers Licences and Recognizances, DCRMB; WYAS, Wakefield: Borough and Liberty of Ripon, Alehouse Keepers Recognizances, QT. 1. 6/2, 11, 24 and 51.

50 Lancashire Record Office, Preston: Alehouse Recognizances, QSB/3; WYAS, Wakefield: West Riding Alehouse Recognizances, QE 32 and Parson and White, *Directory of the Borough of Leeds, the City of York and the Clothing District of Yorkshire* (Leeds, 1830); Jennings, *Public House*, pp. 21–2.

51 Clark, *English Alehouse*, pp. 57–8; East Riding Archives, Beverley: Alehouse Recognizances, QDT1/1 and QDT2/1-15; North Yorkshire Record Office, Northallerton: Alehouse Recognizances, QDL/5.

52 George, *London Life*, pp. 27–42; Clark, 'Mother Gin'; Davison, 'Gin Legislation'; Warner, *Craze*; J. White, 'The "Slow but Sure Poyson": The Representation of Gin and Its Drinkers, 1736–1751', *Journal of British Studies*, vol. 42, 2003, pp. 35–64.

53 *Gentleman's Magazine*, September 1736, vol. VI, p. 537, January 1739, vol. IX, p. 8 and October 1754, vol. XXIV, pp. 461–2; *Monthly Review*, December 1759, vol. XXI, pp. 575–6 and January 1773, vol. XLVIII, pp. 19–26.

54 Webb, *Parish and County*, pp. 541–2.

55 F.G. Stokes (ed.), *The Blecheley Diary of the Rev. William Cole M.A. F.S.A. 1765–67* (Constable: London, 1931), pp. 111–12.

56 A. Fletcher, *Reform in the Provinces: The Government of Stuart England* (Yale University Press: New Haven and London, 1986), p. 278; A. Young, *A Six Months Tour Through the North of England* (Kelley: New York, 1967, first published 1771), vol. 2, pp. 98–104.

57 J. Disney, *Thoughts on the Great Circumspection Necessary in Licensing Public Ale-Houses* (London, 1776).

58 H. Zouch, *Hints Respecting the Public Police* (London, 1786).

59 Webb, *Liquor Licensing*, ch. III and appendix; J. Innes, 'Politics and Morals: The Reformation of Manners Movement in Later Eighteenth-Century England', in E. Hellmuth (ed.), *The Transformation of Political Culture in England and Germany in the Late Eighteenth Century* (Oxford University Press: Oxford, 1990).

60 Harrison, *Drink*, pp. 63–72 and for what follows.

61 Maitland, *History*, pp. 519–20; Shwarz, *London* for population estimate; Clark, *English Alehouse*, pp. 52 and 55; SCHC on Inquiry into Drunkenness among Labouring Classes of UK; PP 1834 (559) VIII.315, Appendix 5, excluding beershops.

62 Clark, *English Alehouse*, p.286.

63 PP 1816 (510), pp. 67–70; PP 1817 (233), pp. 2–14; SCHC on Public Breweries; PP 1818 (399) III.295, pp. 1–5 and PP 1819 (220) V.453.

64 4 Geo. IV, c. 51 and 5 Geo. IV, c. 54; Account of Number of Brewers and Licensed Victuallers in England, Wales and Scotland; PP 1826–27 (74) XVII.353 and 1830 (190) XXII.161; PP 1830 (253), pp. 9–12.

65 3 Geo. IV, c. 77.

66 9 Geo. IV, c. 61; Burn, *Justice of the Peace*, (1830), pp. 48–9; 2 *Hansard*, New Series vol. XVIII, cc. 1149–50 (14 March 1828); S. Anderson, 'Discretion and the Rule of Law: The Licensing of Drink in England, c. 1817–40', *Legal History*, vol. 23, 2002, pp. 45–59.

CHAPTER 4 FREE TRADE IN BEER 1830–1869

1   The best account of the Act is in Harrison, *Drink*, pp. 63–84; also T.R. Gourvish
     and R.G. Wilson, *The British Brewing Industry 1830–1980* (Cambridge University
     Press: Cambridge, 1994), pp. 3–22; and N. Mason, '"The Sovereign People Are
     in a Beastly State": The Beer Act of 1830 and Victorian Discourse on Working-
     Class Drunkenness', *Victorian Literature and Culture*, vol. 29, 2001, pp. 109–27.

2   N. Longmate, *The Waterdrinkers: A History of Temperance* (Hamish Hamilton:
     London, 1968), p. 31; *BO*, 24 May 1849.

3   Webb, *Liquor Licensing*, pp. pp. 115–16; Wilson, *Alcohol*, p. 101; S.G. Checkland,
     British Public Policy 1776–1939: An Economic, Social and Political Perspective
     (Cambridge University Press: Cambridge, 1983), p. 105.

4   Harrison, *Drink*, p. 73.

5   Anon., 'Licensing of Alehouses', *Edinburgh Review*, vol. XLIV, 1826, pp. 441–457.

6   P. Jupp, *British Politics on the Eve of Reform: The Duke of Wellington's Administration
     1828–30* (Macmillan: Basingstoke, 1998), pp. 143–4, 274 and 286.

7   2 *Hansard*, New Series vol. XXIV, cc. 323-5, 387–9, 401–22 and 951–65 and vol.
     XXV, cc. 862–70 and 990–7 (1830).

8   PP 1830 (253), pp. 16–17.

9   *LM*, 20 March and 1 May 1830; *Hansard*, vol. XXV, c. 990 (6 July 1830);
     Harrison, *Drink*, p. 76.

10   *Hansard*, vol. XXIV, c. 325 (3 May 1830).

11   PP 1830 (253), p. 16.

12   *Hansard*, vol. XXIV, c. 324 (3 May 1830); *LM*, 17 April 1830.

13   *Hansard*, vol. XXV, cc. 990–2 (6 July 1830).

14   11. Geo. IV & 1 Will. IV, c. 64. At the time it was generally referred to as the
     Beer Act, but was later given the short title of the Beerhouse Act.

15   *Hansard*, vol. XXIV, c. 1334 (3 June 1830).

16   4 & 5 Will. IV, c. 85 and 3 & 4 Vict., c. 61.

17   Pottle, *Boswell*, p. 119.

18   SCHC on Sale of Liquors on Sunday Bill; PP 1867–68 (402) XIV.1, p.8; J.
     Burnett, *Liquid Pleasures: A Social History of Drinks in Modern Britain* (Routledge:
     London, 1999), p. 218, n. 55; SCHC on Sale of Beer; PP 1833 (416) XV.1, pp.
     250 and 403; Crowther, *Sharp*, p. 422.

19   J. Wright, *English Dialect Dictionary* (English Dialect Society: Oxford, 6 vols, 1898–1905); Douch, *Cornish Inns*, pp. 25–6 and 182.

20   Jennings, *Public House*, p. 96.

21   Number of Brewers, Victuallers and Retailers of Beer; PP 1831 (60) XVII.67; Account of Number of Persons in UK licensed as Brewers, and Victuallers; PP 1831–32 (223) XXXIV.27; Return of Beer-Houses in Manchester and Salford; PP 1839 (182) XXX.251; SCHC on Regulation of Public Houses; PP 1852-53 (855) XXXVII.1, p. 577.

22   PP 1833 (416), pp. 145 and 160; Crowther, *Sharp*, pp. 281, 458 and 469.

23   Return of Number of Licensed Victuallers and Keepers of Beer-Shops charged before Police Magistrates with Breaches of Laws, 1830–38; PP 1839 (173) XXX.435; B. Bennison, 'Drink in Newcastle' in R. Colls and B. Lancaster (eds), *Newcastle upon Tyne: A Modern History* (Phillimore: Chichester, 2001); J.J. Rowley, 'Drink and the Public House in Nottingham, 1830–1860', *Transactions of the Thoroton Society*, vol. XXIX, 1975, pp. 72–83; RC of Inquiry into Municipal Corporations of England and Wales; PP 1835 (116) XXIII.1, p. 585.

24   PP 1834 (559), Appendix 5.

25   PP 1839 (173); Jennings, *Public House*, pp. 81–5; PP 1839 (182).

26   Mrs Austin (ed.), *A Memoir of the Rev. Sydney Smith by his daughter Lady Holland with a Selection from his letters* (Longmans, Green, Reader, and Dyer: London, 1869); *LM*, 23 October 1830; Douch, *Cornish Inns*, p. 104.

27   3 *Hansard,* vol. IV cc. 502–12 (30 June 1831).

28   PP 1833 (416), pp. 3, 7 and 45.

29   E.J. Hobsbawm and G. Rudé, *Captain Swing* (Lawrence and Wishart: London, 1969), pp. 88 and 212; Harrison, *Drink*, p. 83.

30   W.R. Lambert, *Drink and Sobriety in Victorian Wales c.1820–c.1895* (University of Wales Press: Cardiff, 1983), p. 18; D.G. Wright, *The Chartist Risings in Bradford* (Bradford Libraries and Information Services: Bradford, 1987), p. 17.

31   PP 1833 (416), pp. 11 and 71.

32   Ibid., pp. 44 and 177–82.

33   Ibid., pp. 53–4, 206 and 224.

34   Crowther, *Sharp*, pp. 422 and 456; *BO*, 4 May 1837.

35   SCHL to consider Operation of Acts for Sale of Beer; PP 1850 (398) XVIII.483, p. iv; SCHC on Regulation of Public Houses; PP 1854 (367) XIV.231, p. ix.

36   PP 1850 (398), p. v; Burn, *Justice of the Peace*, (1830), pp. 48–9; PP 1817 (233), p.7.

37   Annual Account of Number of Persons in UK licensed as Brewers and Victuallers 1831–1868–69.

38   PP 1833 (416), pp. 10, 16, 94, 109–11, 224 and passim.

39   PP 1850 (398), pp. v and 38; PP 1852–53 (855), p. 460.

40   Return of Rental of Houses occupied by Publicans and Licensed Sellers of Beer; PP 1839 (365) XXX.242; PP 1852–53 (855), Appendix 1.

41   R.C. Riley and P. Eley, *Public Houses and Beerhouses in Nineteenth Century Portsmouth* (Portsmouth City Council: Portsmouth, 1983), p. 8; Jennings, *Public House*, pp. 91–3.

42   Lord Askwith, *British Taverns: Their History and Laws* (Routledge: London, 1928), pp. 59–60; Harrison, *Drink*, pp. 228–31; 23 & 24 Vict., c. 27; 24 & 25 Vict., c. 91.

43   Wilson, *Alcohol*, pp. 331–3 and 395–6; Return of Number of Licences for Sale of Beer, Wine and Spirits; PP 1868–69 (429) XXXIV.307.

44   J. Scarisbrick, *Beer Manual (Historical and Technical)* (Revenue Series 1: Wolverhampton, 2nd ed. 1892), p. 17; 42 Geo. III, c. 38; SCHL on Bill for regulating Sale of Beer and other Liquors on Lord's Day; PP 1847-48 (501) XVI.615, p. 6.

45   Webb, *Liquor Licensing*, p 115, n. 2; Wright, *Dialect Dictionary*.

46   PP 1833 (416), p. 172; PP 1850 (398), p. 185.

47   *LM*, 12 August 1843; *BO*, 30 January 1845, 7 September and 19 October 1848, 3 May and 6 December 1849; PP 1850 (398), p. 123; PP 1847–48 (501), p. 6.

48   24 & 25 Vict., c. 21; Wilson, *Alcohol*, pp. 395–6.

49   Return of Number of Licences for Sale of Beer and Cider in England and Wales granted or refused in each County and Borough at Brewster Sessions; PP 1870 (215 and 215–1) LXI. 177 and 261, pp. 44–5.

50   Gourvish and Wilson, *Brewing Industry*, p. 30; *BO*, 11 February 1841; PP 1868–69 (429).

51   Bills to amend Laws relating to General Sale of Beer and Cider by Retail in England; PP 1857 Session1 (13) I.385 and Session 2 (10) IV.487.

52   Harrison, *Drink*, pp. 231–2.

53   32 & 33 Vict., c. 27.

54   PP 1870 (215 and 215–1) and Return of Number of Licences for Sale of Beer and Cider in Middlesex and Surrey granted or refused at Brewster Sessions of March 1870; PP 1870 (434) LXI.277. For a number of reasons these returns are not easy to interpret, see P. Jennings, "' … One of the Most Mischievous

Acts that Ever Passed the British Legislature": The 1830 Beer Act and Its Consequences' in M. Hewitt (ed.) *Unrespectable Recreations* (Leeds Centre for Victorian Studies, Leeds, 2001), pp. 67–8.

55　*BO*, 26 August 1869 and succeeding editions to 30 September and 7 October.

56　SCHL for inquiring into Prevalence of Habits of Intemperance, and Effects of Recent Legislation; PP 1878–79 (113) X.469, pp. xxx–xxxi.

57　Wilson, *Alcohol*, p. 236.

CHAPTER 5　THE LICENSED TRADE 1830–1869

1　As ch. 4, n. 37.

2　South Cave: see ch. 3, n. 51 and I. Slater, *Directory of Yorkshire* (Manchester, 1875); Chester: RC into Municipal Corporations; PP 1835 (116) XXVI.1, pp. 2,631–2 and SCHL on Intemperance; PP 1877 (171) XI.1, p. 389; Manchester: PP 1852–53 (855), pp. 162–3 and PP 1877 (171), p. 338; Norwich: PP 1835 (116) XXVI.1, p. 2,470 and PP 1877 (171), p. 391; Birmingham: PP 1839 (173) and PP 1877 (171), p. 343; Derby: PP 1835 (116) XXVI.1, p. 1,853 and Return of Number of Public Houses and Beerhouses proceeded against and convicted of Offences against License; PP 1868–69 (94) LI.159; Newcastle: PP 1835 (116) XXVI.1, p. 1,650 and PP 1868–69 (94).

3　PP 1852–53 (855), pp. 42–8, 67–80 and 92.

4　PP 1877 (171), pp. 19, 21–3 and 41; A. Mutch, 'Magistrates and Public House Managers, 1840–1914: Another Case of Liverpool Exceptionalism?', *Northern History*, vol. XL, 2003, pp. 325–42.

5　PP 1877 (171), pp. 87-8; SCHL on Intemperance; PP 1877 (271) XI.357, p. 81.

6　PP 1835 (116) XXIII, p. 480.

7　PP 1833 (416), p. 109.

8　*BO*, 25 August 1853 and 25 August 1859.

9　Riley and Eley, *Portsmouth*, pp. 3–11.

10　PP 1877 (171), pp. 180–2.

11　Census of 1851, Bradford Borough, HO 107/2305-10 and see P. Jennings, 'Occupations in the Nineteenth Century Censuses: The Drink Retailers of Bradford, West Yorkshire', *Local Population Studies*, no. 64, 2000, pp. 23–37.

12　PP 1854 (367), p. xi.

13   PP 1852–53 (855), pp. 131–59, 177–80, 234–40, 503–11 and 571–2.

14   Return for Metropolitan District of Number of Licensed Victuallers whose Licenses have not been renewed in consequence of Misconduct; PP 1856 (222) LV.479.

15   PP 1839 (173); SCHC on Sale of Liquors on Sunday Bill; PP 1867–68 (402) XIV.1, pp.12 and 414.

16   PP 1834 (559), p. 19.

17   PP 1852–53 (855), pp. 349–53 and Appendix 8; PP 1856 (222).

18   Riley and Eley, *Portsmouth*, p. 10; *LM*, 5 September 1840.

19   As n. 10 above.

20   *Jackson's Guide to Leeds*, pp. 88–9; F. Finnegan, *Poverty and Prejudice: A Study of Irish Immigrants in York 1840–1875* (Cork University Press: Cork, 1982), p. 39.

21   *BO*, 25 September and 16 October 1834.

22   Hart, 'Sherman and the Bull and Mouth'; M. Neesam, *Harrogate Great Chronicle 1332–1841* (Carnegie: Lancaster, 2005), pp. 285–368.

23   R. Thorne, 'Places of Refreshment in the Nineteenth-Century City' in A.D. King (ed.), *Buildings and Society: Essays on the Social Development of the Built Environment* (Routledge & Kegan Paul: London, 1980), pp. 232–43.

24   Clark, *English Alehouse*, p. 10; Jennings, *Public House*, p. 211; M. Winstanley, 'The Rural Publican and His Business in East Kent Before 1914', *Oral History*, vol. 4, 1976, pp. 63–78.

25   Douch, *Cornish Inns*, p. 170; RC on Liquor Licensing Laws, Second Report; PP 1897 [C.8523] XXXV.1, p. 40.

26   Municipal Corporations Act 1882; Local Government Act 1894; Licensing Act 1902; G.E. Evans, *The Days That We Have Seen* (Faber and Faber: London, 1975), p. 146.

27   *BO*, 5 February 1874; Jennings, *Public House*, pp. 100 and 210–11.

28   J.P.D. Dunbabin, 'Electoral Reforms and their Outcome in the United Kingdom. 1865–1900' in T.R. Gourvish and A. O'Day (eds), *Late Victorian Britain 1867–1900* (Macmillan: Basingstoke, 1988); Ballot Act 1872; Corrupt and Illegal Practices Prevention Act 1883; Municipal Elections (Corrupt and Illegal Practices) Act 1884.

29   *Times*, 1 December 1829.

30   PP 1834 (559), pp. 15 and 115.

31   Ibid., p. 274.

32   Girouard, *Victorian Pubs*, pp. 20–32.

33   C. Dickens, 'Gin-shops' in *Sketches by Boz*.

34   J.C. Loudon, *An Encyclopaedia of Cottage, Farm, and Villa Architecture and Furniture* (Longman, Orme, Brown, Green & Longmans: London, 1839, first published 1833), pp. 675–90.

35   H.B. Fearon, *Suggestions and Correspondence Relating to Magistrates Licences* (1830) quoted in Girouard, *Victorian Pubs*, pp. 28–9.

36   PP 1834 (559), pp. 53, 92, 130, 152 and 374–5.

37   L. Faucher, *Manchester in 1844: Its Present Condition and Future Prospects* (Frank Cass: London, 1969, first published 1844), pp. 48–9.

38   PP 1850 (398), p. 78.

39   *BO*, 24 August 1865; J. Burnley, *Phases of Bradford Life* (T. Brear: Bradford, 1870), pp. 145–56; Jennings, *Public House*, pp. 114–19.

40   *LM*, 9 September 1837.

41   PP 1834 (559), pp. 3 and 274–5.

42   PP 1877 (271), p. 11.

43   *Times*, 14 December 1829.

44   PP 1852–53 (855), pp. 165–6; PP 1877 (171), pp. 147 and 184.

45   *BO*, 24 August and 19 October 1865, 23 August 1866, 5 October 1882, 30 August and 15 and 16 October 1884.

46   Girouard, *Victorian Pubs*, pp. 44–5.

47   Murray, *York Pubs*, pp. xvi and 36.

CHAPTER 6   RUNNING A PUB

1   'The Diary of Joseph Rogerson' in W.B. Crump, *The Leeds Woollen Industry 1780–1820* (Thoresby Society: Leeds, 1931), p. 144; OBP t18250519-168 and t18300114-134.

2   J.C. Hotten, *A Dictionary of Modern Slang, Cant, and Vulgar Words* (Hotten: London, 1859), p. vi.

3   *BO*, 15 November 1889.

4   J. London, *The People of the Abyss* (Arco: London, 1963, first published 1903).

5   RC into Municipal Corporations, Second Report; PP 1837 (239) XXV.1, p. 163; Unwin, *Wetherby*, p. 61.

6   Clark, *English Alehouse*, p. 286; A Gentleman of the Middle Temple, *The Publican Protected*.

7   Morris, *Fiennes*, p. 79.

8   Jennings, 'Occupations'.

9   J.A. Chartres, 'The Place of Inns in the Commercial Life of London and Western England 1660–1760' (PhD thesis, Exeter College, Oxford, 1973), p. 158; North Yorkshire Record Office, Northallerton: Richmond Borough Alehouse Recognizances, DCRMB/3/3/3 (2); Everitt, *English Urban Inn*, pp. 18–6; PP 1833 (416), p. 229.

10   Ibid., pp. 53, 112, 183, 253 and passim; Webb, *Liquor Licensing*, p. 117.

11   East Riding Archives, Beverley: Hedon Innkeepers Licences Book, DDHE 16/64.

12   Southampton Archive Services: A List of Persons Applying for Licences, D/PM 5/3/22/3.

13   Chartres, 'Place of Inns', p. 166; Census of Great Britain, Population Tables Part II, vol. 1; PP 1852-53 (1691-I) LXXXVIII, p. lxxxii; T.S. Ashton, *An Eighteenth-Century Industrialist: Peter Stubs of Warrington 1756–1806* (Manchester University Press: Manchester, 1939), pp. 1–4.

14   M. Beresford, *East End, West End: The Face of Leeds During Urbanisation 1684–1842* (Thoresby Society: Leeds, 1988), p. 414; PP 1850 (398), p. 22.

15   Information from S. Howe, for which thanks; Winstanley, 'Rural Publican'.

16   C.B. Hawkins, *Norwich: A Social Study* (Warner: London, 1910), p. 132; for the undercounting of second occupations in 1851 see Jennings, 'Occupations'; Jennings, *Public House*, pp. 182–3.

17   YO, 15 March 1917; WYAS, Bradford: Deeds to Upper Croft Hotel, 53D84, which contain the tenancy agreement.

18   B. Harrison, 'Pubs' in H.J. Dyos, and M. Wolff (eds), *The Victorian City: Images and Realities, vol. 1* (Routledge & Kegan Paul: London, 1973), p. 173; L..F. Pearson, *The Northumbrian Pub: an Architectural History* (Sandhill Press, Morpeth, 1989), p. 66.

19   T. Collins and W. Vamplew, *Mud, Sweat and Beers: A Cultural History of Sport and Alcohol* (Berg: Oxford, 2002), p. 10; Collins and Vamplew, 'The Pub, The Drinks Trade and the Early Years of Modern Football', *Sports Historian*, vol. 20, 2000, pp. 1–17; T. Mason, *Association Football and English Society 1863–1915* (Harvester: Sussex, 1980), pp. 118–19.

20   Girouard, *Victorian Pubs*, p. 14; *BO*, 26 August 1875.

21   George, *London*, p. 301; D. Philips and R.D. Storch, *Policing Provincial England*
      1829–1856: The Politics of Reform (Leicester University Press: London, 1999), p.
      12; D. Eastwood, *Governing Rural England: Tradition and Transformation in Local*
      Government 1780–1840 (Clarendon Press: Oxford, 1994), pp. 87 and 227; 3 Geo.
      IV, c. 77 and Parish Constables Act 1842; *BO*, 18 November 1898.

22   *Licensee*, 4 January 1913; WYAS, Wakefield: Bradford Borough Police Registers
      of Beerhouse Keepers, A124/110 and 111.

23   WYAS, Wakefield: West Riding Alehouse Recognizances, QE 32/7; Clark,
      English Alehouse, pp. 203 and 285.

24   D.W. Gutzke, 'Mrs John Bull, Proprietor: Women Publicans in Victorian and
      Edwardian England' (unpublished paper, 1987); RC on Liquor Licensing Laws,
      Statistics; PP 1898 [C.8696] XXXVII.205, pp. 41–2.

25   A.F. Part, *The Art and Practice of Innkeeping* (Heinemann: London, 1922), p. 271;
      W. Cudworth, *Rambles Round Horton* (T. Brear: Bradford, 1886), p. 153; Burke,
      English Inn, p. 153.

26   Everitt, *English Urban Inn*, pp. 193–8; Jennings, *Public House*, p. 40; W.B. Johnson,
      Hertfordshire Inns Part One (Hertfordshire Countryside: Letchworth, 1962),
      pp. 18–19.

27   Markham, *Beverley Arms*, p. 6; Bradford Borough Census Returns; L. Stanley,
      The Diaries of Hannah Cullwick Victorian Maidservant (Virago: London, 1984), p.
      36; J. Burnett (ed.), *Useful Toil: Autobiographies of Working People from the 1820s to*
      the 1920s (Allen Lane: London, 1974), pp. 71–2.

28   V. Padmavathy, 'The English Barmaid, 1874–1914: A Case Study of Unskilled
      and Non-unionized Women Workers' (PhD thesis, Miami University, 1989), pp.
      229–30 and 232; P. Bailey, 'Parasexuality and Glamour: the Victorian Barmaid as
      Cultural Prototype', *Gender and History*, vol.2, 1990, pp. 148–72.

29   *LM*, 15 February 1817; above, n. 28; Girouard, *Victorian Pubs*, p. 12.

30   Bradford Borough Census Returns; A. Mutch, 'Managing Birmingham's Public
      Houses in the Nineteenth Century', *Birmingham Historian*, no. 18, 1999, pp. 21–4.

31   Thale, *Place*, pp. 20–37.

32   Girouard, *Victorian Pubs*, p. 13; *Licensee*, 14 June 1913 and passim; R. Kaye, *The*
      Meeting Place: A Guide to the Past History of Huddersfield and District Pubs, vol. 2
      (the author: Huddersfield, 2001), pp. 10–12.

33   Wilson, *Alcohol*, p. 209; *Telegraph & Argus*, 18 June 1993; O. Anderson, *Suicide in Victorian and Edwardian England* (Clarendon Press: Oxford, 1987), p. 95; *BO*, 2 December 1858.

34   Using my earlier estimates and Mathias, *Brewing Industry*, pp. 542–3.

35   Ibid., pp. 117–38.

36   Ibid, pp. 542–3 and my estimate of 49,000 publicans; Account of Number of Brewers and Licensed Victuallers in England and Wales; PP 1822 (571) XXI.139.

37   Mathias, *Brewing Industry*, p. 129; Johnson, *Hertfordshire Inns*, p. 17.

38   Gourvish and Wilson, *Brewing Industry*, pp. 70–5; A. Crawford, M. Dunn and R. Thorne, *Birmingham Pubs 1880–1939* (Alan Sutton: Gloucester, 1986), p. 4.

39   Gourvish and Wilson, *Brewing Industry*, p. 68.

40   PP 1850 (398), p. iv; Gourvish and Wilson, *Brewing Industry*, pp. 134 and 149.

41   D.W. Gutzke, *Protecting the Pub: Brewers and Publicans Against Temperance* (Boydell Press: Woodbridge, 1989), pp. 11–29; PP 1877 (418), pp. 193–4; P.W. Robinson, *The Emergence of the Common Brewer in the Halifax District* (Halifax Antiquarian Society: Halifax, 1982).

42   Gourvish and Wilson, *Brewing Industry*, pp. 250–83.

43   Ibid., pp. 68–9.

44   PP 1897 [C.8356], pp. 93, 227–32, 239, 309, 327, 364 and 447; PP 1897 [C.8523], p. 73.

45   C.C. Owen, *The Greatest Brewery in the World: A History of Bass, Ratcliff & Gretton* (Derbyshire Record Society: Chesterfield, 1992), pp. 83 and 128; Gutzke, *Protecting the Pub*, pp. 23–4; Gourvish and Wilson, *Brewing Industry*, pp. 268–73; Girouard, *Victorian Pubs*, pp. 89–94; D.M. Knox, *The Development of the Tied House System in London* (Oxford Economic Papers, New Series, vol. 10, 1958).

46   J. Vaizey, *The Brewing Industry 1886–1951: An Economic Study* (Pitman and Sons: London, 1960), p. 17.

47   Gutzke, *Protecting the Pub*, pp. 24 and 182; E.A. Pratt, *The Licensed Trade: An Independent Survey* (Murray: London, 1907), pp. 97–105 and 305–8; Deeds to Upper Croft Hotel; PP 1897 [C.8356], pp. 447–9.

48   Pratt, *Licensed Trade*, pp. 106–28 and 308–13; PP 1897 [C.8356], pp. 239, 309 and 447–9; PP 1898 [C.8694], p. 4; A. Mutch, 'Shaping the Public House, 1850–1950: Business Strategies, State Regulation and Social History', *Cultural and Social History*, vol. 1, 2004, pp. 179–200; 'Magistrates and Public House Managers, 1840–1914: Another Case of Liverpool Exceptionalism?', *Northern History*, vol.

XL, 2003, pp. 325–42; 'Public Houses as Multiple Retailing: Peter Walker & Son, 1846–1914', *Business History*, vol. 48, 2006, pp. 1–19; Bass North, Leeds: Hammonds Bradford Brewery Company Ltd, Directors' Meetings Minute Book 1897–1920, 23 March and 9 May 1898; Jennings, *Public House*, pp. 156–7.

49   PP 1897 [C.8523], pp. 73 and 93; PP 1898 [C.8696], pp. 40–1; Jennings, *Public House*, pp. 156–7.

50   Ibid., pp. 155–6; Gutzke, *Protecting the Pub*, p. 25.

51   Ibid., pp. 181–7; *YDO*, 21 March 1907; Jennings, *Public House*, pp. 157–9; Hammonds Minute Book, 26 September 1899.

52   Girouard, *Victorian Pubs*, pp. 94–100 and 110–97.

53   Crawford et al., *Birmingham Pubs*, pp. 7–39.

54   Pearson, *Northumbrian Pub*.

55   Riley and Eley, *Portsmouth*, pp. 14–27.

56   Ibid., pp. 25–6.

57   *BO*, 28 June 1898, 29 August 1878, 27 August 1885, 23 August 1888 and 19 September 1895; City of Bradford Metropolitan Council: Deeds to Ancient Druids' Inn; Jennings, *Public House*, pp. 170–6.

58   Part, *Innkeeping*, pp. 197–203.

59   Clark, *English Alehouse*, pp. 288–90.

60   *Licensed Victuallers' Official Annual 1894*, p. 43 and *1900*, p. 140.

61   Defoe, *Tour*, vol. 2, p. 181; Everitt, *English Urban Inn*, p. 167; Unwin, *Wetherby*, p. 67.

62   Clark, *English Alehouse*, pp. 201 and 284.

63   Hyland, *London Spy*, pp. 263–9; H. Fielding, *Tom Jones*, Book VIII, ch. VII.

64   Clark, *English Alehouse*, p. 292.

65   WYAS, Wakefield: Alehouse Recognizances, QE 32/22; Clark, *English Alehouse*, pp. 203 and 292; P. Earle, 'The Middling Sort in London' in J. Barry and C. Brooks (eds), *The Middling Sort of People: Culture, Society and Politics in England, 1550–1800* (Macmillan: Houndmills, 1994), pp. 143–5.

66   P. Colquhoun, *Observations and Facts Relative to Public Houses* (Dilly: London, 2nd edn, 1796), pp. 11–16; B. Hilton, *A Mad, Bad and Dangerous People? England 1783–1846* (Oxford University Press: Oxford, 2006), pp. 126–8.

67   *Northern Star*, 19 October 1839.

68   *BO*, 6 September 1838.

69   *LM*, 1 September 1849.

70   R. Roberts, *The Classic Slum: Salford Life in the First Quarter of the Century* (Penguin: Harmondsworth, 1973), pp. 17–18 and 120–1.

71   F.W. Thornton, *How To Purchase and Succeed in a Public House* (Griffith, Farran, Okeden & Welsh: London, 1885).

72   *BO*, 10 September 1873, 7 November 1888, 27 February 1894 and 24 October 1895; W. Cudworth, *Condition of the Industrial Classes of Bradford and District* (Bradford, 1887), pp. 40–1.

73   PP 1897 [C.8356], pp. 305 and 311.

74   Southampton Archive Services: Compensation Authority Minutes 1905–1932, SC/MAG 6; Lancashire Record Office, Preston: Compensation Reports 1907–1909, QAD6/1.

CHAPTER 7   CUSTOMERS AND THEIR WORLD

1   J. Lawson, *Progress in Pudsey* (Caliban Books: Firle, 1978, first published 1887), p. 83; Roberts, *Classic Slum*, p. 120.

2   Thale, *Place*, p. 27; Lawson, *Pudsey*, pp. 53–4; PP 1834 (559), pp. 173–4.

3   Girouard, *Victorian Pubs*, pp. 74–7; British Library of Political and Economic Science, Charles Booth Online Archive, www.booth.lse.ac.uk (September 2005): Police Notebooks B347, p. 199; Roberts, *Classic Slum*, pp. 120–1; Winstanley, 'Rural Publican', pp. 73–5.

4   R. Hyde, 'Cartographers versus the Demon Drink', *Map Collector*, vol. 3, 1978, pp. 22–7; C. Booth, *Life and Labour of the People in London: Final Volume Notes on Social Influences and Conclusion* (Macmillan: London, 1902); B.S. Rowntree, *Poverty: A Study of Town Life* (Macmillan: London, 1903).

5   W.M. Bramwell, *Pubs and Localised Communities in Mid-Victorian Birmingham* (Occasional Paper 22, Department of Geography and Earth Science, Queen Mary College, University of London: London, 1984), pp. 7–22; *BO*, 5 and 7 July 1880; *YO*, 5 July 1919.

6   H. Mayhew, *London Labour and the London Poor* (Frank Cass: London, 1967, first published 1851), vol. 1, p. 87; Evans, *Days That We Have Seen*, pp. 169–70; Booth Notebooks B346, p. 147; R. Samuel, *East End Underworld: Chapters in the Life of Arthur Harding* (Routledge & Kegan Paul: London, 1981), pp. 17 and 146.

7   Colquhoun, *Observations*, p. 25; Booth, *Final Volume*, p. 59.

8   A. Shadwell, *Drink, Temperance and Legislation* (Longmans, Green, and Co: London, 1902), p. 89.

9   Warner and Ivis, 'Gin and Gender'.

10   WYAS, Wakefield: QS/10 31 May 1792; Ratcliffe and Chaloner, d'*Eichtal*, pp. 27–8.

11   PP 1834 (559), p. 3; PP 1852–3 (855), pp. 212–15.

12   Chaloner, *Bamford*, pp. 143–4 and 154.

13   RC on Children's Employment in Mines and Manufactories, Second Report; PP 1843 (432) XV.1, p. Q62.

14   RC on Employment of Children in Trades and Manufactories not regulated by Law, Fourth Report; PP 1865 [3548] XX.103, pp. 271–2; PP 1817 (233), pp. 47 and 52; Mayhew, *London Labour*, vol. 4, pp. 228–30.

15   Riley and Eley, *Portsmouth*, pp. 12–13; Harrison, *Drink*, p. 321.

16   Jennings, *Public House*, p. 104; *BO*, 9 October and 24 December 1856 and 15 October 1857.

17   H. Cook, *The Long Sexual Revolution: English Women, Sex, And Contraception 1800–1975* (Oxford University Press: Oxford, 2004), p. 73.

18   *BO*, 7 March 1850; PP 1850 (398), Appendix A, p. 121; for the same story see PP 1854 (367), p. 189.

19   Warner and Ivis, 'Gin and Gender'; T. Hitchcock, *English Sexualities 1700–1800* (Macmillan: Basingstoke, 1997), p. 10.

20   R. Norton, *Mother Clap's Molly House: The Gay Subculture in England 1700–1830* (GMP: London, 1992), pp. 54–64; *Times*, 23 August 1825, 10 July 1827 and 19 April 1830; H.G. Cocks, 'Safeguarding Civility: Sodomy, Class and Moral Reform in Early Nineteenth-Century England', *Past & Present*, 190, 2006, pp. 121–46.

21   J. Walkowitz, *Prostitution and Victorian Society: Women, Class and the State* (Cambridge University Press: Cambridge, 1980); *Manchester Guardian*, 10 September 1897 cited in J. Parke, 'The Social Functions of Public-Houses in Manchester and Preston, c. 1840–1900' (MA Dissertation, University of Lancaster, 1977), p. 64; Rowntree, *Poverty*, pp. 311–13.

22   WYAS, Bradford: Temperance Reports, DB16/Case 39/4.

23   B. and R. Anstis (eds), *The Diary of a Working Man 1872–1873: Bill Williams in the Forest of Dean* (Allan Sutton: Stroud, 1994), p. 43.

24   Stanley, *Cullwick*, p. 210.

25   E. Ross, 'Survival Networks: Women's Neighbourhood Sharing in London
      Before World War 1', *History Workshop*, vol. 15, 1983, pp. 4–27; Booth Notebooks
      B346, p. 41 and B347, p. 121; Booth, *Life and Labour*, vol. 1, p. 54, vol. 5, p. 19 and
      Final Volume, pp. 61–4.

26   RC on Liquor Licensing Laws, Third Report; PP 1898 [C.8694] XXXVI.9, p. 171.

27   Ibid., p. 172; C.M. Parratt, *"More Than Mere Amusement": Working-Class Women's
      Leisure in England, 1750–1914* (Northeastern University Press: Boston, 2001), p.
      141; C. Chinn, *They Worked all Their Lives: Women of the Urban Poor in England,
      1880–1939* (Manchester University Press: Manchester, 1988), pp. 66 and 120–1;
      PP 1897 [C.8356], pp. 330–1.

28   Roberts, *Classic Slum*, p. 175; Rowntree, *Poverty*, p. 325; R. Thorne, 'The
      Movement for Public House Reform 1892–1914' in D.J. Oddy and D.S. Miller,
      Diet and Health in Modern Britain (Croom Helm: London, 1985), pp. 236-7;
      Winstanley, 'Rural Publican', p. 73.

29   Parratt, *"More Than Mere Amusement"*, p. 127.

30   Metropolitan Police Act 1839; in bye laws under the Municipal Corporations
      Act 1835, for example; Licensing Act 1872; Intoxicating Liquors (Sale to
      Children) Acts 1886 and 1901; H.M. Johnson, *Children and Public-Houses*
      (Church of England Temperance Society: London, 4th edn 1897).

31   G.R. Sims, *The Cry of the Children* (Tribune: London, 1907).

32   Home Office, Information Obtained From Certain Police Forces as to the
      Frequenting of Public-Houses by Women and Children; PP 1908 [Cmnd 3813]
      LXXXIX.625.

33   G.P. Williams and G.T. Brake, *Drink in Great Britain 1900–1979* (Edsall: London,
      1980), p. 181.

34   A. Clark, *The Struggle for the Breeches: Gender and the Making of the British Working
      Class* (Rivers Oram Press: London, 1995), p.30.

35   Ross, 'Survival Networks'; '"Fierce Questions and Taunts": Married Life in
      Working-Class London 1870–1914', *Feminist Studies*, vol. 8, 1982, pp. 575–602;
      Love and Toil: Motherhood in Outcast London, 1870–1918 (Oxford University Press:
      Oxford, 1993).

36   Metropolitan Police Act 1839; PP 1847-8 (501) for the beneficial effects; 11
      & 12 Vict., c. 49; 17 & 18 Vict., c. 79; 18 & 19 Vict., c. 118; B. Harrison, 'The
      Sunday Trading Riots of 1855', *Historical Journal*, vol. 2, 1965, pp. 219–45; the

precise details of the variations in opening times produced by all these statutes are usefully tabulated in Harrison, *Drink*, pp. 315–18; Forbes-Mackenzie Act 1853; Welsh Sunday Closing Act 1881.

37 PP 1834 (559), pp. 262–3; *LM*, 7 February 1824; F. Engels, *The Condition of the Working Class in England* (Oxford University Press: Oxford, 1993, first published 1845). p. 138; Scurrah survey in Temperance Reports, using the 1871 census population.

38 Ibid.; E. Ezard, *Battersea Boy* (Willam Kember: London, 1979), cited in Ross, *Love and Toil*, p. 38.

39 PP 1897 [C.8356], p. 393.

40 Ibid., p. 309; Lady Bell, *At the Works: A Study of a Manufacturing Town* (Thomas Nelson & Sons: London, 1911, first published 1907), p. 347.

41 Wilson, *Alcohol*, pp. 55–6, 61–2 and 250–1; Harrison, *Drink*, pp. 294–5.

42 Wilson, *Alcohol*, pp. 396–7; Beer Dealers' Retail Licences (Amendment) Act 1882; 24 & 25 Vict., c. 21; PP 1878-79 (113), pp. xlvi–xlvii.

43 Clark, *English Alehouse*, pp. 209–11; Mathias, *Brewing Industry*, pp. 12–21; O. Macdonagh, 'The Origins of Porter', *Economic History Review*, Second Series, vol. 16, 1964, pp. 530–5.

44 R.G. Wilson, 'The Changing Taste for Beer in Victorian Britain' in R.G. Wilson and T.R. Gourvish (eds), *The Dynamics of the International Brewing Industry Since 1800* (Routledge: London, 1998); *BO*, 8 November 1888 and 27 February 1894; Booth Notebooks, B347, p. 199.

45 J.A. Spring and D.H. Buss, 'Three Centuries of Alcohol in the British Diet', *Nature*, vol. 270, 1977, pp. 567–72; G. King, *Two Tracts* (Johns Hopkins Press; Baltimore, 1936), pp. 40–1; Clark, *English Alehouse*, pp. 209-13; Mathias, *Brewing Industry*, p. 345; M.D. George, 'The London Coal-Heavers: Attempts to Regulate Waterside Labour in the Eighteenth and Nineteenth Centuries', *Economic History* supplement to *Economic Journal*, vol. 1, 1926–1929, pp. 229–48.

46 Gourvish and Wilson, *Brewing Industry*, pp. 27–40 for discussion of statistics and reasons for the trends; J. Rowntree and A. Sherwell, *The Temperance Problem and Social Reform* (Hodder and Stoughton: London, 7th edn, 1900), pp. 5–7.

47 Harrison, *Drink*, pp. 38–40; W. James, *The Varieties of Religious Experience: A Study in Human Nature* (Longmans, Green and Co: London, 1941, first published 1902), p. 387; Roberts, *Classic Slum*, p. 102.

48   Adler, 'Symbolic Exchange to Commodity Consumption'; J. Dunlop, *The Philosophy of Artificial and Compulsory Drinking Usage in Great Britain and Ireland* (Houlston and Stoneman: London, 6th edn 1839); Harrison, *Drink*, pp. 40–5.

49   D.H. Lawrence, *Sons and Lovers*, ch. II.

50   Lawson, *Progress in Pudsey*, pp. 83–4; *BO*, 2 February 1886; Evans, *Days That We Have Seen*, pp. 154–5; C. Dickens, *Great Expectations*, ch. 18; Bramwell, *Pubs*, p. 28.

51   Lawson, *Progress in Pudsey*, pp. 83–4; Jennings, *Public House*, pp. 57–8; Winstanley, 'Rural Publican', p. 71; Evans, *Days That We Have Seen*, p. 142; PP 1852–53 (855), p. 13.

52   Collins and Vamplew, *Mud, Sweat and Beers*, pp. 1 and 8–9; Mayhew, *London Labour*, vol. 1, p. 12.

53   *BO*, 4 November 1841 and 12 December 1861; J.K. Walton and A. Wilcox (eds), *Low Life and Moral Improvement in Mid-Victorian England: Liverpool Through the Journalism of Hugh Shimmin* (Leicester University Press: Leicester, 1991), pp. 65–70; *BO*, 8 June 1854 and 15 July 1870; Mayhew, *London Labour*, vol. 1, pp. 15 and 451–2 and vol. 3, pp. 5–11.

54   Collins and Vamplew, *Mud, Sweat and Beers*, pp. 18-20; Jennings, *Public House*, p. 205.

55   Hawkins, *Norwich*, p. 314; Collins and Vamplew, *Mud, Sweat and Beers*, pp. 18–19.

56   *YDO*, 25 September 1902.

57   Collins and Vamplew, *Mud, Sweat and Beers*, pp. 12–15.

58   M.J. Huggins, 'The First Generation of Street Bookmakers in Victorian England: Demonic Fiends or "Decent Fellers"?', *Northern History*, vol. XXXVI, 2000, pp. 129–45; Jennings, *Public House*, p. 205; but see also Booth, *Life and Labour*, Final Volume, p. 56.

59   *YO*, 27 August 1912; Jennings, *Public House*, pp. 205–6.

60   M. Hilton, *Smoking in British Popular Culture 1800–2000: Perfect Pleasures* (Manchester University Press: Manchester, 2000), pp. 49 and 83–4.

61   Thale, *Place*, pp. 57–9; Evans, *Days That We Have Seen*, pp. 147–53.

62   Jennings, *Public House*, pp. 101–2; Mayhew, *London Labour*, vol. 3, pp. 200–4.

63   L. Senelick (ed.), *Tavern Singing in Early Victorian London: The Diaries of Charles Rice for 1840 and 1850* (Society for Theatre Research: London, 1997), pp. 14–15 and passim. Jennings, *Public House*, pp. 122–4.

64   Ibid.; R. Poole, *Popular Leisure and the Music Hall in Nineteenth Century Bolton* (Centre for North-West Regional Studies, University of Lancaster, Occasional

Paper 12: Lancaster, 1982); D. Russell, *Popular Music in England 1840–1914: A Social History* (Manchester University Press: Manchester, 1987), pp. 72–5.

65   25 Geo. II, c. 36; D. Kift, *The Victorian Music Hall: Culture, Class and Conflict* (Cambridge University Press: Cambridge, 1996), pp. 99–110; Jennings, *Public House*, pp. 206–7.

66   A. Plowright, *John Henry's Walk: A Journey from Clapham to Scarborough in 1875* (Moorfield Press).

67   PP 1850 (398), p. 22; Bradford Borough Census Returns; PP 1897 [C.8523], p. 212; Winstanley, 'Rural Publican', p. 68.

68   Pratt, *Licensed Trade*, pp. 122–4; Jennings, *Public House*, pp. 98 and 212; Mayhew, *London Labour*, vol. 1, pp. 166–73 and 344–6; J. Walton, *Fish and Chips and the British Working Class, 1870–1920* (Leicester University Press: Leicester, 1992); Roberts, *Classic Slum*, p. 112.

69   A. Everitt, 'Country Carriers in the Nineteenth Century', *Journal of Transport History*, New Series, vol. III, 1976, pp. 179–201.

70   T.M. Hull, 'The Social Significance of the Public House in the Liverpool Economic System c. 1840–1900' (MA Dissertation, University of Lancaster, 1979), pp. 24–7; PP 1834 (559), pp. 40–6; George, 'London Coal-Heavers'; Mayhew, *London Labour*, vol. 3, pp. 233–44; G.W. Hilton, *The Truck System Including a History of the British Truck Acts 1465–1960* (Heffer & Sons: Cambridge, 1960), pp. 81–7.

71   George, *London Life*, pp. 286–90; 5 & 6 Vict., c. 99; Payment of Wages in Public Houses Prohibition Act 1883; Bell, *At the Works*, p. 348; Jennings, *Public House*, pp. 213.

72   Roberts, *Classic Slum*, p. 88; Evans, *Days That We Have Seen*, p. 144.

73   Harrison, 'Pubs', pp. 175–9; Unlawful Societies Act 1799; Clark, *English Alehouse*, pp. 324–5.

74   Rowley, 'Nottingham', pp. 77–8.

75   E.A. Pratt, *The Policy of Licensing Justices* (King & Son: London, 1909), p. 22; Rowntree, *Poverty*, p. 310.

76   Hawkins, *Norwich*, pp. 313–15.

77   G. Stedman Jones, 'Working-Class Culture and Working-Class Politics in London, 1870–1900; Notes on the Remaking of a Working Class', *Journal of Social History*, vol. 7, 1974, pp. 460–508.

78 A.E. Dingle, 'Drink and Working Class Living Standards in Britain 1870–1914', *Economic History Review*, Second Series, vol. XXV, 1972, pp. 608–22.

79 Rowntree, *Poverty*, pp. 312–13; *YO*, 21 April 1914; Jennings, *Public House*, pp. 225–7.

80 J. Taylor, *From Self-Help to Glamour: The Working Men's Club* (History Workshop Pamphlet 7: Oxford, 1972); Booth, *Life and Labour*, First Series, vol. 1, pp. 94–106; Pratt, *Licensing Justices*, pp. 33–51; Licensing Act 1902; Wilson, *Alcohol*, p. 384; Gutzke, *Protecting the Pub*, pp. 195–6; Jennings, *Public House*, pp. 227–30; the RC of 1896–9 has lots of evidence on clubs.

CHAPTER 8 POLICING THE PUB

1 M. Daunton, *Trusting Leviathan, The Politics of Taxation in Britain, 1799–1914* (Cambridge University Press: Cambridge, 2001), pp. 35 and 305.

2 Clark, *English Alehouse*, pp. 24–30; Iles, 'Public House Regulation'; J.M. Bennett, *Ale, Beer and Brewsters in England: Women's Work in a Changing World 1300–1600* (Oxford University Press: Oxford, 1996).

3 Clark, *English Alehouse*, p. 145; Wrightson, 'Alehouse, Order and Reformation'.

4 Burn, *Justice of the Peace*; Hunter, 'Legislative Framework'; 1 Ja. I, c. 9; 4 Ja. I, c. 5; 48 Geo. III, c. 143.

5 R.B. Shoemaker, *Prosecution and Punishment: Petty Crime and the Law in London and Middlesex, c. 1660–1725* (Cambridge University Press; Cambridge, 1991), pp. 20–2; D. Carlile, '"A Common and Sottish Drunkard You Have Been" – Prosecutions For Drunkenness in the York Courts', *York Historian*, vol. 16, 1999, pp. 32–44; A. Redford, *The History of Local Government in Manchester, Volume 1; Manor and Township* (Longmans, Green: London, 1939), p.43; R. Fieldhouse and B. Jennings, *A History of Richmond and Swaledale* (Phillimore: London, 1978), pp. 431–2.

6 Shoemaker, *Prosecution and Punishment*, pp. 30–1; WYAS, Wakefield: West Riding Quarter Sessions Indictment Books and specifically at Pontefract 8 April 1771; information from P. Rushton, with thanks.

7 P. King, 'The Summary Courts and Social Relations in Eighteenth-Century England', *Past & Present*, vol. 183, 2004, pp. 125–72; information from N. Landau, with thanks, records cited in N. Landau, 'The Trading Justice's Trade' in N. Landau

(ed.) *Law, Crime and English Society 1660–1830* (Cambridge University Press: Cambridge, 2002), p. 66; North Yorkshire Record Office, Northallerton: Registers of Convictions 1781–1815, QDX.

8   J. Warner and F. Ivis, '"Damn You, You Informing Bitch": Vox Populi and the Unmaking of the Gin Act of 1736', *Journal of Social History*, vol. 33, 1999, pp. 299–330.

9   G. Morgan and P. Rushton (eds), *The Justicing Notebook (1750–64) of Edmund Tew, Rector of Boldon* (Boydell Press for the Surtees Society: Woodbridge, 2000); E. Crittall (ed.), *The Justicing Notebook of William Hunt 1744–1749* (Wiltshire Record Society: Devizes, 1982), p. 29; R. Paley (ed.), *Justice in Eighteenth-Century Hackney: The Justicing Notebook of Henry Norris and the Hackney Petty Sessions Book* (London Record Society: London, 1991).

10   North Yorkshire Record Office, Northallerton: North Riding Quarter Sessions Minute and Order Book, Thirsk 12 July 1787.

11   J. Brewer, *The Sinews of Power: War, Money and the English State, 1688–1783* (Unwin Hyman: London, 1989); D. Phillips and R.D. Storch, *Policing Provincial England 1829–1856: The Politics of Reform* (Leicester University Press: Leicester, 1999), pp. 12–13 and 22–5.

12   Johnson, *Carrington*; Crowther, *Sharp*, p. 535.

13   PP 1833 (416), p. 99 and passim.

14   Ibid., p. 52.

15   Chaloner, *Bamford*, vol. 2, pp. 68–73; Clark, *English Alehouse*, p. 262.

16   *Bradford and Huddersfield Courier*, 23 November 1826 and 11 January 1827; LM, 24 and 31 October 1829; Jennings, *Public House*, pp. 37–8.

17   PP 1847–8 (501), pp. 43–6 and 71; PP 1852–3 (855), pp. 255, 367, 397, 461 and 469; PP 1854 (367), pp. 206–7.

18   Harrison, *Drink*, p. 305; M. Turner, 'Drink and Illicit Distillation in Nineteenth-Century Manchester', *Manchester Region History Review*, vol. IV, 1990, pp. 12–16; Jennings, *Public House*, pp. 214–15.

19   C. Winslow, 'Sussex Smugglers' in D. Hay, P. Linebaugh and E.P. Thompson, *Albion's Fatal Tree: Crime and Society in Eighteenth-Century England* (Allen Lane: London, 1975), p. 127; D. Hay, 'Crime, Authority and the Criminal Law: Staffordshire 1750-1800' (PhD thesis, University of Warwick, 1975), pp. 158–9.

20   SCHC on the Police of the Metropolis; PP 1828 (533) VI.1, pp. 18–19 and e.g.
     PP 1816 (510), pp. 21 and 38.

21   C. Emsley, *The English Police: A Political and Social History* (Pearson Education:
     Harlow, 1996), p. 5; Phillips and Storch, *Policing Provincial England*; J. Styles,
     'The Emergence of the Police – Explaining Police Reform in Eighteenth
     and Nineteenth Century England', *British Journal of Criminology*, vol. 27, 1987,
     pp. 15–22.

22   R. Paley, '"An Imperfect, Inadequate and Wretched system"? Policing London
     Before Peel', *Criminal Justice History*, vol. 10, 1989, pp. 95–130; PP 1817 (233)
     Appendices 2–18; PP 1839 (173).

23   Ibid.; PP 1849–50 (398), pp. 8 and 13.

24   PP 1839 (173); E.W. Clay, *The Leeds Police 1836–1974* (Leeds City Police: Leeds,
     1974), p. 10.

25   B.J. Davey, *Lawless and Immoral: Policing a Country Town 1838–1857* (Leicester
     University Press: Leicester, 1983), p. 64 and passim.

26   P. Bramham, 'Policing Keighley – a Northern Industrial Town in the Mid-
     Nineteenth Century', *Craven History*, 2003, pp. 40–50; Keighley Local Studies
     Library: Diary of James 'Pie' Leach 1848–1853, BK309.

27   R.B. Storch, 'The Plague of Blue Locusts: Police Reform and Popular
     Resistance in Northern England, 1840–1857', *International Review of Social
     History*, vol. 20, 1975, pp. 61–90 and 'The Policeman as Domestic Missionary:
     Urban Discipline and Popular Culture in Northern England', *Journal of Social
     History*, vol. 9, 1976, pp. 481–509.

28   S. Inwood, 'Policing London's Morals: The Metropolitan Police and Popular
     Culture, 1829–1850', *London Journal*, vol. 15, 1990, pp. 129–45; PP 1839 (173);
     R.E. Foster, 'A Cure for Crime? The Hampshire Rural Constabulary 1839–
     1856', *Southern History*, vol. 12, 1990, pp. 48–67; PP 1850 (398), p. 57.

29   E.C. Midwinter, *Law and Order in Early Victorian Lancashire* (Borthwick Institute
     of Historical Research: York, 1968), p. 26.

30   WYAS, Bradford: Bradford Corporation Watch Committee Minute Book;
     Metropolitan Police Act 1829 and Town Police Clauses Act 1847.

31   PP 1847–48 (501), p. 9.

32   PP 1850 (398), pp. v and 42.

33   Ibid., pp. 42 and 57; PP 1839 (173).

34   Annual Reports of the Chief Constable of Bradford in *BO*, 22 November 1855, 9 October 1856, 15 October 1857 and 7 October 1858.

35   PP 1816 (510), pp. 42 and 58; PP 1817 (233), p. 64; PP 1828 (533), pp. 9 and 46; Thale, *Place*, p. 82; Chaloner, *Bamford*, vol. 1, p. 132.

36   Harrison, *Drink*, pp. 41 and 92; M.J.D. Roberts, *Making English Morals: Voluntary Association and Moral Reform in England, 1787–1886* (Cambridge University Press: Cambridge, 2004), pp. 293–4.

37   PP 1878–79 (113), pp. xxxii–xxxviii.

38   Ibid., p. xxxi.

39   S. Petrow, *Policing Morals: The Metropolitan Police and the Home Office, 1870–1914* (Clarendon Press: Oxford, 1994), p. 192; PP 1877 (171), pp. 338 and 343; PP 1877 (271), p. 385.

40   Petrow, *Policing Morals*, pp. 202–3; PP 1897 [C.8523], pp. 89–90; WYAS, Bradford: Annual Reports of Chief Constable of Bradford.

41   Petrow, *Policing Morals*, p. 192; PP 1897 [C.8523]. p. 509.

42   Judicial Statistics of England and Wales; PP 1901 (Cd 659) LXXXIX; C.P Sanger, *The Place of Compensation in Temperance Reform* (King: London, 1901), p.117.

43   J. Crowther, *Beverley in Mid-Victorian Times* (Hutton Press: Beverley, 1990), p. 119; G.W.E. Russell (ed.), *Sir Wilfred Lawson: a Memoir* (Smith, Elder: London, 1909), p. 124.

44   Petrow, *Policing Morals*, pp. 194–203; PP 1878–79 (113) p. xxxiv; PP 1897 [C.8356], p. 134.

45   Jennings, *Public House*, p. 221.

46   SCHC on Sale of Beer Act First Report; PP 1854–5 (407) X.339, pp. 1.20; Second Report; PP (427) X.505, p. iii.

47   W.R. Lambert, 'The Welsh Sunday Closing Act, 1881', *Welsh History Review*, vol. 6, 1972, pp. 161-89; G. and W. Grossmith, *The Diary of a Nobody*, ch. II.

48   Askwith, *British Taverns*, p. 129; RC on Liquor Licensing Laws Final Report; PP 1899 [C.9379] XXXV.1, pp. 17–19 and 145–7; PP 1897 [C.8356], pp. 209 and 393; PP 1897 [8523], pp. 79 and 262–6.

49   M. Clapson, *A Bit of a Flutter: Popular Gambling and English Society c. 1823–1961* (Manchester University Press: Manchester, 1992), pp. 27–9.

50   Jennings, *Public House*, p. 221; Southampton Archive Services: Southampton Register of Licences 1903–1923, SC/MAG 3/2.

51   B.S. Rowntree, *Betting and Gambling, A National Evil* (Macmillan: London, 1905), p. 136; *YO*, 27 August 1912.

52   As no. 50. Pratt, *Licensing Justices*, pp. 151–6.

53   J. Kneale, '"A Problem of Supervision": Moral Geographies of the Nineteenth-Century British Public House', *Journal of Historical Geography*, vol. 25, 1999, pp. 333–48.

54   *BO*, 2 February 1886.

55   Booth, *Life and Labour*, First Series, vol. 1, pp. 113–14.

CHAPTER 9   POLITICS AND THE PUB

1   J. Greenaway, *Drink and British Politics Since 1830: A Study in Policy Making* (Palgrave Macmillan: Basingstoke, 2003), pp. 1–2.

2   Wilson, *Alcohol*, p. xi.

3   *BO*, 9 August 1855.

4   Harrison, *Drink*; A.E. Dingle, *The Campaign for Prohibition in Victorian England: The United Kingdom Alliance 1872–1895* (Croom Helm: London, 1980); J. Greenaway, 'The Local Option Question and British Politics, 1864–1914' (PhD thesis, University of Leeds, 1974).

5   Harrison, 'Sunday Trading Riots'.

6   Harrison, *Drink*, pp. 242–73.

7   Account of Number of persons in UK licensed as Brewers, and Victuallers; PP 1870 (187) LXI.281; Wilson, *Alcohol*, p. 236.

8   Return of Number of new Licences granted by Justices in each County of England and Wales; PP 1881 (135) LXXXIII.387 and 1882 (33) LXIV.489; PP 1898 [C.8869], pp. 33–6 and 43–91.

9   Riley and Eley, *Portsmouth*, pp. 13–21.

10   Based on reports of brewster sessions in *BO* and in particular 3 December 1874 and 28 August 1879.

11   D.W. Gutzke, *Pubs and Progressives: Reinventing the Public House in England 1896–1960* (Northern Illinois University Press: DeKalb, 2006), pp. 75–6.

12   PP 1897 [C.8523], pp. 71–2 and 509.

13   Brewster sessions reports and WYAS, Wakefield: List of Licences Refused 1877–92, in records of Bradford Borough Police.

14   PP 1877 (418), p. 170; PP 1878 (338), pp. 39–40 and 543; frequently found in the deeds to Victorian properties.

15   Askwith, *British Taverns*, pp. 76–7.

16   Sir R. Ensor, *England 1870–1914* (Oxford University Press: Oxford, 1936), p. 360; Greenaway, *Drink*, pp. 43–8; for the temperance view see J. Newton, *W.S. Caine, MP: A Biography* (Nisbet and Co: London, 1907).

17   Sanger, *Place of Compensation*.

18   *Kendal and County News*, 4 January 1896; J. Scott, *A Lakeland Valley Through Time: A History of Staveley, Kentmere and Ings* (Staveley and District Historical Society: Kendal, 1995), pp. 42 and 98–9; Sharp v. Wakefield and Others, reported 1891, AC 173, *All England Law Reports 1886–1890* (London, reprint 1963); *Times*, 31 January 1891; the case is also cited as Sharpe.

19   Askwith, *British Taverns*, pp. 131–73; PP 1899 [C.9379], pp. 6–7 and 49-56; D.M. Fahey, 'Temperance and the Liberal Party – Lord Peel's Report, 1899', *Journal of British Studies*, vol. X, 1971, pp. 132–59.

20   Gutzke, *Protecting the Pub*, pp. 153–5; *YDO*, 19 March 1903.

21   Ensor, *England 1870–1914*, pp. 360–1; K. Young, *Arthur James Balfour: The Happy Life of the Politician, Prime Minister, Statesman and Philosopher* (Bell and Sons: London, 1963), p. 249.

22   C. Wrigley, *Lloyd George* (Blackwell: Oxford, 1992), p. 35; Gutzke, *Protecting the Pub*, pp. 155–6; Yorkshire Brewers' Association, Tadcaster: Minute Books of the Bradford and District Brewers' Association, 30 June 1904; *YDO*, 24 April and 21 May 1904, 2 February and 4 November 1905.

23   Wilson, *Alcohol*, p. 381.

24   Gutzke, *Protecting the Pub*, pp. 155–6; A. Sherwell, *Licence Reduction Under the Act of 1904* (Temperance Legislation League: London, 1911); *Times*, 25 July 1906; WYAS, Wakefield: City of Bradford, Report of the Licensing Committee and Compensation Authority, P16/2; Jennings, *Public House*, pp. 167–9.

25   Southampton Archive Services: Compensation Authority Minutes 1905–1932 SC/MAG 6; Lancashire Record Office, Preston: Compensation Reports 1907–1909 QAD6/1; *YDO*, 17 February 1906; B. Bennison, 'The Scramble for Licensed Houses: Some Evidence From Newcastle Upon Tyne', *Journal of Regional and Local Studies*, vol. 15, 1995, pp. 1–13; Douch, *Cornish Inns*, pp. 116–17; D.J. Butler, 'Defeating the Demon Drink – The 1904 Licensing Act and

its Implementation in Durham City, 1906–1939', *Durham County Local History Society Bulletin*, 1995, vol. 54, pp. 52–65.

26 R.G.Wilson, *Greene King: A Business and Family History* (Bodley Head: London, 1983), pp. 142–3; T. Gourvish, *Norfolk Beers from English Barley: a History of Steward & Patteson, 1793–1963* (Centre for East Anglian Studies, University of East Anglia: Norwich, 1987), p. 79.

27 Wilson, *Alcohol*, pp. 111 and 381; P. Eley and R.C. Riley, *The Demise of Demon Drink? Portsmouth Pubs 1900–1950* (Portsmouth City Council: Portsmouth, 1991), p. 8.

28 Shadwell, *Drink*, p. 161.

29 Kneale, 'A Problem of Supervision'; RC of 1896–99 passim.

30 Jennings, *Public House*, pp. 115–17 and 176–8; PP 1897 [C.8356], pp. 307–9.

31 Ibid., pp. 128 and 312–13; PP 1897 [C.8523], pp. 104 and 136.

32 Harrison, *Drink*, p. 296; Bennison, 'Drink in Newcastle', pp. 176–7; BO 24 and 26 April 1871, 31 March and 22 July 1873 and 3 January and 20 March 1876; PP 1878–79 (113), p. ix.

33 Thorne, 'Places of Refreshment', pp. 244–5; M. Elliott, ' The Leicester Coffee-House and Cocoa-House Movement', *Transactions of the Leicestershire Archaeological and Historical Society*, vol. XLVII, 1971–2, pp. 55–61; Jennings, *Public House*, p. 228.

34 Greenaway, *Drink*, pp. 38–9; A.Shadwell, 'A Model Public-House And Its Lessons', *National Review*, no. 149, July 1895; J. Rowntree and A. Sherwell, *British Gothenburg Experiments and Public-House Trusts* (Hodder & Stoughton: London, 1901); Gutzke, *Pubs and Progressives*, pp. 23–48; Thorne, 'Public House Reform'; B. Bennison, 'Earl Grey's Public House Reform', *Journal of the Northumberland Local History Society*, vol. 48, 1994, pp. 68–73.

35 Harrison, *Drink*, p. 255.

36 Gutzke, *Protecting the Pub*, pp. 167–8; Minute Books of the Bradford and District Brewers' Association, December 1907.

37 Clark, *English Alehouse*, p. 286; Gutzke, *Protecting the Pub*, pp. 63–4.

38 Jennings, *Public House*, pp. 90–1, 128–30 and 187–95.

39 Gutzke, *Protecting the Pub*, pp. 102–3, 120–3 and 167–8.

40 Ensor, *England 1870–1914*, pp. 21–2; Rowntree and Sherwell, *Temperance Problem*, ch. 11.

41 Gutzke, *Protecting the Pub*, pp. 9–10 and 230–45; Jennings, *Public House*, pp. 187–95.

42 Greenaway, *Drink*, pp. 29–90; Gutzke, *Protecting the Pub*, p. 241.

CHAPTER 10   THE FIRST WORLD WAR AND THE PUB

1   J.M. Winter, *The Great War and the British People* (Macmillan: Basingstoke, 1985), p. 210.

2   *YO*, 17 September, 8 October and 8 December 1914.

3   H. Carter, *The Control of the Drink Trade in Britain: A Contribution to National Efficiency During the Great War 1915–1918* (Longmans, Green: London 2nd edn, 1919), pp. 17–37; this key work from a temperance point of view should be read alongside A. Shadwell, *Drink in 1914–1922: A Lesson in Control* (Longmans, Green: London, 1923).

4   Carter, *Control*, pp. 37–52; Greenaway, *Drink*, pp. 91–5; S. Mews, 'Urban Problems and Rural Solutions: Drink and Disestablishment in the First World War' in D. Baker (ed.), *The Church in Town and Countryside: Studies in Church History vol. 16* (Blackwell: Oxford, 1979).

5   Carter, *Control*, pp. 53–76 and 123–34; J. Turner, 'State Purchase of the Liquor Trade in the First World War', *Historical Journal*, vol. 23, 1980, pp. 589–615; D.H. Aldcroft, 'Control of the Liquor Trade in Great Britain, 1914–21' in W.H. Chaloner and B.M. Ratcliffe (eds), *Trade and Transport: Essays in Economic History in Honour of T.S. Williams* (Manchester University Press: Manchester, 1977); M.E. Rose, 'The Success of Social Reform? The Central Control Board (Liquor Traffic) 1915–21' in M.R.D. Foot (ed.), *War and Society: Historical Essays in Honour and Memory of J.R. Western 1928–1971* (Elek: London, 1973); I. Donnachie, 'World War I and the Drink Question: State Control of the Drink Trade', *Journal of the Scottish Labour History Society*, vol. 17, 1982, pp. 19–26.

6   Carter, *Control*, pp. 135–71.

7   Ibid., pp. 200–33; Greenaway, *Drink*, pp. 102–7.

8   Carter, *Control*, p. 169.

9   I. Dewhirst, *The Story of a Nobody: A Working Class Life 1880–1939* (Mills & Boon: London, 1980), pp. 65–6; *Licence Holder*, 15 January and 11 March 1916; *YO*, 1 March and 7 October 1916.

10 Offences recorded in Borough of Bradford Police Registers of Licensed Victuallers and Beerhouse Keepers.

11 *YO*, 15 May 1915.

12 Wilson, *Alcohol*, p. 275; Carter, *Control*, pp. 240–1; Gourvish and Wilson, *Brewing Industry*, pp. 318–23; Shadwell, *Drink in 1914–1922*, pp. 81–7.

13 *Licence Holder*, 7 and 21 April 1917; *YO*, 3 and 14 April 1917 and 5 January and 6 February 1918.

14 Gourvish and Wilson, *Brewing Industry*, pp. 332–5.

15 Ibid., p. 323; Greenaway, *Drink*, pp. 116–17.

16 Wilson, *Alcohol*, pp. 58–9.

17 Greenaway, *Drink*, pp. 117–25; Askwith, *British Taverns*, pp. 203–4; Intoxicating Liquor (Sale to Persons Under Eighteen) Act 1923. State control in Carlisle continued until 1972.

18 *YO*, 14 October 1914; Mews, 'Urban Problems'; Shadwell, *Drink in 1914–1922*, p. 105; D.W. Gutzke, 'Gender, Class and Public Drinking in Britain During the First World War', *Histoire Sociale / Social History*, vol. 27, 1994, pp. 367–91.

19 Shadwell, *Drink in 1914–1922*, pp. 102–5; Carter, *Control*, pp. 113–14.

20 Gutzke, 'Gender'; Roberts, *Classic Slum*, p. 204.

21 Gutzke, *Pubs and Progressives*, pp. 67–8.

22 Ibid., p.67; S.O. Nevile, *Seventy Rolling Years* (Faber and Faber: London, 1958), pp. 123–4; Greenaway, *Drink*, p. 128.

23 Wilson, *Alcohol*, p. 333; Gourvish and Wilson, *Brewing Industry*, pp. 335–9.

24 Greenaway, *Drink*, pp. 114–15.

CHAPTER II IMPROVED PUBS AND LOCALS 1920–1960

1 Gourvish and Wilson, *Brewing Industry*, pp. 337–9 and 363–9.

2 Ibid., pp. 335–6 and 358.

3 A. Davies, *Leisure, Gender and Poverty: Working-Class Culture in Salford and Manchester, 1900–1939* (Open University Press: Buckingham, 1992), pp. 48–54; R. Hoggart, *The Uses of Literacy* (Penguin: Harmondsworth, 1958, first published, 1957), pp. 94–6; E. Roberts, *A Woman's Place: An Oral History of Working-Class Women 1890-1940* (Basil Blackwell: Oxford, 1984), p. 123; B.S. Rowntree, *Poverty and Progress: A Second Social Survey of York* (Longmans,

Green and Co: London, 2nd edn, 1942), pp. 363–4; RC on Licensing (England and Wales) Report; PP 1931–2 (Cmd 3988) XI, pp. 13 and 22.

4   Davies, *Leisure*, pp. 31–7; J.N. Reedman, *A Report on a Survey of Licensing in Sheffield* (Sheffield Social Survey Committee: Sheffield, 1931), pp. 29–32; Mass Observation, *Pub and the People*, p. 114.

5   Gourvish and Wilson, *Brewing Industry*, pp. 340, 357 and 365.

6   Rowntree, *Poverty*, pp. 368–9; S.G. Jones, *Workers at Play: A Social and Economic History of Leisure 1918–1939* (Routledge & Kegan Paul: London, 1986), pp. 3 and 10–20.

7   J. Richards, 'The Cinema and Cinema-going in Birmingham in the 1930s' in J.K. Walton and J. Walvin (eds), *Leisure in Britain 1780–1939* (Manchester University Press: Manchester, 1983), p. 32; Roberts, *Woman's Place*, p. 123.

8   Jones, *Workers at Play*, pp. 44–7; Clapson, *Bit of a Flutter*, p. 162; A.J.P. Taylor, *English History 1914–1945* (Penguin: Harmondsworth, 1970, first published 1965), pp. 384 and 391.

9   C.L. Mowat, *Britain Between the Wars 1918–1940* (Methuen: London, 1955), pp. 458–9 and 509.

10   City of Bradford Licensing Committee and Compensation Authority; *YO*, 16 January, 10 April, and 15 May 1930.

11   D.C. Jones (ed.), *The Social Survey of Merseyside, vol. 3* (University Press of Liverpool and Hodder & Stoughton: London, 1934), p. 286; Reedman, *Sheffield*, pp. 24–5; A. Hughes and K. Hunt, 'A Culture Transformed? Women's Lives in Wythenshawe in the 1930s' in A. Davies and S. Fielding (eds), *Workers' Worlds: Cultures and Communities in Manchester and Salford 1880–1939* (Manchester University Press: Manchester, 1992), pp. 80 and 85.

12   Eley and Riley, *Demise*, pp. 11–16.

13   Report of the Departmental Committee on Liquor Licensing; PP 1972–73 (Cmnd 5154) XIV.939, p. 26.

14   G.R. Sims, *The Old Public-House and the New* (True Temperance Association: London, 1917).

15   Gutzke, *Pubs and Progressives*, pp. 67–8 and 141.

16   Ibid., pp. 102–4 and 140–1.

17   Report of the Committee on the Disinterested Management of Public Houses; PP 1927 (Cmd 2862) X, p. 22; Nevile, *Seventy Rolling Years*, pp. 168–70; Gutzke, *Pubs and Progressives*, pp. 110–13 and 138.

18   Ibid., pp. 85–113; Crawford et al. *Birmingham Pubs*, pp. 48–57 and 92–3; Oliver, *Renaissance of the English Public House*, pp. 80–92.

19   Gutzke, *Pubs and Progressives*, pp. 144–57.

20   Ibid., pp. 204–7.

21   This is a particularly well documented episode in the history of the pub, for example: Oliver, *Renaissance*; E.E. Williams, *The New Public-House* (Chapman and Hall: London, 1924); C. Aslet, 'Beer and Skittles in the Improved Public House', *Thirties Society Journal*, vol. 4, 1984; R. Elwall, *Bricks and Beer: English Pub Architecture 1830–1939* (British Architectural Library: London, 1983); Crawford et al. *Birmingham Pubs*; R. Thorne, 'Good Service and Sobriety: The Improved Public House', *Architectural Review*, vol. 159, 1976, pp. 107–11; Eley and Riley, *Demise*; Report of the Committee on War Damaged Licensed Premises and Reconstruction; PP 1943–44 (Cmd 6504) IV.259, pp. 45–6.

22   Gutzke, *Pubs and Progressives*, pp. 210–11 and 246–8, figure is 10 per cent of full on-licences; City of Bradford Licensing Committee and Compensation Authority 1920–39.

23   OBP t18300114-134; *LM*, 9 September 1848; Jennings, *Public House*, p. 33; Gutzke, *Pubs and Progressives*, p. 9; Bradford Metropolitan Council: Report of Public Local Inquiry into the White Abbey Improvement Scheme, 1923, pp. 12 and 42.

24   Sir H.L. Smith, *The New Survey of London Life and Labour, vol. IX, Life and Leisure* (P.S. King & Son: London, 1935), pp. 261–2; Rowntree, *Poverty*, pp. 351–2.

25   B. Bennison, 'Not So Common: The Public House in North East England Between the Wars', *Local Historian*, vol. 25, 1995, pp. 31–42; RC on Licensing (England and Wales) 1929–31, Minutes of Evidence, p. 405 (these were printed although never officially published).

26   Wilson, *Alcohol*, pp. 384 and 134–47; Gourvish and Wilson, *Brewing Industry*, p. 414, n. 12.

27   Smith, *London Life*, p. 259.

28   M. Race, *Public Houses, Private Lives: An Oral History of Life in York Pubs in the Mid-Twentieth Century* (Voyager: York, 1999), p. 121.

29   Gourvish and Wilson, *Brewing Industry*, pp. 346, 409 and 441–45.

30   Part, *Innkeeping*, pp. 27–8 and 51.

31   RC on Licensing 1929–31, Evidence, p. 394; Race, *York Pubs*, pp. 27–30.

32 Calculated from Borough of Bradford, Police Registers of Licensed Victuallers and Beerhouse Keepers; Mass Observation, *Pub and the People*, p. 223; Race, *York Pubs*, pp. 31–7; Eley and Riley, *Demise*, p. 21.

33 E. Selley, *The English Public House As It Is* (Longmans, Green and Co: London, 1927), p. 18.

34 Mass Observation, *Pub and the People*, pp. 90 and 128–31.

35 J.N. Mogey, *Family and Neighbourhood: Two Studies in Oxford* (Greenwood Press: Westport, Connecticut, 1974, first published, 1956), pp. 102–5 and 141.

36 P. Willmott, *The Evolution of a Community: A Study of Dagenham after Forty Years* (Routledge & Kegan Paul: London, 1963), pp. 87–8; M. Young and P. Willmott, *Family and Kinship in East London* (Penguin: Harmondsworth, 1962, first published 1957), pp. 121, 142 and 153–4.

37 Mass Observation, *Pub and the People*, p. 336.

38 Smith, *London Life*, pp. 253–4; J. Stevenson, *British Society 1919–45* (Penguin: Harmondsworth, 1984), p. 166; C. Harris, *The Use of Leisure in Bethnal Green: A Survey of Social Conditions in the Borough 1925 to 1926* (Lindsey Press: London, 1927), p. 48; M. Chamberlain, *Growing Up in Lambeth* (Virago: London, 1989), p. 24.

39 Mass Observation, *Pub and the People*, pp. 134–5; Rowntree, *Poverty*, p. 353; Selley, *English Public House*, pp. 123–4 and 129; Roberts, *Classic Slum*, p. 222; Roberts, *Woman's Place*, p. 122; Davies, *Leisure*, pp. 61–73.

40 C. Langhamer, '"A Public House is For All Classes, Men and Women Alike": Women, Leisure and Drink in Second World War England', *Women's History Review*, vol. 12, 2003, pp. 423–43; Mogey, *Family and Neighbourhood*, p. 105.

41 Mass Observation, *Pub and the People*, pp. 137–8; Smith, *London Life*, pp. 252–4; T. Cauter and J.S. Downham, *The Communication of Ideas: A Study of Contemporary Influences on Urban Life* (Chatto and Windus: London, 1954), p. 94; Mogey, *Family and Neighbourhood*, p. 103.

42 Gutzke, *Pubs and Progressives*, pp. 156–86; Selley, *English Public House*, pp. 51–2.

43 Smith, *London Life*, p. 253; Selley, *English Public House*, p. 21.

44 Mass Observation, *Pub and the People*, pp. 20, 186–91 and 255–62; Mogey, *Family and Neighbourhood*, p. 105; N. Dennis, F. Henriques and C. Slaughter, *Coal is our Life: an Analysis of a Yorkshire Mining Community* (Eyre & Spottiswoode: London, 1956), pp. 154–6; Race, *York Pubs*, pp. 93–101.

45 Girouard, *Victorian Pubs*, pp. 196–7; Race, *York Pubs*, pp. 93–101.

46   Gorham, *The Local*, p. x.

47   M. Houlbrook, *Queer London: Perils and Pleasures in the Sexual Metropolis, 1918–1957* (University of Chicago Press: Chicago, 2005), pp. 71–7, 88–9 and 160.

48   B. Glover, *Brewing for Victory: Brewers, Beer and Pubs in World War II* (Lutterworth Press: Cambridge, 1995), pp. 14–28.

49   B. Beaven, *Leisure, Citizenship and Working-Class Men in Britain, 1850–1945* (Manchester University Press: Manchester, 2005), p. 229.

50   Glover, *Brewing for Victory*, pp. 66–84; PP 1943–44 (Cmd 6504), pp. 21–2.

51   Gourvish and Wilson, *Brewing Industry*, pp. 356–64; Glover, *Brewing for Victory*, pp. 85–123; Race, *York Pubs*, p. 106.

52   Glover, *Brewing for Victory*, pp. 82 and 167; Race, *York Pubs*, pp. 102–4; Gorham, *Back to the Local*, p. 78.

CHAPTER 12   CONCLUSION: MODERN TIMES

1   Mass Observation, *Pub and the People*, pp. 17, 74 and 218.

2   A. Franklin, *Pub Drinking and the Licensed Trade: A Study of Drinking Cultures and Local Community in Two Areas in South West England* (University of Bristol, School for Advanced Urban Studies Occasional Paper 21: Bristol, 1985), p. 33; G.P. Williams, and G.T. Brake, *The English Public-House in Transition* (Edsall: London, 1982), p. 21.

3   P. Haydon, *The English Pub: A History* (Robert Hale: London, 1994); *What's Brewing*, December 1994.

4   PP 1972–73 (Cmnd 5154), p. 61.

5   Ibid., p. 26; Wilson, *Alcohol*, p. 236; note that the figures for 1921 are not quite the same in the two sources.

6   Bradford Central Library: Annual Reports of the Chief Constable of Bradford 1940–70 and Reports of the Chairman of the Licensing and Compensation Committee of Bradford, 1965–72.

7   Ibid., Eley and Riley, *Demise*, p. 26.

8   Finance Act 1942; Licensing Planning (Temporary Provisions) Act 1945; Eley and Riley, *Demise*, pp. 25–6.

9   As n. 6 above.

10   *Statistical Bulletin Liquor Licensing, England and Wales, July 2003–June 2004*
     (Department for Culture, Media and Sport: London, 2004), pp. 8, 10 and 25.

11   R. Sedgley, 'The Village Inn' in Binney and Milne (eds), *Time Gentlemen
     Please*; J.C. Everitt and I.R. Bowler, 'Bitter-Sweet Conversions: Changing
     Times for the British Pub', *Journal of Popular Culture*, vol. 30, 1996, pp.
     101–22.

12   Reports of the Chairman of the Licensing and Compensation Committee of
     Bradford, 1966 and 1969.

13   Gourvish and Wilson, *Brewing Industry*, pp. 581–4.

14   Bradford Magistrates Court: Licensing Statistics 1981; British Beer and Pub
     Association, Pub numbers, www.beerandpub.com (February 2007).

15   DCMS, *Statistical Bulletin*, pp. 8 and 25.

16   Gourvish and Wilson, *Brewing Industry*, p. 566.

17   Everitt and Bowler, 'Bitter-Sweet Conversions'; Hutt, *Death of the English
     Pub*, pp. 122–6; D. White, 'The Pull of the Pub'. *New Society*, vol. 16, 1970,
     pp. 317–18; A. Williams, 'The Postmodern Consumer and Hyperreal Pubs',
     Hospitality Management, vol. 17, 1998, pp. 221–32.

18   D.E. Vasey, *The Pub and English Social Change* (AMS Press: New York, 1990),
     pp. 49–73 and 148–52; M.A. Smith, *The Pub and the Publican* (Centre for
     Leisure Studies, University of Salford: Salford, 1981).

19   D. Gamston, (ed.) *The CAMRA National Inventory: Pub Interiors of
     Outstanding Historic Interest* (CAMRA: St Albans, 2nd edn, 2003); see also G.
     Brandwood, A, Davison and M. Slaughter, *Licensed to Sell: The History and
     Heritage of the Public House* (English Heritage: London, 2004).

20   P. Hadfield, *Bar Wars: Contesting the Night in Contemporary British Cities*
     (Oxford University Press: Oxford, 2006), pp. 44–76; K. J. Brain, *Youth, Alcohol,
     and the Emergence of the Post-Modern Alcohol Order* (Institute of Alcohol
     Studies, Occasional Paper No. 1, New Series: London, 2000).

21   P. Jones, 'Enter the Superpub', *Town & Country Planning*, vol. 65, 1996, pp.
     110–12; Burnett, *Liquid Pleasures*, p. 150.

22   Selley, *English Public House*, pp. 31–2; Williams, *New Public-House*, pp. 48–50;
     Jones, *Merseyside*, p. 286; Race, *York Pubs*, pp. 108–13; R. Graves and A.
     Hodge, *The Long Weekend: A Social History of Great Britain 1918–1939* (Sphere:
     London, 1991, first published 1940), pp. 231–2.

23   R. Mansukhani, *The Pub Report: British Pubs in the 1980s* (Euromonitor, 1985), pp. 113–23; J. Burnett, *England Eats Out: A Social History of Eating Out in England from 1830 to the Present* (Pearson Education: Harlow, 2004), p. 291.

24   Everitt and Bowler, 'Bitter-Sweet Conversions'; G. Crompton, '"Well-Intentioned Meddling": The Beer Orders and the British Brewing Industry' in Wilson and Gourvish, *International Brewing Industry*, p. 175; Williams, 'Postmodern Consumer'.

25   The Monopolies Commission: A Report on the Supply of Beer; PP 1968–69 (216) XL, pp. 50–1.

26   Gourvish and Wilson, *Brewing Industry*, pp. 447–97.

27   Ibid., pp. 457–8; Monopolies and Mergers Commission: The Supply of Beer; PP 1988–89 (Cm. 651) L, p. 10.

28   Gourvish and Wilson, *Brewing Industry*, pp. 596–8; Punch Taverns.

29   PP 1968–69 (216), pp. 52–4; PP 1988–89 (Cm. 651), p. 40.

30   A. Mutch, 'Trends and Tensions in UK Public House Management', *International Journal of Hospitality Management*, vol. 19, 2000, pp. 361–74; British Beer and Pub Association.

31   White, 'Pull of the Pub'; P. Hyde, 'The Occupational Role of Publican' (MPhil thesis, University of Kent, 1974); Franklin, *Pub Drinking*, pp. 31–43 and 59.

32   A. Mutch, 'Where do Public House Managers Come From? Some Survey Evidence', *International Journal of Contemporary Hospitality Management*, vol. 13, 2001, pp. 86–92; 'Trends and Tensions'.

33   M. Bradley and D. Fenwick, *Public Attitudes to Liquor Licensing Laws in Great Britain* (HMSO: London, 1974), pp. 3 and 13; J. Leigh, *Young People and Leisure* (Routledge & Kegan Paul: London, 1971), p. 92; Social Trends 27 (HMSO: London, 1997), p. 220.

34   E. Roberts, *Women and Families: An Oral History, 1940–1970* (Blackwell: Oxford, 1995), pp. 62–3; P. Wilson, *Drinking in England and Wales* (HMSO: London, 1980), pp. ix and 50.

35   Annual Reports of the Chief Constable of Bradford, e.g. to 31 December 1960; Race, *York Pubs*, pp. 27–8.

36   L. Gofton and S. Douglas, 'Drink and the City', *New Society*, vol. 74, 1985, pp. 502–4; Hadfield, *Bar Wars*, p. 83; S. Winlow and S. Hall, *Violent Night: Urban Leisure and Contemporary Culture* (Berg: Oxford, 2006), pp. 103–4 and 176; M. Jayne, S.L. Holloway and G. Valentine, 'Drunk and Disorderly: Alcohol,

Urban Life and Public Space', *Progress in Human Geography*, vol. 30, 2006, pp. 451–68.

37 Hadfield, *Bar Wars*, p. 1; P. Marsh, 'Violence at the Pub', *New Society*, vol. 52, 1980, pp. 210–12.

38 Bradley and Fenwick, *Public Attitudes*, pp. 13 and 55; Williams and Brake, *Public-House*, pp. 51–4.

39 A. Whitehead, 'Sexual Antagonism in Herefordshire' in D.L. Barker and S. Allen (eds), *Dependence and Exploitation in Work and Marriage* (Longman: London, 1976); M.A. Smith, 'An Empirical Study of a Rough Working Class Pub' in E. Single and T. Storm (eds), *Public Drinking and Public Policy* (Addiction Research Foundation: Toronto: 1984), p. 143; M.A. Smith, *Sex, Gender and Power: The Enigma of the Public House* (author: Hebden Bridge, 2003), pp. 75 and 97; G. Hunt and S. Saterlee, 'Darts, Drink and the Pub: The Culture of Female Drinking', *Sociological Review*, vol. 35, 1987, pp. 575–601.

40 Franklin, *Pub Drinking*, pp. 54–6; *Social Trends 27*, p. 220; M. and M. Plant, *Binge Britain: Alcohol and the National Response* (Oxford University Press: Oxford, 2006), pp. 36, 41–4 and 51.

41 Bradley and Fenwick, *Public Attitudes*, pp. 4–5.

42 Mansukhani, *Pub Report*, p. 131; Deregulation and Contracting Out Act 1994; *What's Brewing*, March and April 1995; DCMS, *Statistical Bulletin*, pp. 7 and 12.

43 Ibid., p. 2; Licensing Act 1961.

44 Greenaway, *Drink*, p. 180; Licensing (Restaurant Meals) Act 1987; Licensing Act 1988; Licensing (Sunday Hours) Act 1995.

45 Gourvish and Wilson, *Brewing Industry*, pp. 577–9; Williams and Brake, *Public-House*, pp. 35–7.

46 Vasey, *The Pub*, pp. 97–115; Mansukhani, *Pub Report*, pp. 127–33; Franklin, *Pub Drinking*, pp. 38 and 49.

47 Ibid., pp. 20 and 57; O. Gill, *Luke Street: Housing Policy, Conflict and the Creation of a Delinquent Area* (Macmillan: London, 1977), pp. 77–9; Smith, *Sex, Gender and Power*, p. 75; Williams and Brake, *Public-House*, p. 181.

48 Punch Taverns.

49 Hadfield, *Bar Wars*, pp. 42–4.

50 Greenaway, *Drink*, pp. 150–82; Plant, *Binge Britain*.

51 Ibid., pp. 28–9.

Note on Sources

I have provided full references to the sources consulted for this book, but a short note on sources generally for the history of the pub and drink may be useful.

PRIMARY SOURCES

So central a place have the pub and drink occupied in our history that information on them may be found in a very wide range of sources: including the census, commercial directories, newspapers, local government records and personal records such as diaries. Directories, in addition to listings of pubs and publicans, provide such information as coach and carriers' timetables, or the meeting places of friendly societies, businessmen and trade unions. Local government records comprise in particular those of the police, but also such as building plans or title deeds to former pubs. Local newspapers provide a wealth of information. Until well into the twentieth century they gave detailed reports of brewster sessions and public meetings concerned with drink and the pub. They also have advertisements for pubs for sale or rent, local reaction to proposed or passed legislation, letters to the editor on all kinds of related topics and details of the meetings of groups and societies based at pubs. Their coverage of crime, which frequently provides incidental detail on the world of the pub and its customers, is also invaluable.

More specifically to the subject, licensing records are usefully described and their location given in J. Gibson and J. Hunter, *Victuallers' Licences: Records for Family and Local Historians* (Federation of Family History Societies: Birmingham, 2nd edn 1997). Parliamentary papers for the nineteenth century covering licensing, public houses and drunkenness are listed in P. Cockton, *Subject Catalogue of the House of Commons Parliamentary Papers 1801–1900* (Chadwyck-Healey: Cambridge, 1988), vol. III, pp. 725–56. Trade newspapers held by the British Library are listed in D.W. Gutzke, 'British Trade Newspapers', *Social History of Alcohol Review*, vol. 21–2, 1990, pp. 25–7. For brewing industry records see L. Richmond and A. Turton, *The Brewing Industry: A Guide to Historical Records* (Manchester University Press: Manchester, 1990). The former archive of Allied Breweries has been dispersed to archives around the country, which are listed in the *Pub History Society Newsletter*, Summer 2004. Collections are held at the Bass Brewing Museum and Archive, Burton upon Trent; the Guildhall Library, London; the National Brewing Library at Oxford Brookes University; and in the Library and Archive of the Brewery History Society at Birmingham Central Library. A short guide to sources, finally, which also gives useful websites, is S. Fowler, *Researching Brewery and Publican Ancestors* (Federation of Family History Societies: Bury, 2003).

SECONDARY SOURCES

The following are essential starting points. For the evolution of the public house see P. Clark, *The English Alehouse: A Social History 1200–1830* (Longman: London, 1983). For the inn see A. Everitt, 'The English Urban Inn 1560–1760' in his *Landscape and Community in England* (Hambledon: London, 1985) and J. Chartres, 'The Eighteenth-Century English Inn: A Transient "Golden Age"?' in B. Kümin and B. Ann Tlusty (eds), *The World of the Tavern: Public Houses in Early Modern Europe* (Ashgate: Aldershot, 2002). There is no single, detailed general study of the pub in the nineteenth and twentieth centuries. For the later period see D.W. Gutzke, *Pubs and Progressives: Reinventing the Public House in England 1896–1960*

(Northern Illinois University Press: DeKalb, 2006). There are a number of local studies, of which I would suggest here my own *The Public House in Bradford, 1770–1970* (Keele University Press: Keele, 1995), M. Girouard, *Victorian Pubs* (Yale University Press: New Haven and London, 1984, first published 1975), chiefly on London, and R.C. Riley and P. Eley, *Public Houses and Beerhouses in Nineteenth Century Portsmouth* (Portsmouth City Council: Portsmouth, 1983) and P. Eley and R.C. Riley, *The Demise of Demon Drink? Portsmouth Pubs 1900–1950* (Portsmouth City Council: Portsmouth, 1991). Mass Observation, *The Pub and the People: A Worktown Study* (Cresset Library: London, 1987, first published 1943) on Bolton, is invaluable. For the brewing industry, but also a great deal on the pub and drink, see P. Mathias, *The Brewing Industry in England 1700–1830* (Cambridge University Press: Cambridge, 1959) and T.R. Gourvish and R.G. Wilson, *The British Brewing Industry 1830–1980* (Cambridge University Press: Cambridge, 1994). See also D.W. *Gutzke, Protecting the Pub: Brewers and Publicans Against Temperance* (Boydell Press; Woodbridge, 1989). For the wider issue of drink see B. Harrison, *Drink and the Victorians: The Temperance Question in England 1815–1872* (Keele University Press: Keele, 2nd edn 1994).

The following bibliographies should also be consulted: W.E. Tate, 'Public House Bibliography: Topographical Guide to the Histories of English Inns and Inn-Signs', *Local Historian*, vol. 8, 1968, pp. 126–30; B. Harrison, 'Drink and Sobriety in England 1815–1872: A Critical Bibliography', *International Review of Social History*, vol. XII, 1967, pp. 204–76; D.W. Gutzke, *Alcohol in the British Isles from Roman Times to 1996*, (Greenwood Press: Westport, Connecticut, 1996). A general work of reference finally is J.S. Blocker Jr, D.M. Fahey and I.R. Tyrrell (eds), *Alcohol and Temperance in Modern History: An International Encyclopedia* (ABC Clio: Santa Barbara, 2003) 2 vols.

Index

Individual public houses, publicans and places are indexed only in the case of a substantive reference. There are separate entries for the different types of drinking place, but the main one is for pubs. Similarly, there are separate entries for different types of drinkseller, but the main one is for publicans.

Index